Toward an American Revolution

Toward an American Revolution

Exposing the Constitution
and Other Illusions

Jerry Fresia

98-1594

South End Press

Boston, MA

Cover design by Dan Spock
Produced by the South End Press collective
Printed in the USA
First edition, first printing

Library of Congress Cataloging-in-Publication Data
Fresia, Gerald John.
Toward and American revolution: exposing the Constitution and Other illusions by Jerry Fresia.
p.   cm.
Includes bibliographical references and index.
ISBN 0-89608-298-9: $25.00. ISBN 0-89608-297-0 (pbk.): $10.00
1. Elite (Social sciences)--United States--History. 2. Social classes--Political aspects--United States--History. 3. United STates--Constitutional history. I. Title.
JK1788.F74 1988
306'.2'0973--dc19   8-14784

South End Press, 116 Saint Botolph St., Boston, MA 02115

In memory of Malcolm X

Table of Contents

Acknowledgements

I would like to thank Kenneth M. Dolbeare, Nancy Netherland, Richard Mansfield, Sandia Siegel, and Bethany Weidner for their criticisms and suggestions, and John McGee for his technical support. I would like to thank the members of South End Press for their work and their confidence in me, especially Cynthia Peters whose editorial support was helpful in many ways. And finally, I would like to thank my parents, Armand and Vera, for their long and unwavering support, their insights, and their criticism.

Rise and demand; you are a burning flame
—**Montreux**

Afraid to Reflect

What I relate is the history of the next two centuries. I describe what is coming, what can no longer come differently: the advent of nihilism. This future speaks even now in a hundred signs; this destiny announces itself everywhere...For some time now, our whole European culture has been moving as toward a catastrophe, with a tortured tension that is growing from decade to decade: restlessly, violently, headlong like a river that wants to reach the end, that no longer reflects, that is afraid to reflect.[1]

—**Frederick Nietzsche, 1888**

Consider certain features of the lives of three men. The first was a very wealthy man. In 1787, many considered him the richest man in all the thirteen states. His will of 1789 revealed that he owned 35,000 acres in Virginia and 1,119 acres in Maryland. He owned property in Washington valued (in 1799 dollars) at $19,132, in Alexandria at $4,000, in Winchester at $400, and in Bath at $800. He also held $6,246 worth of U.S. securities, $10,666 worth of shares in the James River Company, $6,800 worth of stock in the Bank of Columbia, and $1,000 worth of stock in the Bank of Alexandria. His livestock was valued at $15,653. As early as 1773, he had enslaved 216 human beings who were not emancipated until after he and his wife had both died.[2]

The second man was a lawyer. He often expressed his admiration of monarchy and, correspondingly, his disdain and contempt for common people. His political attitudes were made clear following an incident which occurred in Boston on March 5, 1770. On that day, a number of ropemakers got into an argument with British soldiers whose occupation of Boston had threatened the ropemakers' jobs. A fight broke out and an angry crowd developed. The British soldiers responded by firing into the crowd, killing several. The event has since become known as the Boston Massacre. The soldiers involved in the shooting were later acquitted thanks, in part, to the skills of the lawyer we have been describing, who was selected as the defense attorney for the British. He described the crowd as "a motley rabble of saucy boys, negroes, and molattoes, Irish teagues and outlandish jack tarrs."[3]

The life of the third man was more complex, more filled with contradiction than the other two. He was wealthy. He owned over 10,000 acres and by 1809 he had enslaved 185 human beings. States one biographer, "He lived with the grace and elegance of many British lords; his house slaves alone numbered twenty-five." Yet slavery caused him great anxiety; he seems to have sincerely desired the abolition of slavery but was utterly incapable of acting in a way which was consistent with his abolitionist sympathies. He gave his daughter twenty-five slaves as a wedding present, for example. And when confronted with his indebtedness of $107,000 at the end of his life in 1826, he noted that at least his slaves constituted liquid capital. He had several children by one of his slaves and thus found himself in the position of having to face public ridicule or keep up the elaborate pretense that his slave children did not exist. He chose the latter course and arranged, discreetly, to have them "run away."[4]

Who are these three men? We know them well. They are among our "Founding Fathers," or Framers as we shall call them. They are the first three presidents of the United States, George Washington, John Adams, and Thomas Jefferson.

The brief sketches of these men are but glimpses into their personal lives, but some of the details are significantly revealing. They suggest that the Framers, far from champions of the people, were rich and powerful men who sought to maintain their wealth and status by figuring out ways to keep common people down. Moreover, I shall present additional evidence about the lives of the Framers, the Constitution, and the period in which it was written which supports the contention that the Framers were profoundly *anti-democratic* and afraid of the people. Some of the information may be surprising. In 1782, for example, Superintendent of Finance Robert Morris believed that a stronger central government was needed to "restrain the democratic spirit" in the states. Eric Foner tells us that Morris's private correspondence reveals "only contempt for the common people."[5] Benjamin Rush, "the distinguished scientist and physician" from Philadelphia and Framer (although he was not at the Constitutional Convention), would often refer to common people as "scum." Alexander Hamilton called the people "a great beast."[6] Not all the Framers resorted to name calling, but it is clear that they feared and distrusted the political participation of common people. Perhaps even more shocking than the personal opinions of the Framers, is the process by which the Constitution was ratified. As described in more detail in Chapter 3, secrecy, deceit and even violence played key roles in the Constitution's passage. These unsavory tactics were used by the Framers and their allies because the majority of the people were against the ratification of the Constitution. What is striking about this historical fact is its similarity with public policy and elite decision-making today. If not, elites tend to go ahead anyway. And because so much of what corporate-government elites believe to be in the national interest violates accepted standards of decency, many public policies are formulated and carried out covertly. But the point here is that cover and anti-democratic measures are not new developments. They have been the method of guaranteeing class rule ever since the Framers decided that they needed the present political system to protect their power and privilege.

It is contrary to everything we've been taught about the Framers to hear that they felt contempt for common people and that their Constitutional Convention was profoundly undemocratic. Indeed such accusations sound even less familiar in the context of the late 1980s when celebrations of the Constitution's bicentennial have brought adulation of this country's political origins to new and even more mindless heights. In its issue celebrating the bicentennial, *Newsweek* gushed, "The educated men in post-Revolutionary America," (and one must presume that this includes the Framers), "embraced the political tradition of participatory democracy, the social pretense of virtual classlessness and the economic fact of absolute equality of opportunity."[7] The "Founding Fathers" are always the champions of freedom, justice, and democracy. "Reverence is due to those men...," states *Time* magazine in its special bicentennial issue.[8]

Books and celebrity television specials packed with familiar myths
and illusions have been churned out by the dozens. The Constitution
itself is "the greatest single document struck off by the hand and mind
of man" we are told by the the Commission on the Bicentennial of the
the U.S. Constitution. Thus on the 200th anniversary of the completion
of the Constitution, former chief justice Warren Burger, on national TV,
led the nation's school children and teachers in a recitation of the
Preamble ("We the people...") and President Reagan led the country
in a recitation of the Pledge of Allegiance. One of the many books
honoring our Constitution, *We The People* by Peter Spier, begins by stating that the "U.S. Constitution is the oldest and most significant written
document of our history." He goes on to say that the Constitution "has
come to symbolize freedom, justice, equality, and hope for American
citizens as individuals and as a collective, democratic nation. For two
hundred years the Constitution has provided its people with rights,
liberties, and a free society that people of other nations can only dream
of." How familiar Spier's words sound to those of us who have grown
up in the United States. From our earliest days we are taught to glorify
the Framers and the great American "democracy" that is their legacy.
Even as adults we are still expected to accept the same grade-school,
cartoon-like version of our founding.

As citizens we are supposed to be like the nation's school children
who are given no choice but to stand by their desks and mindlessly
recite a pledge of allegiance to a flag, a pledge that was introduced into
schools at the turn of the century to counter the influence of ideas that
immigrant school children had received from their parents and from
distant lands. The fundamental purpose of bicentennial ideology, then,
is to encourage us *not* to explore competing ways of thinking or to ask
hard questions about our heritage. We are not encouraged to think because it is understood that thinking sometimes leads to disagreement,
or worse, to the challenging of some sacred text. Instead we are encouraged to believe. Efforts to transform thinking citizens into believing citizens, we should point out, really began at just about the time
that the Framers were planning the Constitutional Convention. Disturbing symptoms that common people were ignoring customs of social
deference and were beginning to think for themselves led some Framers

such as John Dickinson to urge that political instruments be devised to protect "the worthy against the licentious." Benjamin Rush, in a proposal entitled "The Mode of Education Proper in a Republic," stated: "I consider it possible to convert men into republican machines. This must be done, if we expect them to perform their parts properly, in the great machine of the government of the state." And so it must be done today, if people are to "perform their parts properly." The aim of the ideological manager is, in effect, the creation of millions of "republican machines."[9]

Common sense tells us that people who spend a good deal of time either acquiring or protecting a vast personal empire or defending a king's soldiers against the dispossessed would also have believed that the possession of enormous privilege was just and that protection of that privilege ought to be sought and maintained at considerable cost. Common sense should further compel us to wonder whether such people could write a constitution that would effectively transfer power from their few hands into the hands of the many, that is, into the hands of the poor, the debtors and people without property. Brian Price, an American historian who has spent countless hours studying early American elites' rise to power, asks a similar question: "Is it possible for a class which exterminates the native peoples of the Americas, replaces them by raping Africa for humans it then denigrates and dehumanizes as slaves, while cheapening and degrading its own working class—is it possible for such a class to create democracy, equality, and to advance the cause of human freedom?"[5] The implicit answer is, "No. Of course not."

There is a more specific purpose to all of this, however. If we do accept the illusion—the Constitution as sacred, a "shrine up in the higher stretches of American reverence" as *Time* magazine put it, then the serious problems that we face today would have to be aberrations, or deviations from the sacred text. The fundamental principles embedded within the Constitution, because it is "the greatest single document struck off by the hand and mind of man [sic]" and probably ordained by God at that, are intrinsically good. Only the sins of inept bureaucrats and politicians or the zealotry of ideologues ever get us into serious trouble. It follows from this mythology that there are no fundamental connections between the Constitution and the current crisis. Solving our problems always means going back to the Constitution and, not coincidentally, to the power relationships and privilege in the private sphere (or economy) which the Framers sought to protect.

For example, as Constitutional celebrations were unfolding in the summer of 1987, so too was the tale of government drug-running, assassinations, secret government, and private control of foreign policy known as the Iran-Contra affair. A documentary produced for the public broadcasting system, "The Secret Government: The Constitution in Crisis," and which aired in the fall of 1987, broke new ground by revealing to a mass audience some of the facts regarding the role that the federal government has played in assassinating foreign leaders and in over-throwing democratically elected governments. Yet the documentary was quite explicit in stating that this "secret government," rather than possibly having its roots in the distrust and fear of common people expressed by the Framers or in their protection and elevation of private power, is a violation of Constitutional principles. Of course, the Constitution is never critically examined. Instead, the sense of empowered citizenship is invoked as the hallowed words "We the People" are dragged slowly and dramatically across the screen, patriotic music provides the backdrop of sanctification, and Bill Moyers intones, "Our nation was born in rebellion against tyranny. We are the fortunate heirs of those who fought for America's freedom and then drew up a remarkable charter to protect it against arbitrary power. The Constitution begins with the words 'We the People.' The government gathers its authority from the people and the governors are as obligated to uphold the law as the governed."

So what is missing? Moyers says not a word about corporate power, which the Framers chose to insulate from popular accountability and which has since grown and become concentrated and arbitrary in ways unimaginable to elites of the eighteenth century. The failure of the Constitution to provide checks against corporate (private) power can be directly linked to the private control of foreign policy. This defect, so obviously undemocratic, has become increasingly exposed. Moyer's revelations divert our attention away from this essential flaw and thus serve as a quite sophisticated, albeit ineffective, cover-up. Nor does Moyers tell us that some government officials such as the Director of Central Intelligence, who may spend money "without regard to the provisions of law and regulations relating to the expenditure of government funds," are not obligated to uphold certain laws as are the governed. Could it be that by design the Constitution requires that a few "considerate and virtuous" citizens check and balance the "interested and overbearing" majority? Perhaps, but such subtleties tend to complicate, if not contradict, what must be among the greatest stories ever told, namely that the Constitution begins with the words, "We the People." Stop there, we are told. Do not go any further. For to go beyond the grade-school version of our founding is to raise the possibility that the Constitution might be defective in some fundamental way. Viewers might conclude that U.S.-sponsored terrorism may not be a deviation from Constitutional principles but rather the logical consequence of a system which protects the freedom of a handful of Americans to control a good deal of the earth's resources and, correspondingly, the lives of millions of people scattered around the globe. Similar connections between our founding ideas and the virulent racism that now exists, the subordination of women, the massive inequality that marks our society, and what some are pointing to as irreversible environmental degradation could also be made. To move beyond the history constructed for us, then, would be to admit the possibility that one could expose and call into question the legitimacy of the Framers and the system of elite rule they established through the Constitution. It would be permitting citizens of today to become more intimately familiar and identified with the lives and values of the people—a majority—one must emphasize, who opposed the Constitution at the time it was given to the states for ratification. Of course, if the ideological managers were to permit an honest reassessment of who the Framers really were and what they really did, nothing might come of it. But it is the very intensity itself of the ideological stranglehold over our own history which suggests that it is ruling elites, not you or I, who are afraid that if a candid assessment of the Framers and the Constitution were to become common knowledge, it would help citizens to explain their sense of political powerlessness and that it might invite the kind of self-discovery that underlies effective radical politics. "The monopoly of truth, including historical truth," states Daniel Singer, "is implied in the monopoly of power."

Three Obstacles to Effective Radical Politics

The central theme of this book can be summarized as follows: We live in an undemocratic system that is a major source of terror and repression, both at home and around the world. In large measure this is due to the tremendous concentration of unchecked corporate power. Our responsibility, as citizens and as a people, is to challenge the structure of power within our society, particularly the private power of the corporate-banking community. The Constitution prohibits this. In fact, the Constitution was intended to ensure that only a few people would run the government and that they would be the few who would run the economy. The crisis confronting us, in other words, demands effective radical politics and a departure from many Constitutional values, assumptions, and principles. Effective radical politics, however, is inhibited by our acceptance and glorification of the Constitution and the Framers who engineered its ratification. It is as if we believe the IBM ad which stated, "The Constitution is a political work of art...and...It's also the most important contract of your life." We shouldn't have to depend upon or live by IBM's conception of justice today anymore than we should have to depend upon or live by the conception of justice articulated by rich and powerful white men, many of them slaveowners, who lived 200 years ago. Our values are not their values. The government of the United States does not, in its policies, express the decency of its people. It lacks legitimacy. And we need to confront that fact.

Ideologically, then, there are three obstacles to effective radical politics. They are 1) respect for the Constitution as a fair and equitable and democratic document; 2) the underlying belief that the U.S. government is fair, acts justly, or would under ordinary circumstances; and 3) a reluctance on the part of most citizens whose values are at odds with those expressed by corporate and state policy to engage in confrontation. In Chapters 2 through 4, I discuss why the Constitution is not a fair and equitable document, why it impedes rather than encourages democracy, and why it is, ultimately, a constitution that disrespects its people. In Chapters 4 and 5, I explain why I believe that the government of the United States, in order to meet its obligation of protecting the private empire of corporate elites, cannot meet its obligation to promote the common interest of the majority of its people and cannot, therefore, act justly under ordinary circumstances. I argue in this section that we live in a system of injustice. Finally, in Chapters 6 and 7, I argue that each of us as citizens must develop a sense of self-respect and self-confidence that necessarily challenges the role set for us by the Framers as obedient and dependent "republican machines." We need, as I explain below, to learn a "song without knees." Before moving on, let us discuss each of these obstacles a bit further and then briefly review the lives of the founding fathers so that we get a better sense of just who they were.

A Constitution That Disrespects Its People

I have been suggesting that *at the very heart of our political institutions, at the very core of our way of doing politics is fear and distrust of the political activity of common people*. As we explore more deeply the vision of the Framers and the historical context of their work, we shall find that the Framers repeatedly expressed what they felt was the need to *check and balance* the political expression of people who were not like themselves, who were not involved in the market economy, who did not own much property, and who were not very rich. John Adams believed that "Men in general...who are wholly destitute of property, are also too little acquainted with public affairs to form a right judgment, and too dependent on other men to have a will of their own."[10] In fact, when the Framers used the term "the people" they had in mind the "middling" property owning people or, generally speaking, the middle class. It is the political expression of this middle class which they also distrusted but which they felt they had to permit if property owners were to be free from government interference. The Framers were thus willing to permit the limited participation (through the House of Representatives—remember that the Constitution did not permit the direct election of the Senate and we still do not elect the president directly) of white males who met state property qualifications.

The political expression of classes below the middle class property owners, women, or people of color, indentured servants, or people with no property—in short, the "people in the first instance" as Charles Pinckney called them, or the majority, was simply "nonsense" and "wrong." Political expression by these groups was not permitted and as we shall note, the Constitution was purposefully made to be anti-majoritarian in several ways. Representatives were to be of and among "the better people" who would have a material stake in society, who would be less given to some common impulse of passion, and who would be able to tell us what our real needs and interests are. Amendments have broadened the definition of "the people" to include most of those who were excluded in 1787. But the Constitution's very design, its processes, and its structure still gives life to the eighteenth century elitist belief that rich and powerful people ought to rule. The Constitution stil disrespects the political wisdom of most people, of workers, particularly people of color, of women, and of those who happen to be poor.

A System of Injustice

The vision of the Framers, even for Franklin and Jefferson who were less fearful of the politics of common people than most, was that of a strong centralized state, a nation whose commerce and trade stretched around the world. In a word, the vision was one of empire where property owners would govern themselves. It would be a nation in which ambitious industrious (white Anglo-Saxon) men would be finally free from the Crown and from the Church to do with their property as they pleased and as their talents permitted. It would be a nation organized around private power where there would be freedom to acquire wealth and the function of the state and of its executive would be to protect these freedoms and opportunities, defined as natural rights. Meanwhile, it was perceived that the only real threat, to paraphrase Madison, to the rights of the few virtuous citizens and therefore to the "common good," would come from the overbearing majority, the people without property. For it is the less virtuous and less industrious people, the people in debt for example, who would seek to redistribute property and invade the rights of others.

There is a tension, then, between the elite who privately own productive resources and the multitudes who are made dependent, who, as Karl Marx noted, must sell their lives in order to live. Within this relationship of power, the Constitution protects the power of the more powerful. It does this because the Framers believed that it was the right of a few "better" people to own and control much of the earth's resources. And it does this because the Framers believed that the lives of women, people of color, and the poor ought to be defined in terms of the desires and interests of the rich. Resistance to this tyranny, from the Whiskey Rebellion of 1794 to the revolutionary leaders of today who are genuinely committed to directing meager resources to the majority poor in the Third World, are and have been brutally repressed because the national army created by the Constitution is directed by that document to preserve these relationships of disparity. Of course, relationships of disparity are not referred to as such by elites. They would prefer to call them "our rights" and "our freedom." Thus "our" concepts of rights and of freedom are interwoven with the Framers' vision of conquest and empire and privilege.

A "Song Without Knees"

Eric Foner writes that in the minds of the "founding fathers" was a "view of human nature as susceptible to corruption, basically self-interested and dominated by passion rather than reason. It was because of this natural 'depravity' of human nature that democracy was inexpedient: a good constitution required a 'mixed' government to check the passions of the people, as well as representing their interests." We should add that the "founding fathers" were less worried about checking their own passions. They did not see themselves as depraved. Only common people were depraved.[11]

We are the legacy of that warped view. Thomas Ferguson and Joel Rogers point out that none of the major initiatives of the Reagan administration (tax cuts for the rich, budget cuts in social programs, and increased militarism, particularly increased funding for nuclear weapons and the sponsorship of terrorist armies such as the Contras) followed popular initiatives. Instead they were initiated by business elites.[12] Ours is a system, as Noam Chomsky regularly reminds us, of elite decisionmaking with occasional ratification by an irrelevant public. When one studies the views of the Framers, one discovers that it was never intended to be otherwise. The larger problem, however, is that we have become used to playing a subservient role. We live, politically, *on our knees.*

Martin Luther King, Jr. at times stated that perhaps one of the greatest accomplishments of the Civil Rights movement was that blacks, who had been brought to America in "darkness and chains," had learned to "straighten up their bent backs." "We won our self-respect," he said. An inner sense of dignity had been acquired. Stephen Oates, a King biographer, writes with regard to one particular woman in the movement:

> For her and the others who participated, the movement of 1965 became the central event of their lives, a time of self-liberation when they stood and marched to glory with Martin Luther King. Yes, they were surprised at themselves, proud of the strength they had displayed in confronting the state of Alabama, happy indeed, as Marie Foster said, to be "a new Negro in a new South—a Negro who is no longer afraid." And that perhaps was King's greatest gift to his long-suffering people in Dixie: he taught them how to confront those who oppressed them....[13]

In so many ways all of us live in chains and darkness. Writes Starhawk, "Women, working-class people, people of color, and people without formal education, are conditioned to think of their opinions and feelings as valueless. They are taught to listen to an inner voice that murmurs, 'You shouldn't say that. You only think that because something is wrong with you. Everybody else knows more about things than you do.' "[14] We have yet to learn to straighten our backs. We wish to believe that confronting those who disrespect us is somehow bad or itself disrespectful. But we need to learn that proper confrontation is a source of dignity and a necessary first step to politics. Otherwise politics becomes draining. For without a sense of confidence and purpose we play by the rules the Framers set down, rules that were designed for the "depraved."

In Nicaragua, there is a song called "Song Without Knees." It tells of life under the dictator Somoza and how the revolution was a process in which people learned to get off their knees, learned to stand up and express themselves as healthy and creative people. Here in the United States we too need to learn a "Song Without Knees" so that we can create space for a *politics without knees,* a politics which is rooted not in the fear and distrust of common people, but one which departs fundamentally from the myths and illusions of the founding period which hold many of us hostage in a state of comfort, denial, and unfortunately, irresponsibility.

The "Founding Fathers"

Abraham Baldwin of Georgia *

He was a wealthy lawyer who possessed a few thousand dollars worth of public securities. He wanted the Senate to be composed of men of property so that they could check the House of Representatives which was apt to be composed of men of less substantial wealth and therefore closer to the common people.

---

*Unless otherwise indicated, the following information was drawn from chapters 5 and 7 of Charles Beard, *An Economic Interpretation of the Constitution of the United States* (New York: The Macmillan Company, 1948); Chapter 8 of Clinton Rossiter, *The Grand Convention* (New York: The Macmillan Company, 1966); and Page Smith, *The Constitution* (New York: William Morrow and Company, 1978).

Gunning Bedford of Delaware

He was the son of a "substantial land owner," a lawyer, and was eventually elected governor of his state. He was in favor of a more democratic Constitution than the one we have now which he felt checked the "Representatives of the People" more than was necessary.

William Blount of North Carolina

He was born into a substantial planting family and was very deeply involved in land speculation. He enslaved human beings.

Pierce Bulter of South Carolina

He enslaved thirty-one human beings. He also was a stockholder and director of the first United States bank. He felt that no congressional representatives should be directly elected by the people, that the Senate ought to represent property, and that slavery ought to be protected. He was responsible for the Constitution's fugitive slave law and he also "warmly urged the justice and necessity of regarding wealth in the apportionment of representation."

George Clymer of Pennsylvania

He possessed a large fortune, held public securities, and helped create the Bank of Pennsylvania. He believed that "a representative of the people is appointed to think for and not with his constituents." And later as a member of Congress "he showed a total disregard to the opinions of his constituents when opposed to the matured decisions of his own mind."

John Dickinson of Delaware

He was a member of one of the established landed families of the South, a lawyer, and he married into one of the wealthiest commercial families in Philadelphia. He wanted a monarchy and refused to sign the Declaration of Independence. He seems to have constantly worried about the "dangerous influence of those multitudes without property & without principle."

Oliver Ellsworth of Connecticut

He was the most successful lawyer Connecticut had yet known with a fortune "quite uncommonly large." He held public securities and invested in the Hartford Bank and the Hartford Broadcloth Mill. He was also regarded, perhaps more than any other member at the Convention, as someone who feared "levelling democracy." He argued that voting be limited to those who paid taxes. Regarding slavery he said, "As slaves multiply so fast...it is cheaper to raise than import them....[But] let us not intermeddle. As population increases; poor laborers will be so plenty as to render slaves useless."

Benjamin Franklin of Pennsylvania

He was a printer, scientist, author, diplomat and land speculator who had accumulated a "considerable" fortune. More than anyone at the convention, he was sympathetic to meaningful self-government. Because of this he was known to have serious doubts about the Constitution but signed it anyway. Charles L. Mee, Jr., in *The Genius of the People*, states, "Franklin disliked the document, thinking it cheated democracy."

Elbridge Gerry of Massachusetts

He was a Harvard graduate and a merchant with a considerable estate. In reference to the political unrest at the time of the Convention, he complained that "The evils we experience flow from the excess of democracy." He did not want any members of the new national government to be elected by popular vote, having been taught the "danger of the levelling spirit." Although he was quite active at the Convention, Gerry had numerous objections to the final draft and he refused to sign it.

Nathaniel Gorham of Massachusetts

He was a successful merchant who was involved in land speculation on a large scale. He expressed what was then the general attitude about the one chamber that was popularly elected (given the restricted franchise) when he said, "All agree that a check on the legislative branch is necessary." He was sympathetic to monarchy and during the Convention secretly wrote to European royalty in hope of involving someone with royal blood in governing the United States.

Alexander Hamilton of New York

He was an eminent lawyer who perhaps more than any other delegate was responsible for organizing the Convention, and later, as Secretary of the Treasury under President Washington, for implementing the Constitution and institutionalizing its relation to the private economy. He greatly admired monarchy and time and again emphasized the need to check "the amazing violence and turbulence of the democratic spirit." Hamilton believed that government ought to be an instrument in the hands of creditors, financiers, and bankers. When he later sought to create a national bank, he said that it would help unite "the interest and credit of the rich individuals with those of the state."[15] His statement at the Convention concerning the relationship between government, the rich, and the poor deserves to be quoted at length because it represents what was then a very common attitude among elites:

> All communities divide themselves into the few and the many. The first are the rich and well born, the other the mass of the people. The voice of the people has been said to be the voice of God; and however generally this maxim has been quoted and believed, it is not true in fact. The people are turbulent and changing; they seldom judge or determine right. Give therefore to the first class a distinct, permanent share in the government. They will check the unsteadiness of the Second....Can a democratic assembly who annually revolve in the mass of the people, be supposed steadily to pursue the public good? Nothing but a permanent body can check the imprudence of democracy....It is admitted that you cannot have a good executive upon a democratic plan.[16]

William Samuel Johnson of Connecticut

He was a wealthy and successful lawyer and graduate of Yale who refused to help in the War of Independence because he could not "conscientiously" take up arms against England. Clinton Rossiter describes him as "the nearest thing to an aristocrat in mind and manner that Connecticut had managed to produce in its 150 years." He was one of the few northerners at the Convention who simply did not worry about slavery or the slave trade.

Rufus King of Massachusetts

He was born into and married into wealthy families, was a Harvard graduate, and had extensive mercantile and other business interests. He was also a large holder of government securities and was later director of the first United States bank. King argued in favor of a strong unimpeachable executive and urged that the judiciary be permitted to check the political tendencies of common people whom he felt would use legislatures to attack the privilege of property owners. He was responsible for the clause which prevented any state from passing any law "impairing the obligation of contracts." This clause greatly helped the rich, as we shall see.

John Langdon of New Hampshire

He was "uniformly prosperous" and a "man of great wealth and pressing commercial interests," the "leading merchant" from Portsmouth. He was a large creditor of the new government (the third largest holder of public securities among all the Framers) and a strong supporter of a national bank.

James Madison of Virginia

He was a descendant of one of the old landed families, studied law at Princeton, and at one time enslaved 116 human beings. He has been called the "most active of all the moving spirits of the new government." For this reason he is acknowledged as the "Father" of the Constitution. He greatly feared that the majority of people with little or no property would take away the property of the few who held quite a bit. He very much liked the Constitution because he believed that it would check the majority from establishing "paper money," the "abolition of debts," an "equal division of property," or other "wicked projects." And in general it would prevent the majority from "discovering their own strength" and from acting "in union with each other." His defense of the Constitution in *Federalist No. 10*, found in the Appendix, is the most concise and clearest example of the political thought that undergirds our political institutions. Because his role in the design of the Constitution was so central, I shall quote him frequently; his political thought weighs heavily upon us today.

Luther Martin of Maryland

He was a successful lawyer and graduate of Princeton, but his fortune was never large. He enslaved "only" six human beings. He was in sympathy with poor debtors generally and argued that the government ought to protect the debtor against the "wealthy creditor and the moneyed man" in times of crisis. He refused to sign the Constitution, given its protection of creditors, and fought hard against its ratification.

George Mason of Virginia

He was a speculator in land, owning some 75,000 acres. He also owned $50,000 worth of other personal property and he enslaved 300 human beings. Like many large slaveowners, he feared a strong national government and a standing army. He was a strong proponent of the right of individuals to own property without government interference. Given the lack of a Bill of Rights and the strong central power sanctioned by the Constitution, Mason feared that the new system would result in "monarchy or a tyrannical aristocracy"; he refused to sign it. Mason is a classic example of a Framer for whom "rights" meant the protection of private power and privilege. Mason did not object to the anti-democratic features of the Constitution, rather he objected to the fact that a national government might someday interfere with his individual freedom as a property owner.

John Francis Mercer of Maryland

He enslaved six human beings. He also held a moderate amount of public securities. He stated that "the people cannot know and judge of the characters of candidates. The worst possible choice will be made." He left the Convention early, and strongly opposed the ratification of the Constitution.

Gouverneur Morris of Pennsylvania

He was a lawyer who was born into the landed aristocracy of New York. A rich man, he helped establish the Bank of North America. He was "an aristocrat to the core," once stating that "there never was, nor ever will be a civilized Society without an Aristocracy." He believed that common people were incapable of self-government and that poor people would sell their votes. He argued, "Give the votes to people who have no property, and they will sell them to the rich who will be able to buy them." Voting should be restricted to property owners. He shaped the Constitution more than most men at the Convention (he made 173 speeches, more than anyone) and was responsible for the style in which it was written.

William Patterson of New Jersey

He was a lawyer, graduate of Princeton, and attorney general of New Jersey who was born in Ireland. He resisted the creation of a strong central government and left the Convention early.

Charles Pinckney of South Carolina

A successful lawyer, and a considerable landowner, he enslaved fifty-two human beings. Taking the side of the creditor against the debtor, he had been among the Congressmen who were critical of the Articles of Confederation and sought the creation of a centralized national government. At twenty-nine, he was the youngest member of the Convention. He believed that members of government ought to "be possessed of competent property to make them independent & respectable." He wrote to Madison before the Constitution was ratified, "Are you not...abundantly impressed that the theoretical nonsense of an election of Congress by the people in the first instance is clearly and practically wrong, that it will in the end be the means of bringing our councils into contempt?"

General Charles C. Pinckney of South Carolina

A successful lawyer who worked for the merchants of Charlestown, he was also a large landowner in Charleston, and he enslaved human beings. He felt that the Senate ought to represent the "wealth of the country," that members of the government ought to hold property, and according to Clinton, believed in the need "for stiff measures to restrain the urges of arrant democracy."

Edmund Randolph of Virginia

He was a successful lawyer who owned 7,000 acres of land. He enslaved nearly 200 human beings. He held considerable public securities. He believed that the problems confronting the United States at the time were due to the "turbulence and follies of democracy." The new Constitution, therefore, ought to check popular will. He thought that the best way of doing this would be to create a independent Senate composed of relatively few rich men.

George Read of Delaware

A successful lawyer who "lived in the style of the colonial gentry," enslaved human beings, and was a signer of the Declaration of Independence. He was in favor of doing away with states and wanted the President to be elected for life and have absolute veto power.

John Rutledge of South Carolina

He was a very successful lawyer who also owned five plantations. He enslaved twenty-six human beings. He said that the defects of democracy have been found "arbitrary, severe, and destructive." We see in Rutledge a clear expression of the notion that the general welfare is, in essence, economic development and accumulation. With regard to the issue of objections to slavery, he stated: "Religion & humanity had nothing to do with this question. Interest alone is the governing principle with Nations. The true question at present is whether the Southern states shall or shall not be parties to the Union. If the Northern States consult their interests they will not oppose the increase of Slaves which will increase the commodities of which they will become the carriers."

Roger Sherman of Connecticut

He was a shoemaker, storekeeper, farmer who rose from poverty to affluence and he also owned public securities. A signer of the Declaration and drafter of the Articles of Confederation, Sherman was not terribly enthusiastic about a strong national government. But nor was he enthusiastic about popular sovereignty. He said, "The people immediately should have as little to do as may be about the government. They want information and are constantly liable to be misled."

Caleb Strong of Massachusetts

He was a lawyer and Harvard graduate. He owned public securities and seems to have accumulated considerable wealth. He was in favor of more frequent congressional elections than what the Constitution eventually mandated. He left the Convention early and went home.

George Washington of Virginia

As we have noted, by several accounts Washington was the richest man in the United States and he enslaved hundreds of human beings. He made only one speech at the Convention and seems to have had no particular theory of government. He distrusted popular democratic tendencies and viewed criticism of the government, as Beard notes, as "akin to sedition." He also feared the growth of urban populations, stating that "The tumultuous populace of large cities are ever to be dreaded. Their indiscriminate violence prostates for the time all public authority."

Hugh Williamson of North Carolina

Educated as a medical doctor, he inherited a great trading operation. He also speculated in land and owned public securities. He wrote Madison following the Convention that he thought an "efficient federal government" would in the end contribute to the increase in value of his land. He sided with creditors against debtors in his state. At the Convention he was generally in favor of shifting power away from the states toward the national level.

James Wilson of Pennsylvania

Born in Scotland, he was a successful lawyer whose clients were primarily "merchants and men of affairs." He was one of the directors of the Bank of North America. He was involved in the corrupt Georgia Land Company and held shares "to the amount of at least one million acres." He later became a member of the Supreme Court. He was apprehensive, as were most of his colleagues, about the opportunity that common people would have to express themselves politically though legislatures. But he also believed that the judiciary would be a sufficient check on popular will. He, therefore, was in favor of more popular participation in the selection of government officials (popular election of the President and the Senate) than the Constitution permitted.

Part I

A Constitution That Disrespects Its People

We have probably had too good an opinion of human nature in forming our confederation. Experience has taught us that men will not adopt and carry into execution measures the best calculated for their own good, without the intervention of a coercive power.

—George Washington

Counterrevolutionary Tendencies

When England invaded America—what we usually call "settling" it—The Crown lawyers had consulted their only precedents to rationalize the position of the new American outposts in the structure of the empire. Each colony became in legal theory a collective lord analogous to the barons who had marched into Ireland. When the Americans turned against the Crown they continued an ancient tradition of lords who have marched too far and grown too powerful to accept royal orders gladly. In this perspective the American Revolution was a barons' revolt.[1]

—Francis Jennings

It is useful to think of the Framers as barons who had marched too far and grown too powerful. Sixty-nine percent of the signers of the Declaration of Independence had held colonial office under England. They were, essentially, merchants or businessmen who wanted independence or freedom from the Crown and the Church to run their businesses any way they wanted. Corporate elites would still have us believe that government is "on their backs." But just as today, elites then would not risk altering the relationships of power and certainly would not consider sharing economic and political power with the less privileged classes. What they wanted was to create a new political economy in which they were independent from Great Britain but still in possession of power and privilege in their own society. According to John C. Miller:

> [The Framers]...had no wish to usher in democracy in the United States. They were not making war upon the principle of aristocracy and they had no more intention than had the Tories of destroying the tradition of upper-class leadership in the colonies. Although they hoped to turn the Tories out of office, they did not propose to open these lush pastures to the common herd. They did believe,

however, that the common people, if properly bridled and reined, might be made allies in the work of freeing the colonies from British rule and that they—the gentry—might reap the benefits without interference. They expected, in other words, to achieve a "safe and sane" revolution of gentlemen, by gentlemen, and for gentlemen.[2]

How were the Framers to create a new system in which the many disenfranchised would support, or at least not contest, the privilege of the few?

The Framers' Fear

English merchant capitalists who arrived in America found that whatever wealth was to be had would come from the hard labor of mining, cutting down forests, planting and harvesting crops, and constructing buildings, roads, and bridges. Investors, therefore, arranged to bring "new hands" to the "new world" to exploit its resources. A vast propaganda campaign was launched to lure the poor of Europe to America. Roughly half the immigrants to colonial America were indentured servants. At the time of the War of Independence, three out of four persons in Pennsylvania, Maryland, and Virginia were or had been indentured servants. Of the 250,000 indentured servants that had arrived by 1770, more than a 100,000 had been either kidnapped or released from their prison sentences. And by this time, roughly 20 percent of the colonial population was in slavery. Jefferson was clear about this when he said that "our ancestors who migrated here were laborers not lawyers."[3]

In the hundred years or so prior to the War of Independence, the rich had gotten richer, and the poor, poorer. For example, in 1687 in Boston, the top 1 percent owned about 25 percent of the wealth. By 1770, the top 1 percent owned 44 percent of the wealth. During this same period, the percentage of adult males who were poor, "perhaps rented a room, or slept in the back of a tavern, owned no property, doubled from 14 percent of the adult males to 29 percent." It was during this time that the rich introduced property qualifications for voting in order to disenfranchise the poor and protect their privileges. In Pennsylvania in 1750, for example, white males had to have fifty pounds of "lawful money" or own fifty acres of land. This meant that only 8 percent of the rural population and 2 percent of the population of Philadelphia could vote. Similar situations existed in the other states. It is important to note the way in which voting qualification requirements can be used to curb political expression. Keep in mind also that voting has never been guaranteed in this country, or made a *right*, a point to which we shall return in Chapter 4.[4]

Common people were not taking this abuse sitting down. During the last quarter of the seventeenth century, militant confrontations brought down the established governments of Massachusetts, New York, Maryland, Virginia, and North Carolina. In Virginia, in a dispute over land distribution and Indian policy, white frontiersmen, together with slaves and servants forced the governor to flee the burning capital of Jamestown. England was forced to quickly dispatch 1,000 soldiers to Virginia to put down the armed insurrection. By 1760, there had been eighteen rebellions aimed at overthrowing colonial governments, six black rebellions, and forty major riots protesting a variety of unfair conditions. In addition, women were beginning to speak and write about their inequality and would soon begin fighting the "irresponsibility of men" in family matters, and the denigration of the status of women in the public world.[5]

To be sure, common people were involved in and supported the unfolding struggle for independence from Great Britain, even though Britain's colonial policies would, for them, only end in more severe or permanent forms of subordination. But as Philip Foner points out, for common people, independence meant *freedom from the oppression of colonial aristocracy* as well as freedom from British rule. Stated one slogan, common people must be free from all "Foreign or Domestic Oligarchy."[6] In other words, common people were thinking in terms well beyond "independence." They were thinking in terms of *liberation*.

We see then, that in the context of the struggle for independence, the specific aspirations of common people put them into conflict with the people we think of as the "Founding Fathers" or Framers. The Sons of Liberty, the Loyal Nine, and the Boston Committee of Correspondence and other such groups which the Framers organized were rooted in the "middling interests and well-to-do merchants" and upper classes. They have been wrongly described as revolutionary. The truth is that they took great measures to keep the peace and defuse revolutionary tendencies. As mass resistance to British policies mounted, for example, they urged, "No Mobs or Tumults, let the Persons and Properties of your most inveterate Enemies be safe." Sam Adams agreed. James Otis added, "No possible circumstances, though ever so oppressive, could be supposed sufficient to justify private tumults and disorders..." The Boston Committee of Correspondence actually did its best to contain and control the militancy of activists involved in the Boston Tea Party.[7]

Virtually ignored by most historians is the fact that much of the resistance directed toward Great Britain by common people was an extension of the resistance they felt toward what Dirk Hoerder has described as "high-handed officials and men of wealth whose arrogant conduct and use of economic power was resented." Rioters often damaged coaches and other luxury items of the rich. The homes of the wealthy were sometimes broken into and destroyed. The governor of Massachusetts said in 1765, "The Mob had set down no less than fifteen Houses...the houses of some of the most respectable persons in the Government. It was now become a War of Plunder, of general levelling and taking away the Distinction of Rich and poor."[8]

In the countryside, there was similar class antagonism. In New Jersey and New York, tenant riots led to the carving of Vermont out of New York State. And in North Carolina in 1771 there was the Regulator movement, an armed insurrection which according to Marvin L. Michael Kay was led by "class-conscious white farmers...who attempted to democratize local government." What was the general response to this revolutionary moment by the Framers? The response of Gouverneur Morris, a key co-author of the Constitution, was not atypical: "The mob begins to think and to reason...I see and I see with fear and trembling, that if the disputes with Britain continue, we shall be under the domination of a riotous mob. It is to the interest of all men therefore, to seek reunion with the parent state."[9]

The Threat of Democracy

As the legitimacy of the Crown's government began to collapse, the period of control by extra-legal committees and congresses established by the colonists set in. Reflecting the class hostility described above, urban workers and artisans and country farmers often formed strong alliances in order to protect themselves vis-à-vis the merchant class. For example, in 1768 mechanics from Charlestown, Massachusetts were dissatisfied with the initial non-importation agreement written by merchants because it ignored their demand for the prohibition of the importation of slaves who were being hired out as craftspeople; they decided to elect their own representatives. The *Boston Chronicle* reported that "a number of the leading mechanics of this city assembled under some trees in a field adjacent to the ropewalk in order to select six gentlemen to represent the inhabitants of Charles Town in the ensuing General Assembly." Reading the report in the newspaper, mechanics then went to the town meeting, ignored the legal restrictions on their right to vote, and took charge of town government. One aristocrat complained two years later in 1770, "The Merchants in Boston are now entirely out of the question in all debates at their Town Meeting." A group of merchants added, "At these meetings, the lowest Mechanicks discuss upon the most important points of government with the utmost freedom."[10]

The fears of the Framers were being confirmed. The underclasses were not taking orders. They were speaking for themselves. And they were making it quite clear that their vision of a new society was not the same as that of the Framers. This seems to have been particularly true in Philadelphia. In 1770, the first political meeting specifically restricted to mechanics was held and by 1772 craftsmen had organized their own political organization, the Patriotic Society, to promote their own candidates and agenda. Gary Nash notes that "By mid-1776, laborers, artisans, and small tradesmen, employing extralegal measures when electoral politics failed, were in clear command in Philadelphia." In selecting delegates for the 1776 Pennsylvania Constitution, they urged voters to shun "great and overgrown rich men [who] will be improper to be trusted." They also drew up a bill of rights to be considered which included the assertion that "an enormous proportion of property vested in a few individuals is dangerous to the rights, and destructive of the common happiness, of mankind; and therefore every free state hath a right by its laws to discourage the possession of such property."[11]

The constitution which the Pennsylvania backwoods farmers came up with was impressive. Kenneth M. Dolbeare, respected for his knowledge of U.S. political institutions, concludes that "the extent of popular control" put forward by these common people "exceeds that of any American government before or since." Although it was not radical by some twentieth century standards (it ignored women, slaves, servants and the poor but did challenge property rights as we now know them), it dramatically reveals the degree to which our present federal Constitution is elitist *by the eighteenth century standards of common people.* For example, the document began by stating quite explicitly that all men possessed the right of "acquiring, possessing, and protecting property and pursuing *and obtaining* happiness and safety." We will be in a better position to appreciate the egalitarian features of this constitution once we have discussed the meaning of our own federal constitution which the Framers designed, but nonetheless, the attempt to genuinely involve some common people in political decisionmaking was more honest in the document described below:

> A one-house Assembly whose members were elected annually was made the seat of almost all power. The Assembly was required to function in open public sessions, and to keep full records. Legislation had to indicate its purpose clearly in the preamble, and except in emergencies had to be published and distributed publicly by the Assembly before it could be considered for enactment— but only by the next session of that body, after another election had been held. The office of governor and its veto power were eliminated in favor of a weak Supreme Executive Council of 12 members, four of whom were elected each year for three-year terms. Judges were elected for seven-year terms, but were made removable for cause by the Assembly. A council of Censors was

to be elected every seven years to review the government's performance and recommended a new constitutional convention if changes in its structure or powers were required.[12]

The reaction to this radical departure from the aristocratic liberalism of Great Britain by the Framers and their class allies was predictable. They referred to it as "mobocracy of the most illiterate," a constitution written by "coffee-house demagogues," "political upstarts," and "the unthinking many who believed that men of property...men of experience and knowledge were not to be trusted..." Benjamin Rush, a Framer, called it "a tyranny. The moment we submit to it we become slaves."[13]

The kind of system which the Framers generally had in mind was a particular kind of representative system or republic; it was one in which elites or "better people" decide what is best for "common people." This kind of system, in fact the kind we now live under, is often referred to as *classical liberalism*. It is the aristocratic or paternalistic representative system associated with John Locke. Locke, it is important to note, was a wealthy man, with investments in the silk trade and slave trade who also received income from loans and mortgages. He invested heavily in the first issue of the stock of the Bank of England and he also advised the colonial governors of the Carolinas, suggesting a government of slaveowners run by forty wealthy land barons. The purpose of Locke's political theory was to create a political system that would support the development of mercantile capitalism in which property owners, not the Crown, held power. Therefore, the concept of "the people" associated with his theories, and the concept of "the people" used by the Framers, as we saw earlier, meant the people who owned productive property—capital, land, factories, and the like. As one member of the British Parliament made clear, by the people "I don't mean the mob...I mean the middling people of England, the manufacturer, the yeoman, the merchant, the country gentleman." It is also important to note, because it helps explain the views of the Framers and our way of politics today, that Locke and his contemporaries also believed that people who labored and who did not own productive property were thought of as "human capital" to be used, but they were not considered intelligent enough to govern themselves.[14]

We see, then, that as early as the 1760s and 1770s the democratic tendencies of common people had alarmed the Framers. Stated a Pennsylvania newspaper in 1772, it was "time the Tradesmen were checked. They take too much upon them. They ought not to intermeddle in State Affairs. They ought to be kept low. They will become too powerful." Therefore, when the First Continental Congress convened in Philadelphia in the fall of 1774, the members of the Congress were selected from the "ablest and wealthiest men in America." John Jay, who would later become the first Chief Justice of the Supreme Court, was chosen as president. He believed that the upper classes "were the better kind of people, by which I mean the people who are orderly and industrious, who are content with their situation and not uneasy in their circumstances." His theory of government was simple: "The people who own the country ought to govern it."[15]

By 1776, according to Jackson Main, 10 percent of the white population—large landholders and merchants—owned nearly half the wealth of the country and held as slaves one-seventh of the country's people. As Howard Zinn correctly points out, the Framers were a "rising class of important people" who "needed to enlist on their side enough Americans to defeat England, without disturbing too much the relations of wealth and power that had developed over 150 years of colonial history." Unlike the situation in Pennsylvania, efforts of common people to build popular governments in most of the other states were defeated. In Massachusetts, for example, the new Constitutions of 1776 to 1780 increased rather than decreased property qualifications for voting. In Maryland, 90 percent of the population was excluded from holding office because of property qualifications.[16]

But the Framers were not out of the woods. In some respects, the war had exacerbated class conflict (the rich could buy their way out of the draft and officers received much more pay than common soldiers); more than once, common soldiers mounted attacks on the headquarters of the Continental Congress in Philadelphia, once forcing the members to flee to Princeton across the river. And in yet still other states (Delaware, Maryland, North Carolina, South Carolina, Georgia, and to a lesser degree, Virginia), the civil strife which was part of the challenge to elite domination persisted throughout the war. Elites did succeed in adding modifications to the new bills of rights in North Carolina, Maryland, New York, Georgia, and Massachusetts that stated that "nothing herein contained shall be construed to exempt preachers of treasonable or seditious discourses from legal trial and punishment." In other words, even after independence had been achieved, the possibility of a revolution remained.[17]

Military Defeat of the Common People: Shays Rebellion

Technically, Shays Rebellion was a rebellion over tax policies that took place in western Massachusetts. Politically, however, it was much more than that. It encompassed a series of defiant and militant showdowns that took place between the Framers and the common people in twelve of the thirteen states. The battles had less to do with taxes, as we shall see, and more to do with choosing the direction in which the new nation would move. Militarily, the common people were defeated in Massachusetts and in other states where skirmishes took place. In Philadelphia, at the Constitutional Convention, the Framers would consolidate their victory, and the common people would suffer a corresponding political defeat. Their hopes for community, for a moral economy, for localized political power, and for democracy would be dashed.

Although one-fourth of blacks in the North were held in slavery (30,000 blacks were enslaved in the North as late as 1810), during the 1780s the vast majority of white New Englanders, and perhaps the majority throughout the entire North, lived in a largely subsistence culture.[18] That is, as one yeoman farmer stated, a farm "provided me and my whole family a good living on the produce of it. Nothing to wear, eat, or drink was purchased, as my farm provided all." Near self-sufficiency generated feelings of self-mastery and independence, but not the independence of the individualistic "self-made I-pulled-myself-up-by-my-bootstraps" variety. Rather it was it was the sense of independence associated with *community*. Small white farmers lived in a community directed culture. Their sense of independence was linked to the cooperation and interdependence of friends and family at the community level.

Women often labored in the fields along with men. Members of extended families traded labor. Neighbors traded labor and animals. Payment and exchange in nearby towns was often in goods, services, and land. Craftspeople produced not for an abstract market, but in most cases limited production to items specifically needed and required by neighbors.

> Community help even extended to the new farmer in a village. "In America, a man is never alone, never an isolated being," observed Marquis de Chastellux in 1781. "The neighbors, for they are every where to be found, make it a point of hospitality to aid the new farmer. A cask of cider drank in common, and with gaiety, or a gallon of rum, are the only recompense for these services." During the 1780s, community cornhuskings, barn raisings, logrollings, and quilting bees symbolized the overall cooperation among rural New Englanders.[19]

Simply stated, common people within the white community seemed willing to take care of one another. Together, they had a greater appreciation of their common interests. Individual needs were understood, in part, as community needs.

These sets of needs and values were much different than the market-oriented approach to life pressed by the most important economic groups within coastal towns, the merchants, shopkeepers, lawyers, bankers, speculators, and commercial farmers—the class out of which the Framers emerged. The Framers and their allies sought greater economic development, expanded trade, and accumulated personal wealth. Initial gains were reinvested in order to realize increased profits. Sam Adams, for example, speculated in continental and state securities, buying them cheaply and hoping the government would back them with gold. A well known Boston lawyer in 1785 stated, "Money is the only object attended to, and the only acquisition that commands respect." Individualism and competition were accepted and celebrated. Boston wholesaler Thomas Hancock made clear the impoverished sense of community merchants shared when he said, "As to the profit you get on your goods its your look out, not mine. I expect my money of you when it's due."[20]

In the mind of the Framers, it was "every man for himself." This deserves special emphasis because it was this understanding of political and economic (social) behavior that helps us to grasp the meaning of Shays Rebellion and later the Constitution itself. Freedom in the minds of the Framers was both freedom from others and freedom to accumulate wealth. Given this concept of freedom, community, becomes less like a family and more like a market where relations revolve around exchange. The Framers feared communities that were networks of mutual concern and mutual obligation, for when moral considerations based on traditional and community values come into play, the property owners and the money lenders are restricted to what the community has to say about how resources are used. In the Framers' world, the community becomes a set of exchanges between producers and consumers, owners and workers. People are free individuals (free from traditional, moral, or community values) in a free market, freely pursuing self-interest. The social order is held together, not on the basis of tradition or a sense of mutual responsibility but by impersonal *contracts*. With the rise of contractual relations, particularly in a society with great inequality, power is shifted away from people who were recognized as being able to interpret traditional, moral, and community rules (often religious leaders, elders, healers) toward those who owned great amounts of property and money. In addition a coercive agency is required to enforce contracts. As Howard Zinn argues, "To protect everyone's contracts seems like an act of fairness, of equal treatment, until one considers that contracts made between rich and poor, between employer and employee, landlord and tenant, creditor and debtor, generally favor the more powerful of the two parties. Thus, to protect these contracts is to put the great power of the government, its laws, courts, sheriffs, police, on the side of the privilege."[21]

The role of the state in this setting is the key to making the market system work. It's function is to make sure the relations of exchange keep on going, to help expand or create markets (especially with regard to capital and labor), to subsidize or protect key industries, to protect the property of those who have it, to guarantee contracts, to insure that foreign or critical ideologies don't take hold, and to use force, if necessary, in each of these undertakings.

Proponents of the new market political economy argued that it was natural, self-evident, and divinely inspired. But like all systems, it was and is not neutral. It carries with it historically specific biases which have been the source of protest to this day. In the world of individualistic competition, each person confronts every other person as a competitor and potential enemy. The individual freedom to become rich and separated from community is valued more highly than the rewards of family-like bonds found in a cooperative community. Moral standards tend to give way to standards of efficiency and productivity. Nature loses its spiritual significance and becomes a resource. Compassion and a genuine concern for others is too frequently shuffled into and contained within the private sphere, in families or love relations, or in the church. Mutual responsibility and the obligations of family and community—those troublesome, ethical, sticky, personal, emotional realms of human experience—are split off and given to women, generally, to worry about. Egoism, ambition, and upward mobility are encouraged. The stratification of society is viewed as natural, not a product of human actions.

The Framers, by virtue of the Constitution, would finally place the power, legitimacy, and force of the state squarely behind these new market values and the privilege of private elites. But keep in mind that the urgency with which they undertook that task was due to the fact that during an economic downturn during the mid-1780s, when the Framers pushed their market-relations hard, common people held fast to their vision of community, did everything they could to peacefully defend it, and then in a last desperate attempt to hang on, they fought back.

The trouble really started when merchants and coastal wholesalers got stuck, following the War of Independence, in their attempt to re-establish large-scale trade with Great Britain. British officials, who now viewed the United States as a foreign nation (and one with whom they had lost a war), decided to play hard ball. They denied New England merchants access to the lucrative British West Indies market and they demanded that the U.S. merchants pay for imports in specie (hard money or what we might say "in cash"). In other words, British officials stopped giving credit.

The wholesalers then turned around and demanded hard money or cash from retail shopkeepers in inland regions. Country store owners then turned around and demanded that farmers immediately pay back their loans in cash. But farmers, quite accustomed to the cooperative relationships in the community, felt that these demands were unwarranted and rather selfish. Besides, they had been used to paying back their loans in crops, goods, and labor. Farmers found themselves being dragged into debtor court and threatened with the loss of their land. Others were threatened with jail for unpaid debts.

Merchants had difficulty collecting debts so they tried taking legal action. In the farming community of Hampshire County Massachusetts, 32.4 percent of the county's men over sixteen were hauled into court from 1784 to 1786. The jail conditions were often abominable. In one cell, twenty-six prisoners were held without proper food or ventilation. Prisoners developed boils and sores. Some even died. To compound matters, some state governments such as Massachusetts which were practically instruments of the merchant class decided to help merchants out by shifting the tax burden away from the merchants and onto the farmers. Moreover, the increased tax burden had to be paid in hard money. The justification given for this tax policy was that it would help to promote commerce.[22]

Notice the role of the state. It was protecting the interests and values of the merchant class and the market system in general. In Hampshire county, not a single retailer went to jail. This of course was the great issue. One farmer stated that "it cost them much to maintain the *Great Men* under George the 3rd, but vastly more under the Commonwealth and Congress."[23]

The common people started with peaceful protest. They worked through the existing legislatures hoping for a "traditional world in which men are justly dealt with, not a perfect world." Specifically they sought paper money and tender laws (bartering), legislation which would have permitted them to acquire credit and a way to pay it that was compatible with a self-sufficient way of life and community values. In states where the legislature was controlled by mercantile interests, they organized town meetings and county conventions. Easily a majority of the people demanded paper money; the *New Hampshire Gazette* reported that "three-quarters at least, and more likely seven-eights of the people" wished that "paper money on loan be made by government."[24]

Notice the key features of this movement: 1) A *majority* of common people, at least in New England and perhaps across the country wanted a particular piece of legislation. But just as a majority of people today may want an end to Contra funding or a nuclear weapons freeze, such policies continue because they are policies which are considered as imperative in order to protect the interests of the most powerful class. As we shall see, the Constitution was designed to protect the few property owners from the majority. 2) Because of property qualifications and the location of capitals in the coastal areas, the merchant class was given disproportionate influence in most states. The creation of popular assemblies by farmers was a way to make *political power available at the local level.* It was a way to involve the majority in meaningful political decisions. These would-be rebels were doing what they were supposed to be doing—working together and advancing workable and feasible legislation. The Constitution would further weaken local political power and insure that it was centralized at the national level. 3) The issue was not just economic. It was social, cultural, and moral as well. Small landholders in Middleboro, Massachusetts believed that the depreciation that would be created by the issuing of paper money would enable them to escape the "most pressing demands" of the "wealthy and overbearing sets of men who can build up their fortunes on the ruins of the country in its present distressed situation." Other farmers criticized those "who have a greater love to their own interest than they have to that of their neighbors." The Constitution would firmly establish market rules as the law of the land.[25]

In this context it is worth noting the actual plight of most merchants. Few merchants were without assets. Many owned large farms, had assets in stock and trade, investments in factories, and received support from wealthy kin. "Probably most important," writes David Szatmary, "merchants had no legal obligation to discharge postwar debts owed to foreign creditors." In other words, the debt or liquidity problem could have been solved collectively, or democratically, with the full participation of all parties. But it would have meant an entirely different social order, one based more upon respect for all people, and the sharing of political and economic power. For merchants, this was unthinkable. At issue for them was political and economic privilege and how to protect it with the development of a strong, sovereign state. They wanted to protect their credit because they believed that the future success of *their* enterprises depended on it. And they want to protect their political power. Coastal elites, of whom the Framers were a part, strongly condemned the creation of popular assemblies as subverting the principle of "free and rational government." They were, said one elite, "treasonable to the state" in that they "support a government of their own making."[26]

So for elites, there was no question of cooperation or of figuring out a way to help each other. There was no respect for genuine dissent or for a different point of view if it conflicted with their self-interests. They argued that contracts were "sacred things," that the "right of property is a sacred right." The right of property said one Connecticut merchant, who captured the essence of the Framer's thinking, was the "one most religiously to be respected by every society, that in these modern times wishes to flourish."[27]

As tax collectors carried off hogs and horses and as courts seized land, farmers, "living in a community-oriented society...were indignant at the plight of friends and relatives." By the end of 1786, armed uprisings, often directed at stopping court proceedings, involving almost 9,000 militants or roughly one-quarter of the "fighting men" in rural areas, had broken out in Maine, Vermont, New Hampshire, Massachusetts, and Connecticut. David Humphreys of Connecticut dashed off a letter to George Washington: "We have prevented an emission of paper money and tender laws from taking place." By mid-1787, uprisings had spread to Pennsylvania, Virginia, South Carolina, Maryland, and New Jersey. In Rhode Island, debtors had taken over the legislature and were issuing paper money. In North Carolina, New York, and Georgia legislatures passed either tender laws or issued paper money.[28]

Meanwhile, coastal merchants who had in 1785 pressured the Massachusetts legislature to adopt a resolution "to propose to the several states a convention of delegates for the express purpose of a general revision of the Confederation" were moving fast to change the laws of the land and weaken the power of the states through the creation of a national government. By June1786, Rufus King, co-author of the Constitution, noted that "the merchants through all the states are of one mind, and in favor of a national system." In September of 1786, several hundred men had surrounded the legislature in New Hampshire and demanded paper money. Daniel Shays, with 700 armed farmers, closed down court proceedings in Springfield, Massachusetts. And in September of 1786, merchant delegates from five states met at Annapolis to consider plans for a national government. They recommended that they call for a convention in Philadelphia in May of 1787. Eight of the twelve states that sent delegates to the Convention chose their delegates from October 16, 1787 to February 28, 1787, the period when the rebellion was most threatening. George Washington correctly noted that the rebellions had so alarmed state leaders that "most of the legislatures have appointed and the rest will appoint delegates to meet at Philadelphia." James Madison also linked the motivation of the delegates at the Constitutional Convention to Shays Rebellion. He said that the rebellion in the states "contributed more to that uneasiness which produced the Convention…than those…from the inadequacy of the Confederation…."[29]

Early in 1787, Daniel Shays began, in what was the boldest rebel action, a march on Boston with 1,000 men. Militarily, the action, not unlike the insurrection in general, was a failure. The militants fought in several skirmishes in a number of states, but were defeated in each of them, their leaders arrested, several sentenced to death, and several were hanged. But as the Framers convened in Philadelphia, small bands of farmers continued cross-border raids from New York into Massachusetts and attacked the homes of retailers, professionals, and military leaders. As late as June 8, after the Framers had been meeting for three weeks, farmers in Maryland and South Carolina were still blocking the consideration of debt suits, and in one incident forced a sheriff who was serving a writ to "eat it on the spot."

Some Things To Remember

In 1976, the bicentennial year of the "American Revolution," a play was performed in the western Massachusetts town of Northampton about Shays Rebellion which led the audience to believe that the Constitutional Convention which followed gave expression to the values and interests of the common people. It implied that the Constitution was a people's document. It set things right, fixed things up, and let the majority rule. Such was not the case.

The Framers were not simply supporting the merchant class against the common people, they *were* the merchant class. They were the champions of market values. It was against them that the common people fought. It should not surprise us that an issue today which finds currency and which is captured by the slogan "People before Property" was an issue then. Time and again, merchant leaders, the Framers among them, were concerned that the general effort by common people to equalize the burden of an economic crisis and preserve bonds of mutual responsibility would undermine the "security of property." Henry Knox, a Framer who did not attend the Convention, stated that unless the government is "strengthened...there is no security for liberty and property." Edward Rutledge, a Framer who did not attend the Convention, argued that the rebels would "stop little short of a distribution of property—I speak of a general distribution" and that would destroy commercial exchange and lead to economic ruin. Oliver Ellsworth, co-author of the Constitution, felt that it was a "favorable moment to shut and bar the door against paper money" and tender laws which had "disgust[ed]...the respectable part of America." George Washington, co-author, worried that the rebellion "sunk our national character much below par," bringing U.S. "credit to the brink of a precipice." Keep in mind the priority which property has in the mind of the Framers when we examine the Constitution itself.[30]

It is also important to remember how swiftly the Framers turned to repressive measures to curb political expression *when that expression did not accommodate their system of privilege.* When the protest began, for example, Sam Adams engineered a Riot Act which prohibited twelve or more armed persons from congregating in public and which empowered county sheriffs to kill rioters. If convicted under the act, rioters would "forfeit all their lands, tenements, goods, and chattels, to the common wealth" and would be "whipped thirty-nine stripes on the naked back, at the public whipping post, and suffer imprisonment for a term not exceeding twelve months, nor less than six months." Massachusetts suspended the writ of *habeas corpus*. The state was also granted the power to arrest and imprison without bail for an indefinite period "in any part of the Commonwealth any person whom they shall suspect is unfriendly to government." Sam Adams's justification for these measures bears repeating because it underscores the attitude of the Framers toward revolutionaries which prevails to this day: "In monarchy the crime of treason may admit of being pardoned or lightly punished, but the man who dares rebel against the laws of a republic ought to suffer death." The right to revolution (for the middle class) advanced in the Declaration of Independence is here taken back—for good.[31]

At the Constitutional Convention, the Framers made clear their desire to enact coercive measures which would counter the revolutionary impulse that had been bubbling to the surface for twenty-five years. Alexander Hamilton told the Convention in June, "A certain portion of military force is absolutely necessary in large communities. Massachusetts is now feeling the necessity." George Mason added, "If the General Government should have no right to suppress rebellions against particular states, it will be in a bad situation indeed." Mason then argued for national control of the militia. James Madison agreed, "without such a power to suppress insurrections, *our* liberties might be destroyed by domestic faction (emphasis added)." Charles Pinckney, not having faith in the state militia, called for a national army: "There must also be a real military force. This alone can effectively answer the purpose. The United States have been making an experiment without it, and we see the consequences in their rapid approaches to anarchy." John Langdon: "The apprehension of the national force will have a salutary effect in preventing insurrections." In Article I, Section 8 of the Constitution, Congress was given the ability, finally, to "raise and support armies."[32]

Article IV, Section 4 of the Constitution reads that the United States "shall protect" every state "on application of the legislature, or of the executive (when the legislature cannot be convened), against domestic violence." James Wilson explained, "I believe it is generally not known on what a perilous tenure we held our freedom and independence....The flames of internal insurrection were ready to burst out in every quarter...and from one end to the other of the continent, we walked in ashes concealing fire beneath our feet." The guarantee clause (just cited) "is merely to secure the states against dangerous commotions, insurrections, and rebellions." The delegates also agreed that the writ of *habeas corpus* could be suspended "in cases of rebellion" (Article I, Section 9). A clause intended to prevent rebels from hiding in bordering states as the Shaysites had done was also added. Article IV, Section 2 in part reads, "A person charged in any state with treason, felony, or other crime, who shall flee from justice, and be found in another state, shall, on demand of the executive authority of the state from which he fled, be delivered up, to be removed to the state having jurisdiction of the crime." A similar clause relating to fugitive slaves can be found in the same section.[33]

The swiftness of the Framers to quickly and forcibly snuff out the dissent of common people who dare to be equal was demonstrated again in the Whiskey Rebellion of 1794. Western Pennsylvania farmers who understood clearly that the new federal Constitution had taken political power from them, refused to pay a tax on whiskey (which had been used as currency) that had been forced on them by a commercial elite. Some 7,000 western Pennsylvanians marched against the town of Pittsburgh, feigned an attack on Fort Pitt which held a federal arsenal, and destroyed the property of some prominent people there. Washington dispatched Hamilton along with 12,950 troops, the "army of the Constitution, to the troubled area in order to put down the "enemies of order." Because of the measures provided by the Constitution, the Whiskey Rebellion, unlike that of Shays, was immediately crushed.[34]

The rebellions of 1776-1787 were an attempt on the part of the majority of white common people to establish a political and economic system that departed radically from the aristocratic paternalism of the colonial era. Indentured servants, blacks, Native Americans, and women (although women who met property qualifications could vote in New Jersey until 1807) were excluded. Yet small farmers and artisans did resist the vision of the commercial elites of a "splendid empire," of a distant, impersonal, and arbitrary centralized government. Their vision was not that of a wealthy world power, but of community, free from the greed and lust for power that had marked the commercial empire of Great Britain. They placed their hope in retaining and building upon the vitality of local self-government, on town meetings, popular assemblies, recall, and referenda.

Ralph Ketcham summarizes the general attitude of those opposed to the Constitution this way: the decency found amid family, church, school, and other community oriented institutions could "impinge directly and continuously on government" so that it too might be expressive of human decency. Each town or district or ward or region was to have its own and be conscious of its particular identity rather than being some "amorphous, arbitrary geographic entity. Only with such intimacy could the trust, good will, and deliberation essential to wise and virtuous public life be a reality." Anthing else, for them, would not be self-government.[35]

This is not to say that the vision of the common people in question did not embody values that contributed to domination and subordination of various sorts, particularly with regard to race and gender. Yet it is clear that many common people within the white community consciously sought to establish a political economy that would prevent the arrogant and oppressive rule of people who accepted privilege as a natural right. From the point of view of the Framers this was the wrong kind of political economy, the wrong kind of vision. They had never really gone beyond the British vision of empire, of commercial growth, westward expansion, and increased national and international power and prestige. To them, the "levelling tendencies" unleashed by the War of Independence had gone too far. They sought a centralized national government, the ability to coercively suppress internal dissident movements, to regulate trade, to protect private property, and to subsidize industries which would drive the economy and the nation forward to greater horizons of productivity, comfort, and wealth. They wanted, in short, the "essence of the British imperial system restored in the American states." And "in the name of the people they engineered a conservative counter-revolution and erected a nationalistic government whose purpose in part was to thwart the will of 'the people' in whose name they acted."[36]

The Constitution: Resurrection of An Imperial System

> [O]ur...Founding Fathers, knew the ideas, language, and reality of empire....It became...synonymous with the realization of their Dream....Under the leadership of Madison, the...convention of 1787...produced (behind locked doors) the Constitution. Both in the mind of Madison and in its nature, the Constitution was an instrument of imperial government at home and abroad.
>
> **—William Appleman Williams**[1]

We tend to think of the Constitution as having been written with the full blessing and approval of "the people." Such was not the case. The delegates had agreed to a rule of secrecy. Few knew what had gone on at the convention or what anyone had said until 1840. The *Federalist Papers* had been published but they were more a defense of Constitutional principles than a record of what had transpired at the convention. It was fifty-three years after the Constitution had been written that notes of the convention discussions were made public. The reason for secrecy was fairly simple. When the Constitution was completed, "the majority of the people were completely against it."[2] The majority of the people the document which was the constitution of the United States from 1781 to 1789, the Articles of Confederation.

Under the Articles there was no Senate or Supreme Court or President. There was just one branch of government, the Congress. A centralized government that could pass uniform legislation and coerce the states to go along or use force to put down rebellions had disappeared with the Declaration of Independence and the Articles were designed to keep it that way. There was wide agreement, particularly among the middle and lower classes that whatever the new government was to be in the United States, it should not be like the highly centralized, strongly national government of Great Britain. Rather, political power should be as close to the local level as possible; and it should be decentralized, broken down into many parts which could be brought together into a congress. But that was it. Distant, impersonal, centralized government in which a few had power over the many was feared and thought to be counter to the purpose of the struggle for independence.

The states were completely equal, each having a delegation with one vote. Congress settled disputes between the states. Elections were held every year. Declarations of war, military build-ups, or even treaties had to first have the approval of at least nine of the thirteen states. Congress could not stop a state from issuing paper money. On a regular basis, Congress could only tax to raise money for the Post Office. There were severe restrictions on holding office and a conscious effort to limit individual power. No one could be a member of Congress for more than three out of any six years; no one could be president of Congress for more than one year out of any three. Members could be recalled at any time by their respective state governments. States were not permitted to keep vessels of war in peacetime or maintain troops (unless for defense and with the approval of Congress).

Perhaps the greatest defect of the Articles was an inability to enforce or create unity. States could go their separate ways or fail to respond to particular rulings and nothing could be done about it. The Articles were also an obstacle to the development of national and international relations of trade. Congress lacked the power to regulate or coordinate interstate or foreign trade or even develop a uniform currency. Nor did it have the power to tax. The groups most troubled by the weaknesses of the Articles were those whose own private businesses were dependent upon the protection of interstate and international markets. Interstate and international trade barriers, for example, greatly interfered with merchants and producers implicated in the market economy. Emergent manufacturers were interested in protective tariffs. Many of the plantation owners and merchants were also land speculators and moneylenders; hence they were interested in creating a strong military power which could force or use the threat of force to compel Native Americans, slaves, debtors, or similarly disadvantaged people to act in accordance with their interests, both domestically and internationally.

There was generally agreement across classes (that were permitted to express themselves politically) that the Articles needed to be strengthened. The sovereignty of the nation depended upon it. But among the common people of those classes the issue was how best to *amend* the Articles. But for a few very powerful Framers, such as George Washington, John Dickinson, Charles Carroll, Robert Morris, Gouverneur Morris, James Wilson, and Alexander Hamilton, the issue was not how to amend the Articles. They had never supported the Articles to begin with.[3] For them the goal was to restructure the government entirely. The "inferior" people or "men of more humble, more rural origins, less educated, and with more parochial interests"[4] had too much political influence; they had used state legislatures, in some instances, to curb private economic power and expansion in the interest of community. John Lloyd worried that "Gentlemen of property" too frequently lost electoral contests to men from the "lower classes." Elbridge Gerry seems to have had a similar concern when he said that if western farmers obtained influence equal to that of eastern merchants they would "oppress commerce, and drain out wealth into the Western Country."[5]

The Framers preferred a system more like Great Britain in which the "better" people had the authority to use the state to promote the expansion of a private economy independently of what the "inferior" people might think is in their best interest. They believed, paraphrasing John Locke, that "having more in proportion than the rest of the World, or than our Neighbours, whereby we are enabled to procure to ourselves a greater Plenty of the Conveniences of Life" was the end to which the state should be committed. Empire is freedom. It is natural. It is our right.

A Coup d'état

Although it is a misnomer, those who supported the Framers in their effort to ratify the Constitution have been called "federalists." Those who opposed the Constitution and favored the federal form of government provided by the Articles of Con*federation* have been misleadingly referred to as "*anti*-federalists." The Framers who were pushing for a Constitutional Convention wanted a national government, not a federation of states, and would have been more accurately labeled "nationalists." Most people, however, feared a national government so the Framers, in order to align themselves with those who responded well to the idea of a federation of states, began calling themselves federalists and their opponents anti-federalists. Not only did this disguise their intentions but the term "anti-federalist" made opponents of the Constitution seem obstructionist and negative.

The series of meetings that led to the convention were engineered by men who did not like the Articles. They were part of an elite consensus that was forming in reaction to the many rebellions (black and white) and democratic tendencies among excluded people and it was their private meetings that led to the initiative for the Constitutional Convention. At every turn, the popular voice was absent, and elites were increasingly empowered. *No special popular elections were held to select delegates.* Instead, delegates to the Convention were selected by the state legislatures, who were already once removed from the limited electorate. Moreover, the Constitutional Convention had been called to *amend the Articles only* and any proposed changes *had to be approved by all the states before they were adopted.* But the Framers defied these legal stipulations, abandoned their authorization to amend the Articles only, designed an entirely new centralized national government, and inserted in the Constitution that it should go into effect when ratified by *only nine states.* J. W. Burgess has stated that what the Framers "actually did, stripped of all fiction and verbiage, was to assume constituent powers, ordain a constitution of government and liberty and demand a *plebiscite* thereon over the heads of all existing legally organized powers. Had Julius or Napoleon committed these acts, they would have been pronounced *coup d'état.*"

The Constitution of the United States

A National System

At the most fundamental level the Constitution went beyond the Articles in the following way. The new Constitution (Article I, Sections 8 and 10) simply swept away the sovereignty of the states in the areas of war and treaty-making, coining money, emitting bills of credit, and impairing the obligation of contracts. These sections also placed the state militia under control of the national government, authorized the national government to tax directly and raise a national army and navy, and gave the national government the new powers to regulate commerce and establish a national currency. Article IV, Section 3 gave the national government the power to dispose of western territories. And to make clear the supremacy of the national government vis-à-vis the states, and Article III, Section 2 and Article IV stipulated that national laws, treaties, and judicial power are superior to those of the states.

The sweep of these changes is breath-taking. First, note that the national government was now in a position to protect and develop markets (and with a national army and navy this could be done forcibly), protect manufacturers, develop a capital market by paying creditors in full, raise revenue directly, and do all this without having to wait for the approval or compliance of the states. The ability of the states to help out the debtor or disadvantaged by emitting bills of credit or by modifying contracts was outlawed. Consequently, just as so many Framers had wanted,[6] military force was now available and authorized to be used against recalcitrant states or insurgents. Quite plainly, political power at the local level had been significantly reduced. In fact, the Framers "failed to provide any Constitutional guarantees for the lowest level of government, the municipalities...[where] political enthusiasm and activity of the American citizens had developed and flourished."[7] In other words, the development of an economy based upon impersonal market relations and the rational self-interested individual could go forward with full swing.

In short, a major change occurred quickly. Power was shifted from the local and state levels to the national level. This meant that political power was now concentrated in not only a few hands but in those fewer hands that held considerable wealth and economic power. The new national system assured the "commercial and financial interests...that ...potentially unpopular rules and practices would nevertheless be enforced reliably and consistently....The ability to change the economy, to deal with substantive public policy issues such as the distribution of wealth and fiscal and monetary measures, was effectively removed from popular control."[8] With the erosion of a way of life based upon production for use and the encouragement of one based upon production for profit, the space for collective discussion, resistance, or non-compliance was drastically narrowed. Thus the function of the federal government was clarified. Its purpose was to protect property essential to a commercial economy (contracts, bonds, and credit) and promote the expansion and development of market relations. We may say then that the role of the government as established by the Constitution, at least implicitly, was that *of an instrument of private power* both in the political sense of limiting meaningful popular involvement and in the economic sense of imperial expansion. David Smith notes that the "imperial organization designed to advance England's foreign trade, to protect her colonial interests in North America...was the parent...of American Federalism."[9]

Checks and Balances

One indication of how poorly we understand our political system is that we celebrate the concept of checks and balances as a hallmark of democracy. It is not. Checks and balances limits public power (the government), especially the power of the people, and thereby expands private power (owners of productive property and capital) which is left largely unaccountable to the public. It is, if anything, a hallmark of *lack* of democracy and reflects the Framers' admiration of Great Britain and their identification with imperial thinking. The Framers set for themselves the task of designing an imperial system that would be legitimized by the consent of the governed. In the context of eighteenth-century thinking, consent of the governed included constitutional monarchy where the monarch's powers were limited and where the government included an assembly elected by the people. But any influence in the government by common or "inferior" people raised the possibility that the poor could challenge the rich, public power could be used to challenge private power. Note Madison's remarks:

> ...as had been observed (by Mr. Pinckney) we had not among us those hereditary distinctions of rank which were a great source of the contests in the ancient governments as well as the modern States of Europe...We cannot, however, be regarded even at this time as one homogeneous mass....In framing a system which we wish to last for ages, we should not lose sight of the changes which ages will produce. An increase of population will of necessity increase the proportion of those who will labor under all the hardships of life, and secretly sigh for a more equal distribution of its blessings. These may in time outnumber those who are placed above the feelings of indigence. According to the equal laws of suffrage, the power will slide into the hands of the former.

In order to prevent common people from having an equal say in public affairs and to safeguard private power in general by limiting public power, the Framers chose to discard the arrangement under the Articles of Confederation where the important powers of government were vested in a single legislature and resurrect England's aristocratic system of "checks and balances." The purpose of checks and balances was this: public power would be "checked," especially the House of Representatives which was closest to the people. Moreover, the House of Representatives would be "balanced" by the interests of property by giving property owners a greater voice in two ways: 1) the Presidency and the Senate would be elected directly by property owners through the electoral college and state legislatures respectively, and 2) the Presidency and the Senate would be given more power than the House in the government. John Adams, who once stated, "We have been told that our struggle has loosened the bonds of government everywhere; that children and apprentices were disobedient; that schools and colleges were grown turbulent; that Indians slighted their guardians, and negroes grew more insolent to their masters," was the supreme advocate of checks and balances. Although he was not at the convention, many of the delegates shared his desire that the structure of the new government should be modeled closely on the British Constitution.

In the British system, the House of Commons (common people or small property owners) was balanced by the House of Lords (aristocrats or large property owners) and the king. In this way, should "wicked projects" emerge from the "lower" house, such legislation could be checked by the "upper" house or if necessary by the executive, in this case the king. Again we can see that common people, in this model, are distrusted and that property owners are thought of as "better" or more "virtuous." That most of the Framers shared these assumptions and used these terms is well-documented.

The relationship of the Presidency and the Senate to the Congress was intended to parallel the checks and balances built into the British system; property, argued the Framers, was the stabilizing force. People with property are conservative and cautious. People without property have nothing to lose and engage in foolish experiments.[10] Therefore, the Framers chose to have an "upper house" or Senate which could check the House of Representatives, the "lower house." The Senate would represent property by virtue of representing entire states (as Madison correctly noted a very large district such as a state takes in a greater variety of parties and interests making it more difficult for underclass people to sustain a majority, not to mention the greater and prohibitive campaign costs) and by having Senators elected by state representatives (who were far more connected to property than the general electorate). Senators would also be given longer terms than members of the House (six years as opposed to two).

This design reversed the popular trend toward unicameral (single chamber) legislatures, small districts, annual elections, and rotation in office. Stated Edmund Randolph, if the task of the delegates was to "provide a cure for the evils under which the United States labored," then, "in tracing these evils to their origin every man had found it in the turbulence and follies of democracy: that some check therefore was to be sought for against this tendency of our governments: and that a good senate seemed most likely to answer the purpose."[11] Historian Arthur Lovejoy concludes that the intention of the Framers in adding a senate to the legislative branch was to insure that "the poor" could never get a law passed which would be unfavorable to the economic interests of "the rich." But for a general view, we need to come back to Madison, Father of the Constitution:

> The landed interest, at present, is prevalent, but in process of time...when the number of landholders shall be comparatively small...will not the landed interests be overbalanced in future elections? and, unless wisely provided against, what will become of our government? In England, at this day, if elections were open to all classes of people, the property of landed proprietors would be insecure. An agrarian law would take place. If these observations be just, our government ought to secure the permanent interests of the country against innovation. Landholders ought to have a share in the government, to support these invaluable interests, and to balance and check the other. They ought to be so constituted as to protect the minority of the opulent against the majority.

As Veron Parrington states, the "revolutionary conception of equalitarianism, that asserted the rights of man apart from property and superior to property, did not enter into their thinking...."[12]

Separation of Powers

Separation of powers refers to the fact that the Framers scattered each type of national power (legislative, judicial, and executive) among the various branches of government. For example, the President has the legislative power of the veto (Article I, Section 7), the Senate has the executive power of confirming certain appointments made by the President (Article II, Section 2), and the Congress and President are checked by judicial review (Article III, Section 2).[13] The separation of powers accomplishes several things. First we see that it is a continuation of checks. Some of the checks are upon the other branches as well. One reason for this is that the Framers, as elites within the private economy, sought mainly to protect their individual freedom as property owners from state intrusion. So they checked the legislative branch as well as the other branches through the separation of powers to insure protection from a misguided executive (which very well could be an executive responding to the demands of the people). The point is that as the national government was purposefully made inefficient, it would leave private power, or the power of business or corporate elites untouched. As Charles Beard points out, "None of the powers conferred by the Constitution on Congress permits a direct attack on property." Thus Madison argued in *Federalist No. 51*, "The constant aim is to divide and arrange the several offices in such a manner as that each may be a check on the other—that the private interest of every individual may be a sentinel over the public rights."

The check upon the executive branch by the legislative branch is not like the check by the other branches upon the legislative. It is not a distrust or an indictment of the virtue and wisdom of a class of poor people. It is a simple distrust of the government or public power and a belief that private or what we today would call corporate power or business is virtuous. Clearly, fear of the ability of common people to work their way through the legislature was far greater than the potential tyranny of the President. When asked how a system so inefficient could make any progress, Gouverneur Morris appears to have placed his faith in the paternalistic potential of the President: "It is necessary...that the Executive Magistrate should be the guardian of the people, even of the lower classes, against Legislative tyranny, against the great and wealthy who in the course of things will necessarily compose—the Legislative body."

The separation of powers was also intended to prevent the majority from "carry[ing] into effect schemes of oppression," that is, the egalitarian projects many small farmers had in mind. It does this because a majority of common people who gain control of the House can easily be checked by men of property who are (or were) not directly elected by the people: the Senate (elected by state legislatures then, Article I, Section 3), the President (elected by an electoral college appointed by the states, Article II, Section 1), or the Judiciary (appointed by the President and confirmed by the Senate, Article II, Section 2). Here we find full expression given to Madison's well known defense of the Constitution in *Federalist No. 10:* "Extend the sphere and you take in a greater variety of parties and interests; you make it less probable that a majority of the whole will have a common motive to invade the rights of other citizens; or if such a common motive exists, it will be more difficult for all who feel it to discover their own strength and to act in unions with each other." Empowerment of common people was not one of the aims of the Framers.

Representation

Veron Parrington notes that the Constitution represented the first written safeguard against tyranny, "but it was aimed at the encroachments of agrarian majorities rather than at Tory minorities....An honest appeal to the people was the last thing desired by the Federalists...."[14] Similarly, J. Allen Smith has stated that "[I]t was the almost unanimous sentiment of the convention that the less the people had to do with the government the better."[15] This is a terribly important point for it goes to the heart and soul of the Constitution. We know for, for example, that the Framers understood that a very large segment of the voting population, perhaps a majority, had wanted paper money or tender laws. Yet in Article I, Section 10, the impairment clause which we noted above prevents states from emitting bills of credit or interfering with contracts, and therefore quite clearly violates popular if not majority sentiment on this point. The Framers, while hoping to incorporate a broad range of views, wanted to create a political system in which the views of the "virtuous," "more industrious," "better" people—those with "established characters," the rich and wealth property owners, could easily dominate and overcome popular will when necessary. The Framers sought to design a political system that would end the opportunity of the bulk of small property owners to meet at the grassroots level, engage in prolonged discussions, and exercise considerable political influence. This was done through the creation of a system of representation in which, using Madison's words, the "opulent" minority would be protected from the majority by "isolated compartments," "refinement," "enlarged spheres," and "filtration."

Most people were not permitted to vote. The Framers, with some exceptions, particularly Franklin, wanted to restrict the suffrage to those who owned property. But they could not agree on how much or what kind of property should be counted. So in Article I, Section 2, they let the states decide. Women (except in New Jersey), slaves, Native Americans, and many poor people were excluded. One may say that all this has changed, that the exclusion of the majority reflected eighteenth-century thinking. And while it is true that no ethnic group or gender is legally barred from voting, the elitist principles that run through the Constitution and influence it at every turn to favor the propertied class still leave "the people" without a powerful voice. Just how little the people were to be consulted was framed in the following way by Madison: "The danger of disturbing the public tranquility by interesting too strongly the public passions is a still more serious objection against a frequent reference of constitutional questions to the decisions of the whole society." While amendments to the Constitution might empower people superficially in the short-term, they do not change or alter its character, purpose, the general values which it embodies, or its fundamental design.[16] Never has a U.S. president been elected by a majority of the nation's adult citizens. And, to a large degree, this is due to the fact that the Constitution was designed to discourage, not encourage, the participation of the majority.

The Father of the Constitution explains the meaning of representation in *Federalist No. 10* this way: The effect of a representative system, as opposed to a democracy, is "to refine and enlarge the public views by passing them through the medium of a chosen body of citizens, whose wisdom may best discern the true interest of their country and whose patriotism and love of justice will be least likely to sacrifice it to temporary or partial considerations...the public voice, pronounced by the representatives of the people, will be more consonant to the public good than if pronounced by the people themselves...." Understanding that the public good and private rights (or property rights) are equated for Madison, and understanding the value which the Framers placed upon economic development, privilege, and the linkage of individual freedom and affluence, we may conclude that one function of elected representatives is to guard the "better people" against the majority when the majority entertains ideas which challenge inequality, privilege, and/or private property. To put it more simply, representatives were never intended to be among us, carrying our views forward. They were intended (given the checks and balances, separation of powers, and the indirect election of the President and Senate) to be among the "better people" who are above us, who speak and think for us, and tell us what we need.

Whenever "the people" do make demands and become active, it is always a crisis for elites. The demands of the people at the time of the convention were described as "excess democracy" by Elbridge Gerry and "rampant democracy" by James Madison. We shall note in Chapter 5 that after a number of previously disaffected groups such as blacks, students, women, Chicanos, and Native Americans became politically active during the 1960s and 1970s, corporate elites referred to the fuller participation among disadvantaged constituencies as a form of "distemper" and a "crisis of democracy." Elites, quite consistent with the values of the Framers, have always perceived the active political engagement of people without property as a crisis. John Quincy Adams, in a bit of understatement, reminds us that the Framers did not profess to be "slavish adorers of our sovereign lords the people."[17]

The Majority Does Not Rule

Kenneth M. Dolbeare and Murray J. Edelman have identified several ways in which the "Framers built into the Constitution layer upon layer of obstacles to simple majority rule" because they feared the "redistribution of property by the masses." In addition to the built-in checks and balances, separation of powers, the property-biased system of representation, they add: 1) "Amendment of the Constitution is very difficult, requiring a vote of two-thirds of both houses of Congress and ratification by three-quarters of the states," (Article V); and 2) "The electoral college is a device designed to give discretionary power to the elected delegates and deny the people direct choice of the President," (Article II, Section 1).[18]

Note also that the principle found in the Declaration of Independence that revolution is a right of people ("That whenever any Form of Government becomes destructive of these ends [life, liberty, and the pursuit of happiness] it is the Right of the People to alter or to abolish it.") has been eliminated altogether in the Constitution. To be sure, the Framers in 1776 only had the white male middle to upper classes in mind when they framed the right to revolt. The Constitution, however, not only eliminates any encouragement to revolt, it makes revolution virtually impossible. With the state militia under federal jurisdiction, with the creation of a national army, the authorization to suspend *habeas corpus* (or lock people up without giving a reason), and put down domestic insurrections, the risks entailed in challenging political authority are greatly enlarged.

Also, given the system of checks and balances and separation of powers, the Framers believed that the citizen was adequately safeguarded from the abuse of governmental power and therefore the citizen's right to revolt is made invalid. Remember this was the reason Sam Adams gave for suggesting that participants in Shays Rebellion ought to be killed on the spot. It is ironic, although not surprising, that the Framers entertained no safeguards against *private* power or what today is called corporate power. It is ironic also that the Framers would exaggerate to rather hysterical proportions the threat to their privileges posed by the legislative demands put forward by small farmers and the political participation of common people in general. Surely had any of them been enslaved or made to endure the discipline and despotism of the nineteenth-century factories, or the everyday abuse many citizens today experience on the job, they would have found their own justification of withdrawing the right to revolt, namely that the citizen is protected from *public* power, to be wholly irrelevant. In the words of one anti-federalist, because the national government would have its own army and would be able to command the state militia, "the last Resource of a free People is taken away."[19]

Anti-federalist Opposition

Although most common people were against the creation of a national government, opposition to the Constitution extended into all classes. Many slaveowners, for example, feared the creation of a national government, whose power was greater than the states, would be able to interfere with the private practice of human enslavement. In Connecticut the ideas of the nationalists were feared because they were:

founded on Principles Subvertive of a Republican Government
Tending to Destroy that Equallity among the citisans which [is] the
only permanent foundation on which it can be supported to throw
an excessive Power, the constant attendant of property into the
Hands of the Few, to cherish those anti-republican Principles &
feelings which are now predominant in many of the states and
finally to dissolve our present Happy and Benevolent Constitution
& to erect on the Ruins, a proper Aristocracy: wherein the Body
of the People are excluded from all share in the Government, and
the Direction & management of the state is committed to the Great
& Powerful alone.[20]

General comments following the Convention were that the
Framers had gone too far. "The natural Course of Power is to make the
many Slaves to the few." Another objected to the Constitution because
"the bulk of the people can have nothing to say to it. The government
is not a government of the people." The "men of Fortune" would not
feel for the "Common People." An "aristocratical tyranny" would arise,
in which "the great will struggle for power, honor and wealth, the poor
become a prey to avarice, insolence, and oppression." Even John Quincy Adams would write in his diary that the Constitution was "calculated
to increase the influence, power and wealth of those who have any already." In South Carolina, when the "backcountry" learned of ratification, "the people had a Coffin painted black, which borne in funeral
procession, was solemnly buried, as an emblem of the dissolution and
internment of publick Liberty…."

More specifically, anti-federalists felt that the House of Representatives had been made too weak and should control the legislative
process as well as the executive and complained that it was now nothing but an "assistant Aristocratical Branch." They thought that the President had been given too much power, that "he" was an elective king
"vested with power dangerous to a free people" and that the electoral
college was "an aristocratic junto." They complained that the general
structure seemed "to verge too much toward the British plan," that the
relation between the Senate and President looked too much like a king
and a House of Lords, that it equaled an oligarchy, and that the House
was nothing but a "pretended concession to democracy."

They believed that "In a free Government there never will be
Need of standing Armies," that the Framers appropriated both the

"powers of the purse and sword" because they "knew this was not a free government," and that "By far the greater part of the different nations, who have fallen from the glorious state of liberty, owe their ruin to standing armies."

And we find that criticisms of the Constitution were explicit with regard to its failure to respect democracy, although the term was used to mean a variety of political systems. Frequently anti-federalists said that they preferred a "democratick" system to an "aristocratick" and that the Constitution did not erect a "Democratick or Republican," government where democracy was generally defined as a political system that gave space to "the great body of the people, the middle and lower classes," as contrasted with "the few men of wealth and abilities" who comprised the "natural aristocracy."[21]

It is interesting to note that our own complaints of an "imperial presidency," that we feel powerless and that our votes do not count, that the "military-industrial complex" has too much power, that government seems distant and far away, or that corporations seem to dominate all aspects of our lives echo the complaints heard 200 years ago. It is not surprising. After all, it is still the same system, and in so many important respects the debate surrounding the adopting of the Constitution underlies contemporary class and racial divisions as well as debates over militarism, the environment, secret governments, and the spiritual well-being of our country.

Ratification

The majority of the people were against the Constitution. Not suprisingly, those who stood to gain from it directly, the wealthier and more professional, were enthusiastic. Before the Constitution was ratified, Hamilton noted that the supporters of the Constitution were "the good will of the commercial interest...[who want a government] capable of regulating, protecting and extending the commerce of the Union...[and] the good will of most men of property who wish a government of the Union able to protect them against domestic violence and

the depredations which the democratic spirit is apt make on property...." General Knox, in a letter to Washington, wrote, "The new constitution is received with great joy by all the commercial part of the
community." Numerous letters among elites share a similar conclusion.
And it was clear that the Framers understood where the opposition
came from and the nature of that opposition. Rufus King, a member of
the Massachusetts ratifying convention wrote to Madison that the opposition arose chiefly "from an opinion that is immovable, that...the
system is the production of the rich and ambitious, that they discover
its operations and that the consequences will be the establishment of
two orders in the Society, one comprehending the opulent and great
the other the poor and illiterate."

Keep in mind that the Framers, in order to overcome the majority
opposition, first wrote into the Constitution that it would not have to
be ratified by all the states to become law (as stipulated in the Articles)
but that only nine states had to ratify it. That meant that as many as five
states would have to oppose ratification in order for the Constitution
to be rejected. The strategy of the Framers was to move quickly before
opposition could organize properly. The first step was to get the approval of Congress (sitting in New York under the Articles) to approve
the Constitution and to pass it on to ratifying conventions that would
have to be selected. Charles Mee observes that before "opposition could
gather its forces...the plan was slipped dexterously past Congress."
They did this by sending the Constitution to Congress (one-third of
whom who were present had been delegates to the Constitutional Convention) only eight days after it had been signed. They also got Congress to put the words "Resolved unanimously" on the resolution calling
for the ratifying conventions, giving the impression that Congress had
supported the new Constitution unanimously. Richard Henry Lee, a
member of Congress who opposed the Constitution, said that the
Framers had stampeded the Congress and that they had begun the
ratification process with a nasty piece of trickery. There was more to
come.

Even before the Constitution had reached New York, some of the
Framers in Philadelphia were busy at work trying to get the Pennsylvania state legislature or Assembly to quickly set up a ratifying conven-

tion before they adjourned, for their session was about to end. Opponents objected, arguing that there was no rush, that the people had not even seen the Constitution. Nineteen assemblymen who had supported (what was then considered) the radically democratic Pennsylvania Constitution of 1776 decided to block the allies of the Framers by abstaining from the Assembly, thus preventing a quorum and forcing an adjournment. The delaying strategy worked for a time, but when news arrived the following day from New York that Congress had called for the states to select delegates for ratifying conventions, a federalist mob went into the homes of two of the more radical assemblymen and dragged them, protesting, through the streets of Philadelphia and into the Assembly hall, their clothes torn, their faces "white with rage." One of the physically restrained assemblymen tried to escape but they barred his exit. They then voted to set the date for selecting the delegates to the ratifying convention.[22]

Meanwhile in Philadelphia, as Mee observes, "Roving bands of supporters of the new constitution roamed the streets, banging on doors and lobbing rocks through windows."[23] The Constitution was eventually ratified in Pennsylvania. Anti-federalists, in an address to the people, however, noted that members had been "dragged to their seats and kept there against their wills, and so early a day was set for the election of delegates that many a voter did not know of it until it was passed...Of the seventy thousand freemen entitled to vote but thirteen thousand voted."

In Massachusetts, a less forceful but somewhat manipulative strategy was used by Constitutional supporters. When it appeared that the anti-federalists would easily reject the Constitution, federalists came up with a plan called a Conciliatory Proposition. Although the Framers had decided that there would be no second constitutional convention and that the ratification conventions were to simply ratify or reject the Constitution with no changes, the Conciliatory Proposition asked that amendments to the Constitution be proposed. The suggestion was that the amendments would be taken up as the first order of business for the new government. Knowing that their proposals were not binding, but believing that amending the Constitution was feasible, anti-federalists suggested nine amendments that would have, among other things, altered the federal government's power to tax and to govern elections. A proposal stating that Congress could not establish a "company of merchants with exclusive advantages of commerce" was also advanced. The strategy worked. The resistance was broken and Massachusetts ratified the Constitution. The proposed amendments were, for the most part, later pushed aside.[24]

A similar situation unfolded in Virginia when it was pointed out that Massachusetts had proposed amendments to be adopted at a later date. In long and very heated exchanges and with the outcome uncertain, the federalists, perhaps ingenuously, accepted every amendment put forth by the anti-federalists. The federalists won in Virginia by a vote of 89 to 79.

In New Hampshire, a majority of the delegates opposed the Constitution and they indicated that they would vote the way they had been instructed by their constituents even though they had begun to change their minds after having discussions with federalists. The federalists simply adjourned the convention and after a few months work were able to convert their opponents. The Constitution was supported by a vote of fifty-seven to forty-seven.

In New York, two-thirds of the selected delegates were opposed to the Constitution. The strength of the opposition in New York had moved Madison, Hamilton, and Jay to write the now famous *Federalist Papers* urging ratification of the Constitution. In any case, the federalist were able to secure yet another victory (by a vote of thirty to twenty-seven), this time by promising to work at once to call a second constitution convention, at which the Constitution could be revised.

In Maryland, the Constitution was ratified, again with the proposed opportunity for amendments. North Carolina, however, rejected the Constitution and in Rhode Island, where small farmers had gained control of the state, federalists faced formidable opposition. There, copies of the Constitution were distributed among the towns to give the people ample time to study it and unlike all the other states, the question of ratification was submitted directly to the people (who were enfranchised). The result was that 237 votes were cast in favor of the Constitution; 2,708 were cast against it.

In the end the Constitution was ratified by eleven states. But we should note that two states rejected it while in three other states, as measured by delegate strength, voters disapproved of it. Therefore, it appears that there were at least five states (enough to block ratification) in which there was majority opposition among the *active* enfranchised population (which was a minority of the adult population). The emphasis on the "active" voter is important here because the active voter tended to be more conservative. Ratifying conventions were held in the capitals which were mostly coastal towns where merchants and professionals were more numerous and prominent. Rural communities, given the property restrictions, their self-contained spirit and their resentment toward merchant and planter elites, and the cost of travel, often did not send delegates to the conventions. Moreover, their participation rates in delegate elections were low. In Maryland, for example, there were 25,000 eligible voters. Only 6,000 voted in the delegate selection process for the ratification convention and 4,000 of them were from Baltimore. In a study of voter participation and eligibility at the time, Charles Beard concludes that "it seems a safe guess to say that not more than 5 percent of the population in general...expressed an opinion one way or another on the Constitution...[and] it is highly probable that not more than one-fourth or one-fifth of the adult white males took part in the election of delegates to the state conventions. If anything, this estimate is high."[25]

A Great Compromise?

The notion that the Constitution was the result of great compromises suggests, quite inaccurately, that there was great diversity and great debate at the convention. We have seen that the movement toward the Constitutional Convention resembled more the scheming of an elitist cabal than a popular movement anxious to correct the defects of the Articles of Confederation. The "Great Compromise" that historians refer to is the compromise between the large states which sought (in the Virginia Plan) to base congressional representation on population.

It was the Madison-Hamilton conception of a very strong central government in which the states were reduced to the level of provinces. The small states presented the New Jersey Plan which was much more a simple modification of the Articles. There would be no Senate and the states would be represented equally in the unicameral Congress, much the way it was at the time under the Articles. The Great Compromise was the acceptance by the Madison-Hamilton wing of the notion of equal state representation in the Senate. Thus each state is equally represented in the Senate and in the House, state representation is based upon population. We must also note that it was in the context of this "great compromise" that the decision was made to count slaves as three-fifths of a person for the purpose of figuring out the population of the slave states.

The significance of the compromise was that the nationalist cabal that had wanted a strong central state ever since the War of Independence could not quite achieve the kind of national system they had envisioned, at least not entirely. Even among a convention of nationalist minded delegates there was strong sentiment for the idea of federalism in the sense of confederation. Therefore, limited sovereignty of the states was preserved and in at least one congressional chamber there was state equality. Much significance is attached to this compromise because it was around this issue that there was great emotion and division among the delegates. Had a compromise not been worked out, it is quite probable that the convention would have broken up.

But around issues that separated rich from poor, white from black, and men from women, there was considerable agreement. There was no need for compromise when it came to deciding that the suffrage would be restricted to white men with property. There was no need for compromise regarding the unusual authority given to the national government to tax directly, to guarantee contracts, to restore public credit, to regulate commerce, to promote the general welfare (market expansion), to raise a national army, to suspend *habeas corpus* during periods of rebellion, to forcibly put down domestic insurrections, or to use force to compel states to comply with congressional edicts. Indeed, there was a shared understanding that the use of force was a necessary feature of the kind of government they had in mind. Stated George

Washington, "We have probably had too good an opinion of human nature in forming our Confederation. Experience has taught us, that men will not adopt and carry into execution measures that are best calculated for their own good, without the intervention of a coercive power." The idea that there was a need for a federal bill of rights was rejected, *unanimously.*

And that is the rub. There was no debate over whether or not it was the right of the "better," more "virtuous" people to decide what our interests and needs are. There was no debate over the fugitive slave law (Article IV, Section 2). There was no debate over the perceived need to have a Senate, which would represent property, to check the democratic tendencies of common people. *The reason for the Constitution was to empower people of property over common people. Indeed, our definition of self-government and freedom have become linked, if not equated, to the interests of the corporation.* Stated President Carter during the "energy crisis" of the late 1970s, "on the battlefield of energy...we can seize control again of our common destiny...every gallon of oil [saved] gives us more freedom...solutions to our energy crisis can also hep us to conquer the crisis of the spirit in out country....We are talking about the United States of America and those who count this country out as an economic superpower are going to find out just how wrong they are." Spoken like a true Framer.

Finally property owners had secured a document, the Constitution, that would permit them to push ahead with their vision of vast state sponsored markets, expanded state sponsored trade, state assisted development of "cheap" labor and capital, and of state assisted accumulation of material abundance. Property owners were now free from King George, the Catholic Church, from rebellious small farmers, from slaves, people without property with "levelling" tendencies, and debtors who would violate their contracts; in short, property owners were now free from personal relations and the moral constraints that flow from them. Property owners were now free to pursue a fully rationalized, calculating, self-interested quest for empire which, of course, from their point of view was the simple unfettered exercise of self-government. Thomas Jefferson captured the idea quite nicely: "I am persuaded no constitution was never before as well calculated as ours for extensive empire and self-government."

The point of course is that if you wish to become part of the self-governing class, accumulate property. That is your freedom. That is the American dream and by all accounts corporate executive officers such as Lee Iacocca stand as an example of the kind of opportunity the Constitution affords the common person. But there are other visions of opportunity which conflict with those of empire and the kind of self-government which accommodates it. They form the basis of oppositional politics today as they did then. Some anti-federalists advanced alternatives to the Constitution, alternatives which they argued embodied true federalist principles. They said, why don't we have something more like the Swiss Confederation or the United Dutch Provinces. They had local liberties, virtuous citizens, a republican self-defense coupled with a love of peace. They are not powerful nations but republicanism on a small scale may avoid the political rule by a few that comes with continental expansion. And then they asked of the Framers, "What, fellow citizens, are your true aims: are they liberty and republicanism; or are they, perhaps, expansion and glory?"[26]

Part 2

A System of Injustice

What shall we think of a government to which all the truly brave and just men [and women] in the land are enemies, standing between it and those whom it oppresses? A government that pretends to be Christian and crucifies a million Christs every day!

—Henry David Thoreau

Chapter 4

The Lie

I do not think, for example, that it is too much to suggest that the American vision of the world—which allows so little reality, generally speaking, for any of the darker forces in human life...owes a great deal to the battle waged by Americans to maintain between themselves and black men a human separation which could not be bridged. It is only now beginning to be borne in on us—very faintly, it must be admitted, very slowly, and very much against our will—that this vision of the world is dangerously inaccurate, and perfectly useless. For it protects our moral high-mindedness at the terrible expense of weakening our grasp of reality. People who shut their eyes to reality simply invite their own destruction, and anyone who insists on remaining in a state of innocence long after that innocence is dead turns himself into a monster.

—James Baldwin, 1953

James Baldwin's warning is not specific to racism. It can and should be made applicable to a more general claim. Racism is one form of domination and subordination and in 1787 domination by a few and the subordination of the many was made the law of the land. A battle was waged by the Framers to maintain between themselves as property owners and common people as non-property owners a political separation which could not be bridged. We call this relationship democracy and it is this vision of the world that is dangerously inaccurate.

This is not a widely held interpretation, to be sure. In fact, most of us believe quite the reverse, that in 1787 a political system of, for, and by the people was given life. It is somewhat odd, however, that the more sympathetic view is so strong. It is odd because many of the same people who accept this view will complain, if given the opportunity, that they feel powerless. How often do you hear people say in one way or another, "Voting doesn't really do anything?" Or, "Why bother, you really can't change anything. Look at the 60s." Or, the famous, "You can't change city hall." Most revealing is the fact that those of us who are really outraged by what our government is doing in our name spend quite a bit of time asking the question, "But what can we do?" This is hardly the refrain of an empowered people who believe that they govern themselves.

A theme which I shall draw out in this chapter is that far from being a government of "the people," ours is a government which rests on the assumption that "the people," especially when they become politically excited, interested, and alive, are thought of as subversive. Any serious student of political surveillance and repression in this country knows this to be true.[1] But we seem to prefer to protect our moral high-mindedness by permitting elites, virtually at every chance they get, to persist in the lie that it is "we the people," and not "we the largest property owners," who govern this country. In so doing we risk weakening our understanding of the ways in which our lives are systemically made subordinate to the interests of the rich and politically powerful. And in so doing, we invite our own destruction.

"We the People"

The most familiar part of the Constitution is the preamble:

> We the people of the United States, in order to form a more perfect union, establish justice, insure domestic tranquility, provide for the common defense, promote the general welfare, and secure the blessing of liberty to ourselves and our posterity, do ordain and establish this Constitution for the United States of America.

Since the bicentennial year, the preamble appears on postage stamps and is everywhere raised up as evidence of this nation's "democratic" beginnings. Yet the "ordaining" and "establishing" of the Constitution was perhaps one of our history's most *un-democratic* moments. Remember many common people openly resisted the principles which were to be embodied in the Constitution and most had no idea that the Constitutional Convention meant to scrap the Articles of Confederation.

While the Preamble did not reflect the truth, it did serve two important political goals for the Framers. One is it signaled that the Articles had been replaced by a national system. If the confederation had been left alone, it may have begun "We the States." The committee of detail had suggested a preamble which read as follows: "We the People of the States of New Hampshire, Massachusetts...and Georgia, do ordain, declare and establish the following Constitution for the government of ourselves and our posterity." However, Gouverneur Morris, who was the chair of the committee of style, went over the entire first draft and gave the Constitution the style that it has today. He was responsible for the preamble's final form. And although it was intended to signal to its readers that a national system had been established, the word "national" was never used (much in the same way Madison, as slaveowner, saw to it that the word "slave" was never used).

Secondly, Morris, the undisputed champion of aristocracy, anticipated the broad opposition to the Constitution and sought to begin the document with a little phrase that might give the document broader appeal. There is multiple irony in this. Morris, the great egalitarian phrase-maker, may have had more contempt for the common person than anyone at the convention. The phrase which is most well known and which is used to color the Constitution is *legally meaningless* and it falsely suggests that the Framers were either common people themselves or identified with them to the degree that they respected, even celebrated their political wisdom. The suggestion is totally false. However, perhaps the greatest irony stemming from this almost mythic phrase is that it was originally coined by the Iroquois, a people against whom the Framers were committing genocide.

For the Iroquois, the concept of "the people" meant something very different from what the Framers had in mind. Their law and custom provided for the relatively equitable distribution of wealth, universal suffrage, and a confederation of states similar to the one described in the Articles. An observer in 1727 noted, they "allow no kind of Superiority of one over another, and banish all Servitude from their Territories." Iroquois leaders were regarded as servants of their people and were generally "poorer than the common people, for they affect to give away and distribute all the presents or Plunder they get in their Treaties or War, so as to leave nothing for themselves." The Framers, who approved the enslavement of human beings and who sought to prevent the political participation of the poor, women, and Native Americans, are considered by many as terribly progressive for the eighteenth century.[2] Ideological managers would have us forget that the phrase borrowed from the Iroquois by the Framers, and exploited, ("We, the people, to form a union, to establish peace, equity and order...") was taken from the Iroquois Treaty of *1520*.[3]

The Bill of Rights

Following the colonial experience, both the Framers and the common people shared a fear of tyranny or oppressive government and the tyranny of an imperial power which exploited the productive and trade opportunities of its colonies. It is upon this fear that the Bill of Rights rests. The Bill of Rights guarantees individuals *protection* from the government but it is the kind of protection that individual entrepreneurs, merchants, creditors, property owners, and speculators sought after having escaped the grip of British capitalists. As Staughton Lynd reminds us, "The First Amendment was not intended to protect the rights of wage workers...Rather the amendment sought to safeguard the rights of property-owning middle-class citizens to read, speak, meet and publish, prior to the formation of public policy."[4] Therefore, once the Framers had created a government that protected their interests as property owners, it seemed to many of them that a Bill of Rights was unnecessary. "Why, for instance," argued Hamilton, "should it be said that the liberty of the press shall not be restrained, when no power is given by which restrictions may be imposed?"

But some of the Framers, particularly as property owners, still feared the potential power of government. In a republic, the threat posed to private power by common people could not, apparently, be overstated. After all, argued Madison, if there were to be an invasion of private rights, the injury would result "not from acts of Government contrary to the sense of its constituents [owners of property], but from acts in which the Government is the mere instrument" of a popular majority. Jefferson seemed to share this view when he said that he appreciated the "legal check it [the Bill of Rights] puts into the hands of the judiciary."[5] In addition, there was support in the House of Representatives for a Bill of Rights. Remember that some anti-federalists endorsed the Constitution believing that their suggested amendments were to be taken up by the House of Representatives. But several of the proposed amendments, because they challenged private power, clearly ran counter to the purpose of the Constitution. In Massachusetts, for example, a proposed amendment urged that no monopolistic "company with exclusive advantages of commerce" be erected by Congress. In Maryland, a proposed amendment suggested that "in all actions on debts or contracts and controversies respecting property, trial of the facts shall be by jury if either party choose; and that it be expressly declared that state courts have concurrent jurisdiction…"[6] In order to keep decisionmaking regarding contracts and property in private hands and out of the hands of the people, a motion in the House to consider all proposals of the states during the ratification process was defeated.

The first ten amendments to the Constitution that were eventually adopted, or the Bill of Rights, did encompass many of the proposals regarding protection that had been put forward by anti-federalists during the ratification process. Proposals which attempted to make private power accountable, even in limited ways, however, were rejected. Consequently, while we have protection as individuals from the government (in principle but not in practice), the Bill of Rights does not protect us from corporations or from our employers. *The point here is that the Bill of Rights is quite consistent with the enhancement of private power intended by the Constitution*. Corporations, themselves considered individuals (given a 1943 ruling by the Supreme Court), are

---

*The richer and the whiter "we" are the more the principle holds. If you wish to look into the reality of "Amerikan" justice, see *Assata* by Assata Shakur (Westport, CT: Lawrence Hill and Co., 1987).

often shielded by the Bill of Rights from public demands. The recent effort by the tobacco industry to prevent the government from prohibiting their advertisements in magazines by pointing to the Bill of Rights is a case in point.[7]

While few would disagree that the Bill of Rights affords certain individuals important protection from the government and therefore ought to be celebrated and carefully guarded, one could also argue that there is more to citizenship than protection. *The Bill of Rights says not a word about guaranteeing participation.* This is especially true with regard to investment decisions, the use of national resources, and workplace practices (there is no right to strike, for example). It is also true with regard to simple political participation. Despite all the talk about our "right to vote," voting is not a right guaranteed by the Constitution. It is a privilege granted by the state for which we must qualify, and much of U.S. political history has been the struggle of the underclasses to do just that. As Sheldon Wolin points out, the Bill of Rights is "couched in such a language that was less suggestive of what a citizen might actively do than what government was prohibited from doing. ('Congress shall make no law…abridging the freedom of speech…' 'No person shall…be deprived of life, liberty, or property, without due process of law…')"[8] Indeed, the protection afforded by the Bill of Rights is quite conditional as we shall see in a moment.

First let us put all the parts together. A political-economic document, the Constitution was supposedly designed to "preserve the spirit and form of popular government" (Madison) even as the *substance* of popular government was taken away and the participatory politics flourishing at the local level was destroyed. This was done out of fear and distrust of the political tendencies of common people or what Madison called an "unjust and interested majority." Having established the political supremacy of property owners, the Constitution was then able to authorize the state to encourage economic expansion through the regulation of commerce, the protection of industry, trade, and private property the guarantee of contracts, and the development of a capital market. In other words the state was placed at the service of private elites and made an instrument of private power. The token usage of such egalitarian phrases as "we the people," as Wolin correctly points out, was "a formula to give the Constitution a legitimate basis, not to encourage an active citizenry." The vitality of the state would come not from a politically astute and engaged citizenry but from a highly productive and efficient economy. "Getting the economy moving again," not "liberation," would become the slogan of candidates running for political office. And here we come to the heart of the crisis which infects our political order. The concept of a reflective, politically active and community oriented citizen (a Ben Linder, discussed in Chapter 7) must be displaced by the concept of the responsible citizen (a Lee Iacocca): one who gives "a due obedience to its [the federal government's] authority" (Hamilton) and who appreciates and longs for the imperial reward for obedience: material wealth and protection.[9]

What does this mean? It means that as long as we value the accumulation and protection of property, and a judiciary to protect us from the government *more than we value playing a meaningful role in the decisions that affect our lives,* we obey. We don't ask questions. We learn to care more about how much we earn than about what we do and even less about the impact that our work has on others. In fact, obedience implicitly means that when we go to work we leave our conscience at home. It also means that we agree not to care so much about the details of politics as long as the form of popular government and the appearance of democracy is maintained. We agree when we consider political issues to think primarily in terms of self-interest and consumer sovereignty. The Middle-East? That means the price of oil. Central America? There is the potential for more Spanish-speaking refugees to pour across our border. Social programs? Unless I am a recipient, they have a bad effect on my taxes and interest rates. We learn to admit that we are selfish and materialistic, as though it could not be otherwise, and then take pride for being honest in this admission. But notice: it is *in the context of this obedience* that I may claim my rights as a responsible citizen and expect the government to deliver to me as a responsible citizen the real opportunity to acquire affluence and comfort. It is in this *context of obedience* that my freedom of speech is protected. For if I don't obey, if I persist in valuing real democracy and community higher than the opportunity to obtain private power and affluence, then I am a subversive and my freedom of speech cannot be protected. The truth is that if we insist that we, the homeless, people of color, women, Native Americans, and workers—the majority—must govern ourselves, or, for example, if we agree that we are willing to do with less in order that we might genuinely share economic resources and power with the peoples of the Third and Fourth Worlds or in order that we might live in a cleaner environment, then we threaten the privilege and power of the few who have it as well as the entire system that makes their privilege possible. The Framers understood this levelling tendency, this distaste of empire. In 1798, the Sedition Act was passed which made it a crime to "write, print, utter or publish...any false, scandalous and malicious writing or writings against the government of the United States, or either house of the Congress of the United States or the President...with intent...to bring them...into contempt or disrepute." A mechanic was sentenced to eighteen months in jail and a $400 fine for writing the following: "Here is the 1,000 out of 5,000,000 that receive all the benefit of public property and all the rest no share in it. Indeed all our administration is as fast approaching to the Lords and Commons as possible—that a few men should possess the whole Country and the rest be tenants to the others...[the few have] invented every means...to destroy the labouring part of the Community..."[10]

When the administration of Thomas Jefferson took power in 1801, the repression of political opponents continued. Over 2,000 were prosecuted including a minister who criticized Jefferson in a Thanksgiving Day sermon. Many served substantial prison terms. A worker who put up a sign that protested the tax laws and urged "peace and retirement to the president" served two years.[11]

Historian Leonard Levy has stated that the Framers "assumed that...freedom should be available only to believers," a kind of *quid pro quo*. One hardly expects free speech to be absolute; as former Supreme Court Justice Vincent has stated, "The societal value of free speech must, on occasion, be subordinated to other values and considerations." Yes, but what values and what considerations? Former Supreme Court Justice Abe Fortas helped answer this question when he declared that the government was permitted by the Constitution to prevent speech which "[interferes] with the preparation of the nation's defense or its capacity to wage war...[damages] property...[or disrupts] work." Yet Howard Zinn points out, the Supreme Court has restricted speech even more severely than that. The symbolic act of burning one's draft card in 1968, for example, was forbidden.[12]

David Kairys points out that "the founding fathers were an economic and political elite who were more interested in promoting commerce and restraining the democratic impulses of the public than in any new notions of free speech. Hamilton, Madison, Washington, Franklin—even Jefferson and Paine—all supported criminalization of seditious libel."[13] The Constitution, it is clear, was erected upon the fear of levelling tendencies. The claim that common people govern ourselves in the United States is a false claim. And the claim that common people can freely and fundamentally criticize our political and economic system *and work to build one that is more democratic without risking reprisal* is a lie.

The Citizen As Subversive

In 1950, George Kennan, head of the State Department planning staff, gave a briefing to Latin American ambassadors in which he said that a major concern of foreign policy must be "The protection of our raw materials"—in fact, more broadly, the material and human resources that are "ours" by right, require that we combat a dangerous heresy which has been spreading through Latin America, namely "the idea that the government has direct responsibility for the welfare of the people."[14] This "heresy " is simply and most often referred to as "communism," whether it bears any realtionship to that particular ideology or not. This condemnation of the idea that government has a direct responsibility for the welfare of the people captures wonderfully the legacy of the vision of empire and the Lockean notion of rights: 1) The globe is up for grabs. It is all potentially private property, suitable for development. *You are free* to try and acquire it and if you do, you own it. And what you do with it once you own it is up to you. It's your right, unless, that is, 2) a group of people, Church-based groups, unions, or popular coalitions who believe in community more than in *free* enterprise, gain control of a government and define limits to acceptable individual activity in accord with ethical standards. 3) The greatest threat to *private power* (free enterprise, the market system, contracts, production for profit and private ownership of productive property) has primarily been *public power* (a government controlled by common people for the welfare of the common people in the interest of community). Noam Chomsky has made the point well: "If segments of the usually irrelevant and apathetic public begin to organize and try to participate in some meaningful fashion in shaping affairs of state, that is not democracy, that is called a crisis of democracy as liberal elites in fact call it and it's a crisis that must be overcome by various means."[15] The common person then who is not responsibly obedient but who is politically active, who is a *citizen*, is subversive. And to an important degree the crisis of democracy has been confronted by elites in the United States, as in many other countries, through reform and through political repression.

Political Repression

Kairys states that, "Our glorification of the history and modern reality of free speech has masked the lack of substantial participation in the decisions that effect our lives...The mythic version of freedom of speech is a central element of our national identity. It can be easily manipulated to legitimize the lack of adequate means of expression or participation, enlarged power for the already powerful and even military intervention abroad."[16] There are two issues, then. One is the clarification of the nature and degree of political repression in the United States and the second is the suggestion that our belief that we live in a country free from political repression is itself a necessary condition of political repression. Our discussion, like all politically engaged intellectual work, must be seen not only as a process of discovery, but as a process of self-discovery, of liberation.

Political repression in the United States, also contrary to popular myth, has been constant and widespread. And the depth and persistence of political repression in the United States, in light of our nation's self-understanding as a free and innocent people, is, in a word, shocking.[17] According to Robert Justin Goldstein, "Political repression contributed significantly to the failure of the labor movement as a whole to achieve major power until the 1930s, the destruction of radical labor movements, the destruction of radical political movements, and the continuing self-censorship which Americans have imposed upon their own exercise of basic political freedoms."[18] Let us look briefly at each of these themes.

The repression of American labor from 1870 to the mid-1930s, which was "massive and continuous," took the form of government toleration of company towns, private police, private armies and private arsenals, the denial of basic political freedoms to millions of workers, the abuse of force by local police, state militia, and federal troops, and used techniques of harassment, mass arrests, and court injunctions. The most severe repression was directed at workers organizing within key sectors of the economy such as in the railroad, steel, textile, mining, lumber, and agricultural industries. In certain instances, such as in the Pullman Strike of 1894 and the Steel Strike of 1919 where these major strikes could not have been broken without repressive measures, political repression prevented labor from becoming "a major power in American society" for at least twenty to forty years.[19]

Radical unions were "literally smashed by political repression or severely adversely affected by it, at the peak of their strengths." Four of the leaders of the communist-anarchist movement which had achieved considerable strength in Chicago by 1886, for example, were hanged "without any reasonable proof" that they were involved in an alleged bombing. The Western Federation of Miners, a socialist-oriented industrial union which by the early twentieth century had 50,000 members was "physically decimated by arbitrary arrests and deportations." The Industrial Workers of the World (IWW) which had a membership of 100,000 workers by 1917 had its entire top leadership jailed due to government raids and conspiracy prosecutions. Goldstein describes the repression of the IWW as "vicious" and states, "Indeed, the entire history of the IWW is simply a history of political repression...." The union movement affiliated with the Communist Party (CP) elicited a legislative response that was openly repressive: the "1947 Taft-Hartley requirement that all union officers swear non-Communist oaths to qualify for Wagner Act benefits, the 1954 Communist control act provisions removing Wagner Act benefits from 'communist-infiltrated' organizations, and the 1958 Landrum-Griffin ban on CP members serving as union officers were all designed to completely destroy CP strength among American workers. Combined with CIO ousters (under strong government pressure) of CP-dominated unions, these measures decimated communist influence in the American labor movement."[20]

Goldstein points out that not just labor movements but basic political movements as well have been damaged because of political repression. The Socialist Party (SP) during World War I suffered intense political repression in the form of "arrests of party leaders, post office bans on SP publications, and physical attacks on party members by police and vigilantes." This repression completely destroyed about 30 percent of local party organizations and generated divisions within the party which led to its demise. The Communist Party, also during the post-World War I era, was driven underground by means of raids and mass arrests, deportations, and criminal syndicalism prosecutions. When it showed signs of renewed strength in the mid-1930s, the CP was targeted by the 1940 Smith Act (the first peacetime sedition act since 1789), and during the 1940 elections, the CP "was barred from the ballot in fifteen states." During 1939-1941, the party was investigated by Congress and three state legislatures. The FBI's counter-intelligence program or COINTELPRO, the program of repression with which most contemporary activists are familiar, was created to destroy the CP in 1956, even though the party was already decimated. Goldstein notes that given the threat posed, "the American repression of the CP exceeded that of any other democratic nation."[21]

During the Vietnam Era, with citizens becoming involved in a very broad range of issues that extended well beyond traditional left/labor oriented frameworks (some of which were environmentalism, animal liberation, gay and lesbian liberation, a multi-faceted feminism, new forms of black nationalism, American Indian liberation, anti-nuclear power, anti-nuclear weapons, and spiritualism) and with citizens often moving from the language of "rights" to the language of "power" and "liberation," the government's response at one level was massive covert surveillance and the use of *agents provocateurs* and burglaries in attempts to foster division and discord within protest organizations.[22] By the mid-1970s the FBI maintained intelligence files on an estimated 6.5 million individuals and groups. The CIA launched domestic surveillance on roughly 10,000 citizens and more than a 100 groups, and kept an index on more than 300,000 citizens and organizations.[23]

Goldstein believes that political repression in the United States has destroyed the continuity of American radical movements, especially during the 1917-1920 and 1947-1954 periods. He also believes that it has chilled political debate and narrowed the range of acceptable ideas: "One of the most startling aspects of American political life is the virtual exclusion of socialism from any serious consideration as a possible solution to American economic or other problems." Proposals for public control of credit and monetary policy which emerged for a time out of the People's Party 100 years ago (echoing the policy proposals of Shayites 100 years before that) were derailed[24] and their advocates purged in much the same way that today's red-baiting and harassment of citizens working in solidarity with the people of Central America helps to legitimize the present Congressional unwillingness to recognize the validity of socialist movements in that region of the world. "The fear of being investigated by the FBI, wiretapped, hauled before legislative committees, deported or prosecuted for sedition has not been unrealistic," notes Goldstein. But it is a reality the obedient and responsible citizen does not know and, perhaps, does not wish to know.[25]

The Ultimate Check: Secret Police

Consider briefly the experience of blacks in this country. The enslavement of human beings continued for seventy-six years after the signing of the Constitution. In 1865 the Black Codes, which were the slave codes revived, legally restored white supremacy as southern states rejoined the union. In the presidential election of 1876, Democrat Samuel J. Tilden received more popular votes than the Republican candidate Rutherford B. Hayes, but the Democrats agreed to allow the electoral commission to declare Hayes the winner so that they could retain political control and white supremacy in southern states. Following that historic "compromise," blacks were disenfranchised and the most severe and extended period of racist violence, excepting slavery itself, began. Between 1882 and 1930, a system of state sponsored terror was in operation that resulted in the lynching of 3,386 blacks.

Racism, of course, still continues. The median household net worth for whites in 1984 was $39,135. For blacks, it was $3,397. The poverty rate for whites was 11.5 percent while for blacks it was 33.8 percent. Infant mortality rate in 1982 for whites was 10.1 percent while for blacks it was 19.6. The male murder rate for blacks that year was four times that of whites. Blacks have been victims of medical experimentation, particularly in prison but not always. The state of Georgia during the early 1970s, for example, sterilized several "mentally deficient" black girls.[26] Numerous other data, measure, and personal testimony could be wheeled into place to further make the case that the systematic denial of the humanity of people of color is taking place in our society. And similar claims could be advanced, and are done so regularly, that other categories of people in our society experience systematic oppression.

The key word here is *systematic.* That is, the oppression in question is linked to the web of ideas, values, beliefs, assumptions, and practices that help to make up the social relationships in which we are all implicated. Or as Hegel has stated, the world which is outside us has its threads in us to such a degree that it is these threads which make us what we really are. The problem is not just that there is *systematic* racism and/or massive inequality in an otherwise free society. If there is systematic racism and/or massive inequality in a society that is believed by most of its members to be basically free, it means that the humanity of the non-oppressed, as well as the oppressed, is diminished. One can hardly be thought of as a healthy person if one has lost the ability to understand (and act on that understanding) the oppression of another.

The legacy of the Framers in this regard, in addition to the remarkable achievement of ideological mangers who have followed them, needs to be highlighted here. We have unreflectively accepted the idea that freedom means the right of a few individuals to control the lives of millons of people by virtue of their private ownership of community, national, and international resources. We have unreflectively accepted the idea that democracy refers to a political system in which the marginal participation of common people is designed to protect the political and economic power of the propertied class. The key political values that emerge from the Constitution are frozen in the ice of eighteenth-century elitism. We allow the privileged to rest comfortably in a set of social relations that call exploitation freedom and the empowerment of the rich democracy. Given these conceptual blinders, the oppression of others becomes harder to see and the corruption of our own humanity, particularly if we are among the privileged, becomes invisible. Lies about who we are and what we do become more palatable than the truth, denial more palatable than confrontation.

In this context, those people who want to expose corruption or who attempt to challenge power are perceived by guardians of the order as very dangerous, as threats to freedom and democracy and the "good life" we share. The voices of blacks and other marginalized but active and critically minded citizens need to be silenced, if the hierarchy of privilege and power in this country is to be preserved. Correspondingly, it is their voices that need to be heard if fundamental change is to come about.

It is not surprising, then, that even the reformist, anti-communist black organization, the National Association for the Advancement of Colored People (NAACP) was infiltrated by the FBI for a twenty-one year period. The government's response to more militant, radical black organizations, such as the socialist Black Panther Party (BPP), suggests that movements by oppressed people that have a real chance of ending that oppression simply is not tolerated. The BPP which attempted to build "survival" or community service programs which included health clinics, children's breakfast programs, busing, as well as police patrols on which BPP members brandished legally-acquired firearms, was smashed by the government in a manner which Donner describes as "all-out warfare" and a "reign of terror." Twenty-eight BPP members were assassinated by the FBI and/or various local police departments.[27] In addition to attacks made by the FBI (which was later found to be "criminally complicit in violence"—including assassination),[28] Internal Revenue Service harassment, CIA surveillance, Internal Security Division of the Department of Justice grand jury abuse, and the harassment of lawyers defending the BPP by federal urban intelligence teams or "red squads" were all brought into play in the government's campaign to eliminate the BPP.

The strategy behind this repression tells us a good deal about the purpose of the repression itself. "The effectiveness of the BPP newspaper, the eloquence of its leaders, the appeal of its children's breakfast program, and the emergence of a sympathetic white constituency, placed a high priority on actions to...discredit them through unfavorable publicity," notes Donner. In other words, they posed the threat of a good example or of an alternative community in which common people demonstrate clearly that they are capable of governing themselves. Similarly Fred Hampton was targeted and then murdered by the FBI because he was a "highly effective leader, his charisma enabled him partially to overcome the Bureau's divisive efforts....He had instituted a number of successful community welfare, medical, and educational programs...he was slated for national leadership." Or sample the remarks made about Martin Luther King, Jr. by William Sullivan, head of the FBI's Domestic Intelligence Division:

> Martin Luther King must, at some propitious point in the future, be revealed to the people...as what he actually is—a fraud, demagogue, and scoundrel. When the true facts concerning his activites are presented, such should be enough, if handled properly, to take him off his pedestal and reduce him completely in influence. When this is done, and it can and will be done, obviously much confusion will reign...The Negroes will be left without a national leader of sufficiently compelling personality to steer them in the proper direction. This is what could happen, but need not happen if the right kind of national Negro leader could at this time be gradually developed so as to overshadow Dr. King and be in

the position to assume the role of leadership of the Negro people when King has been completely discredited.[29]

Sullivan had Samuel Pierce in mind, currently Reagan's Secretary of Housing and Urban Development who has been accused of racism by other blacks in the government. It is clear the government did not want blacks to demonstrate the capacity of self-government, or the converse, to expose the pervasiveness and hideousness of white supremacy. More importantly, the government did not want the lie that we live in a free country to be revealed. In a FBI communication dated March 4, 1968, J. Edgar Hoover stated, in reference to black nationalism and black leaders, that there is a need to "pinpoint potential troublemakers and neutralize them." The names of black leaders discussed in this particular communication have been deleted, but as Perkus notes, the names of Malcolm X and Martin Luther King, Jr. "fit perfectly in the spaces censored by the bureau." The communication issued one month before the King assassination "raises questions about the FBI complicity in the murders" of both black leaders. It also raises questions of our identity as U.S. citizens and our unreflective acceptance of a way of life and a set of ideas which which are celebrated for their encouragement of free expression.[30]

The BPP was just one of 1,100 groups spied on by the FBI in 1975. The FBI's effort to create internal violent disruption within the BPP also was not an isolated effort. Between 1956 and 1971 there were 2,340 COINTELPRO operations. One-third of them were intended to either disrupt the functioning of a particular group or promote conflict between groups. And it has not been just the labor or civil rights movements that have been considered dangerous. J. Edgar Hoover, in the early 1970s, identified a new target, the "WLM." Wrote Hoover, it is "absolutely essential that we conduct sufficient investigations to clearly establish the subversive ramifications of the WLM and to determine the potential for violence presented by the various groups connected with their movement as well as any possible threat they may represent to the internal security of the United States." The WLM was the women's liberation movement.[31]

The women's liberation movement and other political movements pose a threat to the legitimacy of the Constitution. Women, after all, were not thought of as "people" by the Framers, nor were people of color, nor were wage laborers, or anyone for that matter who did not demonstrate their worth by having accumulated specified amounts of property. Even though the concept of "the people" has been broadened since 1787 and the franchise extended, the essential features of the Constitution (centralized power at the national level, a system of checks and balances which strengthens private power, a system of separation of power which prevents simple majority rule, a Bill of Rights which protects property and individuals in their pursuit of property but which fails to guarantee participation) still cohere in a way that continues to express in 1987 terms one fundamental purpose of the Constitution of 1787 which was to effect a "national political system in which commercial and financial interests were assured that new and potentially unpopular rules and practices would nevertheless be enforced reliably and consistently...."[32] Morever, since the Constitution several steps have been taken to further insulate political and economic policymaking processes from public pressure. According to Kenneth M. Dolbeare and Linda Medcalf, Alexander Hamilton "placed the reins of power as far from the people as he could" through the creation of a "centrally guided financial and development system that would be as hard to identify as it would be to reach and change" and by "transferring as much policymaking as possible into the far less visible and apparently neutral and mechanical hands of courts and lawyers." Dolbeare and Medcalf identify several other steps such as the passage of the Federal Reserve Act which shifted monetary policy out of the public arena into the hands of private bankers that serve to update the Framers' design, frustrate popular movements, and protect private power. And once "this system was consolidated in World War I, participation could actually be encouraged because there was little chance that popular majorities could do much damage."[33]

We may read "We the People" convinced that the Framers were truly democrats, but our political institutions are locked within an eighteenth-century celebration of empire. The most important of our public policies are fashioned by private elites and have their origin in impenetrable boardrooms and in places which lie deep within the bowels of a huge and distant bureaucracy. Therefore, ideas or systems of thought which "steer Negroes in a proper direction" (and undermine the privilege of "better" people) or which suggest that workers should control their work lives (and undermine the privilege of "better" people) or which confront the many forms of patriarchy (and undermine the privilege of "better" people) do, indeed, threaten the security and power of privileged elites who define our needs for us. Of course such ideas are subversive. J. Edgar Hoover made the point in 1938: "Subversive alien theories and 'isms' are not only a drastic contrast to American ways of thinking, feeling and acting, but they stand for a complete overthrow of established ideas of American life and philosophy of government to which America is dedicated."[34]

Elites cannot combat citizenship openly any longer. The "We the People" lie has become too big. Thus, the FBI and other governmental agencies slip quietly and covertly away from their jurisdiction, in this case crime fighting, into intelligence gathering and thought control operations, replete with dirty tricks, violence, and assassination.[35] In other words, the Constitutional imperative that a few "better" people rule in the interest of economic development today requires the establishment of covert military operations to check the threat of democracy. The FBI began domestic surveillance during the 1930s when the leftist orientation of many labor unions alarmed J. Edgar Hoover and President Roosevelt. By 1953, 13.5 million persons (or one out of every five workers) were required to pass loyalty/security tests. Today, the new FBI building in Washington devotes 35,000 linear feet to domestic intelligence files. The rest of the FBI's work takes up 23,000 linear feet. Crime fighting, in the case of the FBI one could argue, is a front for political surveillance and repression.

It is ironic but understandable that because we are supposed to be a government of the people, much the work of our government's "secret police" is concerned with making sure that the people do, in fact, support what the government is doing. The early FBI "countersubversive" campaign during the post-World War I era was part of a "public relations" or "educational" effort (which involved working with the press to distribute false information about subversives) to simultaneously rally support for countersubversive operations. The strategy of using thought control emerged out of the government's propaganda campaign during World War I. In the 1920s, Edward Bernays, who served on the government propaganda commission during World War I wrote, "The conscious and intelligent manipulation of the organized habits and opinions of the masses is an important element in democratic society." During the same period, Walter Lippmann devised the term "manufacture of consent" which he also called an essential "art" in "the practice of democracy."[36] Donner states that it was no accident that the congressional anti-subversive committees following World War I "uniformly singled out 'propaganda' as their target...The spoken and written word...became a prime intelligence target..." "Educational" institutions themselves have become centers of indoctrination. From 1952 to 1966, the CIA spent $3,300,000 on the National Student Association in an attempt to favorably influence the student community toward CIA policies. The CIA monitored faculty members under consideration for grants and recruited professors, administrators, and other covert allies within the university community for purposes of political control. The CIA also funnelled $12,442,925 to labor, business, church, and cultural groups. One million dollars was directly given over to "intellectuals, writers, and artists." Between 1949 and 1972, the CIA spent $25,000,000 on mind-control and brain-washing experiments. The CIA has recruited journalists, including correspondents for the *New York Times*, "CBS News," *Time* magazine, and other organizations, in order to plant stories (many of which are false) and popularize policies which might otherwise enjoy little public approval.[37]

John Stockwell, who worked for the CIA thirteen years, was Chief of the Angolan Task Force in 1975-1976. In that position he was a sub-committee member of the National Security Council as well as manager of CIA covert operations in Angola. He has stated that one-third of his staff of over 140 personnel consisted of professional propagandists who fed false stories about Cuban and Soviet aggression to the press, the State Department spokesperson, and Ambassador to the United Nations (Daniel Patrick Moynihan, now U.S. Senator from New York). Stockwell, referring to information revealed by the Church Committee investigations of the CIA, noted that the "CIA had co-opted several hundred journalists, including some of the biggest names in the business, to pump its propaganda stories into our media, to teach us to hate Fidel

Castro and Ho Chi Minh and the Chinese and whomever...Leslie Gelb, the heavyweight with the *New York Times*, was exposed for having been working covertly with the CIA in 1978 to recruit journalists in Europe to print stories that would create sympathy for the neutron bomb...Freedom of the press doesn't mean that the *New York Times* is required to print the truth, it means that they have the freedom to print lies if they want to."[38]

That the entire political structure of the United States, including the Bill of Rights, is located within a swamp of contempt by elites for the general public is amply revealed by the MK Ultra Program. This was not a program which targeted specific political constituencies but one which dealt with the development of general social control techniques and one which used the general public, again and again, as guinea pigs. For example, during a twenty year period, the CIA, working through 200 medical schools and mental hospitals including those at Harvard and Georgetown universities, experimented with disease and drugs on citizens without their knowledge. "They [the CIA] dragged a barge through San Francisco Bay," stated Stockwell, again basing his claims on congressional testimony, "leaking a virus to measure this technique for crippling a city. They launched a whooping cough epidemic in a Long Island suburb to see what would it would do to the community if all the kids had whooping cough. Tough shit about the two or three with weak constitutions who might die in the process..."[39]

The secret police operations under the Reagan administration have moved us a step closer to the actual implementation of government run by the military. On April 6, 1984, President Reagan issued National Security Decision Directive #52 authorizing Federal Emergency Management Agency (FEMA) to initiate a secret, nationwide, "readiness exercise" called REX 84. This exercise would test the readiness of a plan to enlist the personnel of the Department of Defense, all fifty state National Guard units, and many state-based "State Defense Force" units (which were to be created at the behest of FEMA by state legislatures) in the event that President Reagan chose to declare a "State of Domestic National Emergency" following a nuclear war, violent dissent or, most probably, national opposition to a military invasion abroad. The exercise also included a plan to take into custody some 400,000 undocumented Central American refugees throughout the United States and to intern them in ten detention centers, already prepared or under construction. Louis Guiffreda, while at the Army War College in Pennsylvania in 1970, had written a paper advocating martial law in the event that resistance by black militants escalate nationally. The 1970 scenario also included the roundup and transfer to "assembly centers or relocations camps" of at least 21 million "American Negroes." Directive #52, of course, is the 1970 plan modified to provide current readiness for martial law. An alarmed and active citizenry always poses the threat of democracy and majority rule.[40]

The Tendency of "Better People"

As we have seen, concepts such as "better" people, or "more virtuous," or "more established" people and other judgements of superiority were concepts shared by the Framers. The design of the Constitution and its attendant rights expresses the notion that only the "better" few are fit to govern themselves and the rest of the people are fit to participate in meaningful political decisions, primarily, in indirect and carefully checked ways. The responsible citizen obeys. The democratic citizen is subversive.

The concept of "better" people, of course, did not begin with the United States. It is a concept which is necessary whenever a society, such as ours, accepts massive inequality as normal. The term "better" people is not used today in just the same way it was when George Washington was the richest man in America. Today we come up with different criteria of "better"—IQ test scores, education levels, credentials, competency and merit tests, various measures of efficiency, productivity, and accumulation, and so on. It follows, obviously, that when there are "better" people (and remember .5 percent own 35 percent of the nation's wealth), there are less than "better" people. That is why our own political history has consisted of repeated and explicit attempts to "purify" the electorate. To mention one example, by the 1920s, when the FBI was being created, many dissidents were called reds (reds are not "better" people) and reds in turn were "attacked as godless, bestial, dirty, and depraved…" Attorney General Palmer, in 1920, referred to his program of illegal mass deportation as the removal of "alien filth." J. Edgar Hoover referred to radicals as "termites."[41] As Governor of California, Ronald Reagan called political activists "mad dogs." We find that citizens with critical ideas are easily described in terms that cast them as enemies of the "freedom" and "democracy" and make their elimination seem natural and desirable. The Constitution, while at one level is designed to protect the citizen from arbitrary authority, embodies within it values, assumptions, and procedures which insure that the government will come down ruthlessly upon those who wish to challenge what the Framers understood as "self-evident" truths. Donner, in reference to the FBI operations directed against blacks, suggests that they "plunge us into a den of horror, a nativist Final Solution, justified as violence prevention and bureaucratically programmed in a stunning gloss on Hannah Arendt's 'banality of evil.'"

In spite of the bicentennial celebrations of our political freedom, it appears that we are a nation where citizens who disturb, upset, disrupt, and challenge the Framers' definition of feedom and democracy are people whose existence is ultimately regarded as an insufferable provocation.

The Constitution and Secret Government

Early in 1934, Irene Du Pont and William S. Knudsen [General Mortors president] reached their explosion point over President Roosevelt. Along with friends of the Morgan Bank and General Motors, certain Du Pont backers financed a coup d'état that would overthrow the President with the aid of a $3 million-funded army of terrorists, modeled on the fascist movement in Paris known as the Croix de Feu...[Roosevelt] knew that in view of the backing from high banking sources, this matter could not be dismissed as some crackpot enterprise...On the other hand, Roosevelt also knew that if he were to arrest the leaders of the houses of Morgan and Du Pont, it would create an unthinkable national crisis...Not for the first or last time in his career, he was aware that there were powers greater than he in the United States.

—**Charles Higham**[1]

The bicentennial year was more than a celebration of the Constitution. It was a year of political crisis in which several congressional investigations and a widely followed law suit filed by the Christic Institute exposed what many have called a "secret team."[2] It is through this secret team, we have learned, that the federal government continues to assassinate political opponents despite declarations and statutes to the contrary, collaborates with transnational criminal organizations in drug dealing for the purpose of covert financing, and systematically promulgates disinformation about its political opponents and its own policies.[3] The general response to the dirty work of the secret team (which we shall detail below), from mainstream and progressive leaders alike, has been that these deeds are a direct violation of the Constitution.[4] Only Congress has the power to declare war

(Article I Section 8) we are constantly reminded. The message is clear: this crisis does not mean that it is time to depart from or transform our political economic structure; it means that it is time to get back to the Constitution.

In light of the secret team revelations, how does one explain the rush to defend the Constitution on the part of progressives? Perhaps it is this: it stems from the desire to protect the liberal ideal which the Framers used to cloak their defense of private power and their quest for private empire by separating it from the structures of private power and the reality of private empire. It emerges, ultimately, from a desire to protect the myth of innocence: we are a self-governed nation of the people, where individual freedom is extended to all, where no one is above the law, and where the right to dissent is guaranteed by the Bill of Rights. But in order to preserve the innocence of the liberal ideal, we must ignore the fact that the Constitution is more than a design for a political system; we must ignore that it is a design for a political *economic* system. As has been shown, the political system which the Constitution created was intended to support private power ("freedom") in a private economy ("free" enterprise) and that today its purpose is to support and protect a capitalist empire, indeed, the largest empire on earth. The vision of the Framers has been realized, and then some. That is the crux of the problem.

The Constitution is not a neutral instrument, it is an active element within a political economic structure organized around private power within a private economy. For example, following Harry Magdoff, we can identify three distinct stages in the drive to empire and in each the state has played a crucial role: during the late eighteenth and early nineteenth centuries, the state was used to help private elites market food and raw materials to the rest of the world, assist the importation of capital, and protect maritime commercial interests. By the late nineteenth century, the state was helping a small number of industrial and financial giants compete internationally in the export of manufactured goods and capital. Following World War II, the function of the state was to protect and support what had become the major, dominant capitalist economy, the largest manufacturer, foreign investor, trader, the world's banker, and the dollar which in turn had become the key international currency.[5]

Furthermore, the expansion of our private economy may be viewed as the expansion of power, the imposition of the will and needs of those who own concentrated wealth upon the lives of those people who do not own land or factories and who live dependent lives (what Rosa Luxemburg has called "capital's blustering violence"). Therefore, the use of military force by the state in the service of private power has been a constant feature of the expansion of our economy. According to a 1969 study, the United States has been engaged in warlike activity during three-fourths of its history (in 1,782 out of 2,340 months).[6] To put this dynamic in a constitutional context, persistent acts of war have been sponsored by the federal government because in order to validate the state debt, protect private property, provide military and diplomatic representation abroad, suppress insurrections and do the other things that the Constitution requires the state to do to help property owners control productive activity and markets on a global scale, the state repeatedly has had to take the side of the few who seek control against the many who resist it. In this defense of "freedom," the probability of state sponsored violence and terror is always high.

Here we come to the heart of the problem of secret government. The United States is nearly always at war because the United States is nearly always using violence to support the few who are rich against the many who are poor. It is the few who are rich (those who own vast amounts of wealth producing property), then, who have real power in our society because it is their private interests (the "national interest") that need to be served if economic expansion is to take place. Working through their own private organizations such as the Council on Foreign Relations, the Trilateral Commission, the Ford and Rockefeller Foundations, the Committee for Economic Development, and such "think tanks" as the American Enterprise Institute, these elites become an unaccountable governing force that can become a secret government if and when they acquire positions within the government which enable them to link military and intelligence capability with specific corporate needs. Fletcher Prouty, a former officer within the Defense Intelligence Agency, describes those who run the secret government this way: they are "security-cleared individuals in and out of government who receive secret intelligence data gathered by the CIA and the National Security Agency..." whose power derives from the "vast intra-governmental undercover infrastructure and its direct relationship with great private industries, mutual funds and investment houses, universities, and the news media, including foreign and domestic publishing houses." During the post-World War II era, states Prouty, "more and more control over military and diplomatic operations at home and abroad" was assumed by elites "whose activities are secret, whose budget is secret, whose very identities as often as not are secret..."[7]

The fundamental issue which underlies secret government (and the secret teams which they field to carry out "special" covert operations) is injustice. The American people must not know that their government acts violently and unjustly on a regular basis. But there is an additional twist. The injustice in question is purposeful. It is a feature of economic expansion, privilege, and private empire. It is in the interest of private elites. All of this is quite consistent with the values of the Framers, the way they understood and explained inequality, and the purposes to which the Constitution was committed. To be sure, the Framers had no way of knowing the dimension of the political problem that would confront their descendants following 1945 when the empire was fully realized. They had no way of knowing that the checks and balances outlined within the Constitution might not be sufficient to protect private power against the rapid upward swell of political activism following World War II and on into the 1960s and 1970s. They had no way of knowing that the suppression of insurrections, shifted to a global scale, would take the form of virulent anti-communism, Nazi collaboration, and state sponsored terrorism. This set of sins was not especially more wicked than the acts of human enslavement and genocide committed by the Framers. But against the standards of decency that had emerged by the mid-twentieth century, the blustering and impersonal violence of capitalist expansion could not be legitimated as easily. Instead, new methods of insulating the policymaking of private

---

*This information was reported by National Public Radio's "All Things Considered" on July 7, 1987. The piece was entitled "Barbary Coast Wars."

elites from interested majorities had to be invented. Thus, the real issue today is not whether the dirty work of the secret team violates the Constitution, it is whether the work of the Framers is sufficient to protect corporate power from the people in the wake of yet another "crisis of democracy," whether called feminism, Black Power, student protest, environmentalism, peace, the New Age or simply the "Vietnam syndrome."

The Power of the President and the Role of Congress

Much has been written about the increasing power of the presidency vis-à-vis Congress since World War II. This is not quite right. What should be said is that the power of the Executive branch vis-à-vis Congress has increased. The distinction is an important one because it suggests that what is increasing is not necessarily the power of the president as much as are the various agencies (primarily military and intelligence) within the Executive branch to which private elites have ready access and insulation from popular pressure (often expressed through Congress). In other words, as the government has been drawn into the economy, private power has been protected from direct public interference from the Congress and from the president, if need be, through the construction of layers of bureaucratic insulation within the Executive branch. Pundits have looked at the Iran-Contra affair and have cried foul play: a private foreign policy has been conducted behind the back of Congress (and possibly the president). What they should have said is that the dependent status of public officials generally with regard to private power and the specific distrust of Congress is nothing new. From the point view of the Framers, it is the correct relationship between public and private power.

Article II states that Executive power is invested in a president. That power is not defined but John Locke in his *Second Treatise on Government* argued that in the conduct of foreign affairs, the executive does not simply execute laws passed by the legislature, rather the executive exercises a wholly separate function, particularly with regard to the "power of war and peace." Thomas Jefferson similarly stated that "foreign affairs are executive altogether." In one instance, Jefferson, by executive order and without consulting Congress, returned to France certain "prizes" taken at sea by American warships. Discussing this action in a letter to Madison, Jefferson stated that "the executive, charged with our exterior relations, seems bound, is satisfied of the fact, to do right to the foreign nations, and take on itself the risque [sic] of justification."[8]

Does this mean that something like the Iran-Contra affair could have happened with someone like Jefferson as president? The answer is yes, because it did. In 1803, the United States found itself at the mercy of fundamentalist Muslims who were holding U.S. citizens hostage. In addition, they were asking and getting ransom from the U.S. government. Jefferson's response was a covert plan to secretly overthrow the government (a state in the region near present day Libya) and replace it with one which would be more congenial to U.S. interests. On December 10, 1803, Jefferson held a secret meeting in the White House with with Captain William Eaton. They worked out a plan in which Eaton would be given $40,000 from the State Department and 1,000 rifles. Eaton was then detached from the State Department and loaned to the Navy where he was given the title "Agent for the United States Fleet in the Mediterranean," a post never heard of before. Covertly and behind the back of Congress, Eaton eventually was sent to Egypt with eleven Marines where he organized a mercenary army and achieved some military success but was unable to destabilize the government in question.*

The essential differences between the "secret team" of 1803 and the secret team of 1987 have less to do with violations of constitutional principles than with the way those principles must be expressed, given the very different stages (from fledgling nation to declining empire) of economic development.

And what has been the role of Congress with regard to covert action? As we noted earlier, Veron L. Parrington has stated that the Constitution represented the first written safeguard against tyranny, "but it was aimed at the encroachments of agrarian majorities rather than at Tory minorities...An honest appeal to the people was the last thing desired by the Federalists..." Allen Smith similarly adds that "[I]t was the almost unanimous sentiment of the Convention that the less the people had to do with the government the better."[9] The Framers would have been pleased, then, if they had watched the congressional investigation of the Iran-Contra affair this summer. Congress limited the scope of the investigation, provided a platform for anti-communist ideologues, covered up the most controversial acts such as drug-running, and effectively kept the public misinformed.[10] This is what Madison meant when he said that the purpose of a representative system was "to refine and enlarge the public views by passing them through the medium of a chosen body of citizens, whose wisdom may best discern the true interest of their country...and if pronounced by the people themselves..." The Constitution states that only Congress shall declare war. But notice it does not say which branch of government can or cannot make war nor does it say that acts of war must be declared. Congress, in defining the true interest of the country, has seen fit to declare war only four times despite nearly 1,800 months of fighting and nearly 200 known instances of United States armed interventions abroad.[11] In addition to formal declarations, however, numerous congressional acts have been intended to legitimize acts of war. The Gulf of Tonkin Resolution which permitted the prosecution of the Vietnam war is one. The repeated funding of the Contras is another. But the task of covering up "capital's blustering violence" since the empire gained world dominance has become considerably more difficult than it was during the early nineteenth century when Congress could, without widespread public protest, open the West to economic penetration and the Native Americans to genocide by passing legislation which called for measures that would lead Native Americans to "agriculture, to manufactures, and civilization." After more than a century and a half of varied social movements, Congress in 1947 felt compelled to create a new level of government that better insulated private elites from the public pressures of policy making. The National Security Act of 1947, which gave birth to the Central Intelligence Agency (CIA) and the National Security Council (NSC) among other agencies and departments, enabled corporate elites to more directly and more secretly control war making policies essential for global economic expansion and stability. It was the stronger centralization, the more severe set of checks and balances *against public power* that many of the more conservative members of the Constitutional Convention such as Hamilton had argued for in 1787. Moreover, the act created a new kind of transnational army within the CIA suitable for suppressing insurrections and overthrowing governments ("such other functions and duties") on a global scale just as the Framers had created a national army in 1787 to suppress insurrections on a state or regional scale.

Funding measures have also kept pace with the Framers' original intentions. Although the Constitution states that "All bills for raising revenue shall originate in the House of Representatives" (Article I Section 7) in the interest of ensuring "perfect secrecy," the Framers provided George Washington with a secret slush fund (see Chapter 6). Thus covert financing originated with the Framers. As the government became more deeply involved in economic matters (a situation the Framers could not foresee), the overriding need to insulate key economic decisions from public pressures forced Congress to pass on revenue decisionmaking to the executive and beyond. Following the "Red Scare" in 1921, the Bureau of the Budget was created which permitted the coordination of departmental funding requests. The Bureau was moved to the Executive Office of the President in 1939 and later became the Office of Management and Budget, enabling private elites and the president to originate revenue bills and use the budget to control executive bureaucracies. Moreover, the NSC sets budgetary guidelines for the Defense Department and in 1949 Congress gave permission to the CIA to "transfer to and receive from other government agencies such sums as may be approved by the Office of Management and Budget, for the performance of any functions or activities authorized...and any other government agency is authorized to transfer or receive from the agency such sums without regard to any provisions of law limiting or prohibiting transfers between appropriations." In other words, much of the actual U.S. war making agencies are above the law because Congress has so stipulated. Indeed, the CIA's real charter, its "secret charter," was not shown to Congressional "oversight" committees until July 1973. The public has no way of knowing if the CIA is exceeding its mandate because there is no way of knowing what the mandate is. We see here that Madison's insight that "the danger of disturbing the public tranquility by interesting too strongly the public passions is a still more serious objection against a frequent reference of constitutional questions to the decisions of the whole society," is one that is shared by elites today. Taking added precaution, presidents have "regularly enlarged the functions of the CIA by executive fiat...And sometimes...have acted without informing...[the] normally indulgent congressional 'watchdogs.' " Periodically members of Congress complain that they are not really involved in the secret government in the way that they should be. But most congressional watchdogs share the view of Senator Leverett Saltonstall who in 1966 said, "It is not a question of reluctance on the part of CIA officials to speak to us. Instead it is a question of our reluctance, if you will, to seek information and knowledge on subjects which I personally, as a Member of Congress and as a citizen, would rather not have."[12] Statements such as these capture well our collective need to deny what we have become. But what is it that our government does that citizens, because they are members of that government, would prefer not to know?

The Secret Government and the Rise of Nazi Germany

I have suggested that the military defeat in 1787 of Daniel Shays and others who resisted the advancement of market relations expressed counter-revolutionary tendencies because it marked a return to the imperial values of Great Britain. As market relations became fully capitalist and spread from Europe and the United States into other parts of the world, resistance was organized by those who, similar to the participants of Shays Rebellion, sought either to defend or create space for an alternative way of life. And like the Framers of 1787, U.S. government leaders together with private elites have often felt compelled to organize counter-revolutionary armies to protect property and market relations or what they prefer to call "freedom." The first counter-revolutionaries or "freedom fighters" were the Framers themselves when they put down Shays Rebellion. The next organized effort to en-list Freedom Fighters to put down a revolution was in response to the overthrow of the Russian czar by the Bolsheviks after World War I.

International bankers and lawyers in the Northeast, alarmed by the Bolsheviks but determined to press on with the expansion of foreign investments and operations, established the American branch of the Round Table Groups, a set of "semicovert policy and action groups" formed at the turn of the century by English aristocrats and bankers who sought to create a federation among the English speaking peoples of the world. The American group, centered in New York and led by the Rockefeller-Morgan financial establishment, has since come to be known as the Council on Foreign Relations (CFR) which was then com-mitted to bringing the government and "all existing international agen-cies...into constructive accord." A second response was to assist the displaced armies and supporters of the czar, or White Russians, who were poised to restore the czar, his court, and his industrialists to power. Fourteen nations, including the United States, placed troops inside the borders of the Soviet Union. And still other responses were combina-tions of the two. But significant for us is the mixture of private interest and public policy particularly with regard to the use of the government for counter-revolutionary measures. With this in mind, let us outline the linkage of private and public power, in the immediate post-war era, of Herbert Hoover.

Hoover, a former mining engineer employed by British concerns, had become a successful entrepreneur in Russian oil wells and mines. He had major investments in eleven Russian oil companies. By 1912, together with British investor Leslie Urquhart, Hoover had formed the Russo-Asiatic Corporation which was worth (in 1912 dollars) $1 billion. After the Russian revolution, Hoover's property was seized and a claim was filed with the British government by Russo-Asiatic Consolidated, a new cartel which Hoover and his partners had formed to protect their Russian interests, for $282 billion for damage to properties and loss of probable annual profits. Hoover, however, was also director of the American Relief Administration for the United States government. And it was in this capacity that he was able to use food relief to covertly support the White Russian army.[13]

The interest of the government of the United States was, by 1917, part of the interests of a North Atlantic class of capitalists. The armistice of 1918 (the Treaty of Versailles) between Germany and the allied powers contained in Article 12, for example, a clause stipulating that German troops should remain, with the consent of the allies, in whatever Russian territory they then occupied. It was understood that these forces would be used against the Bolsheviks. The British directed the remnants of the German army against the Red Army under General Rudiger Vondergoltz and later under the czarist, General Nicolas Yudenitch. In each instance, Hoover placed food supplies, which were intended for the relief of starving Europeans, under the direction of these generals who were proceeding with wholesale executions and campaigns of general terror. The money for the food relief had been in part appropriated by Congress and some of it had been privately donated. The point should not be lost, however, that Hoover was using an Executive branch of the government, covertly, to advance his private interests and the counter-revolutionary interests of his class. But he was not alone. In February of 1922, the *New York Globe* editorialized, "Bureaucrats centered throughout the Department of Justice, the Department of State, and the Department of Commerce...are carrying on a private war with the Bolshevist government..." There was in 1922, in other words, just as there had been earlier, a secret government.

The penetration of the Soviet Union by the allied supported czarist Freedom Fighters was turned back. Moreover, to the horror of Western elites, enthusiasm among peasants and workers for various anti-capitalist ideologies spread throughout the West including the United States. It was in this context that many Western elites believed that their salvation lay in the rearmament of Germany. In other words, a rearmed Germany, together with royalist White Russians, would constitute the ultimate counter-revolutionary force both within Europe and against the Soviet Union.

The first obstacle to overcome in the reindustrialization and rearmament of Germany was the Treaty of Versailles itself. The allies had imposed exorbitant reparations payments on Germany. Therefore, prominent U.S. bankers, such as J.P. Morgan, Charles G. Dawes, and Owen D. Young, with the support of the U.S. government came up with two plans, the Dawes and Young Plans, which would help Germany with its reparations payment problem through very generous international loans. The loans helped strengthen Germany's three largest firms (which had significant U.S. capital participation), IG Farben, United Steel, and German General Electric (30 percent of which was owned by U.S. General Electric) by enabling them to out-produce their competition and develop new product lines. It should be pointed out that IG Farben, a huge chemical and pharmaceutical conglomerate that enjoyed close ties to Standard Oil (now Exxon) even after Pearl Harbor, was, perhaps, the single most important firm in Nazi Germany. In addition it produced the gas for the Final Solution and built a synthetic fuel and rubber plant at Auschwitz, which it had created, in order to create an inexhaustible supply of slave labor.

Two Americans who played a central role in successive secret governments were John Foster Dulles and his brother Allen. John Foster Dulles, as special counsel to the Dawes Committee, had drawn up the Dawes Plan and would eventually become Secretary of State under Eisenhower. Allen Dulles would become Eisenhower's CIA Director. Both Dulles brothers were partners in Sullivan and Cromwell which handled the legal affairs of American IG (the U.S. subsidiary of IG Farben). The Dulles brothers were also deeply involved in a number of U.S. and German firms and banks or their subsidiaries that contributed to the Nazi build-up and in U.S. firms which later traded with the enemy during World War II (such firms as the Chase Bank, Ford, ITT, General Aniline and Film, and Standard Oil).[14]

Numerous other U.S. corporations also were deeply involved in the German military build-up. Hitler's two largest tank producers were Adam-Opel and Ford of Cologne, wholly owned subsidiaries of General Motors and the Ford Motor Company. The Curtis-Wright Aviation Corporation helped the German Air Force develop secret dive bombing techniques and they supplied the German air force critical parts which were desperately needed by U.S. aircraft. The research of Charles Higham is the most exhaustive in this area. Perhaps a brief excerpt from his work will helped us grasp the depth of the U.S. corporate-Nazi collaboration. In noting that his research was made more difficult because the "government smothered everything, during and even (inexcusably) after the war," he speculates as to the reasons why:

> What would have happened if millions of American and British people, struggling with coupons and lines at the gas stations, had learned that in 1942 Standard Oil of New Jersey [part of the Rockefeller empire] managers shipped the enemy's fuel through neutral Switzerland and that the enemy was shipping Allied fuel? Suppose the public had discovered that the Chase Bank in Nazi-occupied Paris after Pearl Harbor was doing millions of dollars' worth of business with the enemy with the full knowledge of the head office in Manhattan [the Rockefeller family among others]? Or that Ford[15] trucks were being built for the German occupation troops in France with authorization from Dearborn, Michigan? Or that Colonel Sosthenes Behn, the head of the international American telephone conglomerate ITT, flew from New York to Madrid to Berne during the war to help improve Hitler's communications systems and improve the robot bombs that devastated London? Or that ITT built the FockeWulfs that dropped bombs on British and American troops? Or that crucial ball bearings were shipped to Nazi-associated customers in Latin America with the collusion of the vice-chairman of the U.S. War Production Board in partnership with Goering's cousin in Philadelphia when American forces were desperately short of them? Or that such arrangements were known about in Washington and either sanctioned or deliberately ignored?[16]

The U.S.-Nazi collaboration, we find, was not strictly a private matter. The tendency was for corporate elites to use their own organizations, private networks, and their positions in the government to form a secret government. Dean Acheson, for example, as Secretary of State and as former Standard Oil lawyer, together with the Treasury department issued licenses permitting Standard Oil and other corporations to trade with enemy collaborators during the war. Higham states that while President Franklin Roosevelt knew that these corporations were trading with the enemy, there was little he could do. "Roosevelt was blackmailed, " states Higham. "You can't run a war without Chase Bank, or Standard Oil of New Jersey, or ITT."[17]

The Secret Government Following World War II

No figure was more important within the secret government during the immediate post-war era than Allen Dulles. Before the war was over, he argued that the German state had to remain in existence to maintain order. He also urged that it was necessary to form a *cordon sanitaire* against bolshevism and Pan-Slavism by "enlarging Poland toward the East and maintaining Romania and a strong Hungary." His ideas about a post-war western capitalist alliance were quite in accord with what some Nazi generals, also hopeful of a post-war western capitalist alliance, were beginning to call "the Fourth Reich."[18]

Hitler's infamous SS (*Schutztaffel,* or defense squads) officers, who were directly involved in the Final Solution, were recruited from the conservative German monarchists (who sought to unite the best of the German racial characteristics of the past with a *Pax Europa* in the future)[19] whose commercial interests extended well beyond the German borders. They were part of the older, more aristocratic or Prussian royalist community of world money. They were not particularly enchanted with the "upstart, working-class Hitler," rather their allegiance inclined more toward the "memory of SS leader Heinrich Himmler's idol, King Henry I of Saxony, and to the Stein bank of Cologne, which financed Himmler's inner circle under the aegis of the international banker Kurt von Schroeder," a close associate of the Dulles brothers. Within the SS was the SD (*Sicherheitsdienst,* or intelligence service) whose first and foremost task was to repel communist infiltration. When it became apparent that all was lost, several officers within the SD plotted to displace Hitler in favor of Himmler. The goal was to set up an international front against the Soviet Union. The vision of a restored German aristocracy tied into a transatlantic hegemony of money and power vis-à-vis the Soviets was called the Fourth Reich.[20]

One of the conspirators who believed that communism was "a force of pure evil" was the head of SD, Walter Schellenberg. Schellenberg was also a director of the U.S. firm, International Telephone and Telegraph. In 1943, Schellenberg, through a representative, entered into direct and secret talks with Allen Dulles who in addition to working for the U.S. government in Switzerland for the Office of Strategic Service (OSS or intelligence forerunner of the CIA), was also legal advisor to and director of a banking (Schroeder) subsidiary which directly financed the "hard-core SS inner circle." His private negotiations had "no support whatever in the White House" according to Higham. In 1944 and early 1945, Dulles had entered into separate negotiations with Waffen SS General Karl Wolff who was high in the Himmler hierarchy as leader of the Military SS in Italy and Walter Rauff (designer and builder of the gas ovens at Auschwitz) whom Dulles later employed on anti-communist operations in Italy.[21] In addition to confessing that he was "sick and tired of listening to stories of...prejudiced Jews," Dulles laid out his conception of a post-war Europe. It would be a "high-income zone" with developed markets. Germany would be restored, without Hitler. Perhaps there would be a political federation. Jews would not be returned to positions of power. "He made the curious assertion that the Americans were only continuing the war to get rid of the Jews..." Dulles revealed (to a German agent) a variety of (top secret) military plans and asserted the need to create a strong front against bolshevism. And he stressed, in this and other meetings like it, that he had the support of Roosevelt, which was, according to Higham, totally false. It is clear that private negotiations were conducted behind the back of a misinformed Roosevelt. In negotiating the surrender of northern Italy, Dulles permitted the Germans to dispatch three divisions form Italy to the Eastern Front to attack Russia. It was, as the SS leader who negotiated with Dulles called it, "part of the proposed police force of the Western powers against Russia." Roosevelt had not been briefed and received an angry cable from Stalin in which Stalin stated that he had been tricked by the Allies.[22]

The post-war policies of the Allies, or perhaps it should be said elements within the Allied internationalist corporate world, did accommodate (consciously or otherwise) the interests of Fourth Reich visionaries in the following ways:

Politically—In Germany, Italy, Japan, as well in other countries that were in danger of being governed by popularly supported socialist partisans that had fought the fascists (such as in Greece where the

British were fighting the partisans before the war's end), the Allies insured that lesser known fascist bureaucratic leaders and government officials, mayors and clerks were returned to power. The process of restoration was initiated with Fourth Reich-minded leaders before the war was over. In West Germany, for example, the new Chancellor was Konrad Adenauer who collaborated with the Nazis as Mayor of Cologne. His Secretary of State was Hans Globke who, as head of the Office of Jewish Affairs under Hitler, drafted the lethal anti-Jewish laws which paved the way for the Final Solution. And Reinhard Gehlen, who had been Hitler's chief of intelligence on the Eastern Front (the Soviet Union), eventually became head of West German intelligence after having first worked with the U.S. government at the Pentagon. Gehlen had also been part of the SD royalist clique that had opposed Hilter in hopes of reassembling a Fourth Reich following the war.[23]

   Economically—Amid a degree of controversy and in violation of several agreements such as the Potsdam Agreement, corporate elites insured that, given the post-war influence of the Soviet Union and the internal threat posed by leftist/partisan movements, German cartels would not be broken up and that concessions would be made to German industrialists for the purposes of rapid development and reconstruction. James S. Martin, who worked for the Economic Warfare Section of the Anti-Trust Division of the Department of Justice and whose job it was to blunt international dealings of German cartels during the war and after the war during the supposed period of "denazification," stated:

> We had not been stopped in Germany by German business…[but] by American business. The forces that stopped us had operated from the United States but had not operated in the open. We were not stopped by a law of Congress, by an Executive Order of the President, or even by a change of policy approved by the President…in short, whatever it was that had stopped us was not 'the government.' But it clearly had command of channels through which the government normally operates. The relative powerlessness of governments in the growing economic power is of course not new…national governments stood on the sidelines while bigger operators arranged the world's affairs.[24]

Among the biggest private organizations that had command of government channels and the ability to set policy was the Council on Foreign Relations which consciously attempted "to organize and control a global empire" in the post-war world. The Council, composed of corporate elites, lawyers, academic and journalistic elites, such as Allen Dulles, set up study groups which interlocked with at least five cabinet level departments and fourteen separate government agencies, bureaus, and offices. In a rationally ordered and impersonal fashion, the study groups divided up the world into blocs and the location, production, and trade of all important commodities and manufactured goods were listed for each area. They concluded that the U.S. "national interest" required "free" access to markets and raw materials in the British Empire, the Far East, and the entire Western hemisphere. These "Grand Areas" were "strategically necessary for world control," as one elite planner put it. The idea was a simple one, the economic integration of sufficient global territory to insure that the United States would be the "hegemonic power in a system of world order."[25] In addition to definitions of our national interests and purpose, this private organization initially conceived of and arranged government ratification of such post-war economic instruments as the International Monetary Fund (IMF) and the World Bank.

Militarily—The military collaboration between the Allies and the Fourth Reich Nazis was extensive. As early as December 1941 key top generals had become disillusioned with Hitler's handling of the war and began to plan ways of rebuilding the German military after the anticipated German defeat.[26] Perhaps the major figure in the post-war collaborative efforts was Hitler's chief of Soviet intelligence, Reinhard Gehlen. As the Russians closed in on Berlin in April 1945, Gehlen, with his staff and crates of intelligence, fled to a hideout in the Bavarian mountains. From there he worked out a deal with the Americans where he would continue to supply intelligence on the Soviet Union and its satellites to the United States provided that he would be permitted to maintain an autonomous organization under his control. The deal was made and Gehlen, accompanied by Allen Dulles, Frank Wisner and others, was brought to the United States three months after VE (Victory in Europe) Day in the uniform of a four-star U.S. Army general. Gehlen's entire intelligence organization was grafted from the Third Reich onto the U.S. government and became the nucleus of the CIA. Gehlen's organization was later sent back to West Germany and became West Germany's intelligence system and largely the intelligence of the North Atlantic Treaty Organization (NATO) as well. It should be pointed out that by April 1961, Adolph Heusinger, the last Deputy Chief of the German General Staff (or number two military man in the Wehrmacht) had become Chairman of the Permanent Military Committee of NATO, *the highest ranking U.S. military office in NATO.*[27]

Gehlen was just one of 5,000 SS and Gestapo Nazis who, with the assistance of key U.S. government officials like Dulles, were able to find safe refuge outside of Germany. Many of the most sadistic killers such as Josepf Mengele were protected by the United States in their effort to escape justice. Many would develop links with neo-fascist elements in the military or interior ministries of Latin American countries (particularly in Chile, Bolivia, Paraguay, Argentina, and Peru) and collaborate with the CIA in repressive operations against the Left. And many found their way into the U.S. intelligence system, including, for a time, Adolf Eichmann and Klaus Barbie. Peter Dale Scott concludes that one legacy of the U.S.-Nazi collaboration "is the system of Death Squads now operative in Central America. Another has been the involvement of men like Barbie and their political clients in the highly organized Latin American drug traffic."[28]

Although Gehlen is not well known, he left an important legacy as well. For example, he initiated the idea of erecting an anti-communist propaganda transmitter called Radio Free Europe. The idea was implemented with the assistance of Allen Dulles and Frank Wisner and private contributions from such groups as the CFR. More important for our purposes was his creation before the war was over of Nazi special forces, called the Werewolves, which were intended to act as a partisan underground army inside Germany during the occupation. Their battle cry was "better dead than red."[29] What is interesting is that Gehlen's expertise with regard to guerrilla tactics was called upon during the early 1950s to create a mercenary army to penetrate eastern Europe and the Soviet Union. The units were called the Green Berets.

The two Americans responsible for bringing the idea to Gehlen of creating a guerrilla army that would infiltrate the Soviet Union was Allen Dulles, director of the CIA by the time the operation began, and Frank Wisner, director of Plans and Operations.[30] The special forces were supposed to collect intelligence and Dulles believed that these captive nations would rise up against communist oppression once the liberators had arrived. These "Green Berets" were recruited from the vast reservoir of war refugees from eastern Europe. *They were trained both in Germany and at Fort Bragg, North Carolina and they were trained by U.S. officers and by German Wehrmacht and Waffen SS NCO's.* Gehlen also chose three special assistants who were knowledgeable about the Soviet Union for the training. They were Dr. Michael Achmeteli, Dr. Franz Alfred Six, and Dr. Emil Augsburgs, all Nazi war criminals.[31]

Achmeteli had written books about the need for "civilizing communist Russia." He was a friend of Alfred Rosenberg, Hitler's chief theoretician of the Nazi Aryan doctrine and advisor to Hitler's high command. Six was a brigadier-general in the SS and received a twenty year sentence for ordering the execution of hundreds of civilians but served only four years. Augsburg was a colonel in the SS heading a section attached to Adolf Eichmann's S-4 department, which handled the "Jewish problem." The operation lasted until 1960 and 5,000 men were trained. One can only speculate on the actual effect which the SS training had on the tactics employed by U.S. special forces (which are now part of the U.S. Army, not the CIA). But we do know that between 1950 and 1975, the U.S. provided training or aid to the police of twenty-two nations that practiced torture.[32] The U.S. also trained military personnel of four additional nations that practiced torture during the same period. We know also that United States the documentation of torture instruction by U.S. special forces in Vietnam, Central America, and other places by such groups as Amnesty International is extensive. Members of the CIA have been present, according to some victims, during torture sessions.[33] The following is a brief excerpt from an interview with a Salvadoran soldier who claims to have been in attendance at one of the torture classes:

The officers said we are going to teach you how to mutilate and how to teach a lesson to these guerrillas. The officers who were teaching us this were the American Green Berets...then they began to torture this young fellow. The took out their knives and stuck them under his fingernails. After they took his fingernails off then they broke his elbows. Afterwards they gouged out his eyes. They took their bayonets and made all sorts of slices in his skin...They then took his hair off and the skin of his scalp. When they saw there was nothing left to do with him they threw gasoline on him and burned him...the next day they started the same thing with a 13 year old girl...[34]

The idea of the "death squad," which is central to the torture network, was suggested in 1962 by U.S. General William Yarborough, head of the Special Warfare Center at Fort Bragg. He urged security forces to "select civilian and military personnel for clandestine training" that would "execute paramilitary, sabotage and/or terrorist activities against known Communist proponents." Used in Vietnam in the Phoenix Program which was responsible for the assassination of more than 20,000 Viet Cong (these are CIA figures, other estimates are as high as 100,000), Yarborough's death squad concept often operates out of the U.S. Office(s) of Public Safety, a division of the Agency for International Development. It is interesting to note that the term *public safety* has been used throughout U.S. history to cover instances of repression. And the term has its roots in the Constitution. The one instance where the Constitution (Article I Section 9) authorizes the state to take people off the street without a writ of *habeas corpus* or due process "when in cases of rebellion or invasion the public safety may require it."[35]

John Stockwell, a former CIA agent, has stated that a woman who had been tortured in Brazil for two years testified, before international tribunals, that "the most most horrible thing beyond the pain and degradation was the fact that the people doing the torturing were not raving psychopaths. She said had they been she might have been better able to break mental contact with them. She said they were normal, everyday, decent people doing these things to her." According to Stockwell, the woman reported that during a torture session conducted by six men in which she was strapped naked to a table, there was an interruption: "The American is called to a telephone in the next room. The rest take a smoke break. And she listens to the conversation as he says, 'Oh hi honey. Yes, I can wrap it up here in another hour or two and pick up the kids and meet you at the ambassador's on the way home.'"[36]

It has often been said that the CIA is the president's private army. But the role of the CIA and other military forces that are shrouded in mystery such as those associated with the Defense Intelligence Agency appear to be less at the command of the president than at the command of those whom the president serves, namely international corporate elites. It appears, then, that the CIA is a special force, trained as professionals to carry out impersonal and anonymous punishment, for international corporate elites. These elites, because of their hidden power and influence within the Executive branch of government, constitute, at any given time, a secret government. And that secret government is capable of fielding secret teams whose job it is to remove political opposition to the expansion of our private economy by any means necessary.

The Secret Government and the First Secret War

Tales of U.S.-Nazi collaboration may, at first reading, appear to be mere sensationalism. Instead, it helps us to better understand the origins of our own present day national security state. Challenges to the private economy, ever since the days of Shays Rebellion, have instilled great fear among the propertied classes. Following World War II, the fear had reached fanatical proportions. It was called anti-communism.

What may have been the very first CIA covert operation came about when James Forrestal, as the first Secretary of Defense, became alarmed that the communists might win the Italian elections of 1948. Forrestal, whose relation to General Aniline Film, Standard Oil, and the banking company of Dillon Read (which had helped finance Hitler) brought him into intimate Nazi collaboration during the war, sought to run a private clandestine operation to alter the electoral outcome with money raised from his wealthy Wall Street colleagues. The ubiquitous Allen Dulles felt that the elections could not be subverted privately so he urged the U.S. government to establish a covert organization that could do the job. (Forrestal, it is worth noting, hanged himself in 1949 in a hospital window; newspapers reported him "screaming that the Jews and the communists were crawling on the floor of his room seeking to destroy him.")[37]

John Loftus writes that "[t]he success of the Italian operation brought demands for similar actions elsewhere...to do worldwide what the OSO [Office of Special Operations] had done in Italy." Naturally, such dirty work could only be effectively carried out if it was hidden, if it was insulated from public pressure. George Kennan, a member of the Council on Foreign Relations (CFR) working through the State Department recommended the creation of a new agency called the Office of Policy Coordination (OPC). Officially created by a National Security Council Directive (NSCD) 10/2, OPC was authorized to "overthrow governments regarded as unfriendly to the United States" and OPC's program, according to Loftus "emanated almost entirely from the State Department's Policy and Planning staff, headed by George Kennan."[38]

Frank Wisner, Wall St. lawyer who had worked with Dulles in the OSS organizing covert guerrilla teams in Rumania, was chosen as the head of OPC. In this position he organized an army of Nazi collaborators (again they were called "freedom fighters") and launched a clandestine guerrilla war against the Soviet Union that lasted well into the late 1950s. By 1952, OPC had 4,000 agents in forty-seven stations with a budget of $82 million. Money for the project was drawn from "untraceable government accounts, such as those of the CIA, and laundered through American corporations whose leaders had expressed a willingness to work with Wisner and OPC." Gehlen who was deeply involved in the project saw to it that Wisner hire Nazi war criminal Dr. Franz Six to head the recruitment and training of the special forces. By 1952, OPC had been brought under the control of the CIA. While the secret war "had not received official sanction from the White House," according to Loftus, "its two most ardent advocates, Dulles and Wisner, were in a position to continue the secret war on their own." Did either Truman or Eisenhower know of these operations? It appears that they did. But as Loftus suggest (Eisenhower had "difficulty in presenting cover stories to the press and generally preferred not to know about Wisner's covert operations"), the real impetus and execution of covert policy seems to have come from corporate organizations and the men they supplied to Washington. For example, during Eisenhower's administration a special group, the Operations Coordination Board, which came to be known as the "Twenty Committee" (and it has had other names in other administrations), oversaw covert operations and would serve as a "circuit breaker" to give the president deniability. It was headed by private elites; in this case by C.D. Jackson, a former Time, Inc. executive and later by Nelson Rockefeller.[39]

The Secret Government and the Assassination of JFK

In 1950 the CFR urged President Truman to create yet another private organization to assist "the government in all phases of national activity." The result was the creation of the Committee on the Present Danger (CPD). Working closely with Secretary of State Dean Acheson, the CPD pressed for a policy review which culminated in the creation of NATO which effectively rearmed Germany within a North Atlantic alliance. The outlines of the policy were made clear in what was then a top secret NSC memorandum, NSC-68. The NSC-68 called for a redefinition of or shift away from Truman's policy of "containment" of the Soviet Union to a policy "intended to check and roll back the Kremlin's drive for world domination" or "in general, to foster the seeds of destruction within the Soviet system that the Kremlin is brought at least to the point of modifying its behavior to conform to generally accepted international standards." The purpose of NSC-68, said Acheson, was "to so bludgeon the mass mind of 'top government' that not only could the President make a decision but that the decision could be carried out." As for common people? The "selling" of foreign policy "to the average man on the street" was not an easy task: "Qualification must give way to simplicity, nicety and nuance to bluntness, almost brutality, in carrying home a point." In other words, Acheson admitted, arguments must be made "clearer than truth."[40]

As it turned out, the problem was less selling foreign policy to the average person than it was selling it to top government officials. The clash between the secret government and the elected government would come as a result of the Cuban Revolution and disagreement over the subsequent U.S.-sponsored invasion at the Bay of Pigs. In a report prepared by CIA analyst for the White House, it was suggested that the Cuban revolution was due largely to the corruption of the Batista regime. Dulles altered the report to reflect his own worldview. The revolutionaries would unleash terror and "blood will flow in the streets," Dulles predicted. Moreover, CIA analysts stressed that Cuba was not a security threat to the United States. Nevertheless, in late 1959, Dulles decided that Cuba did pose a security threat and that the solution was to invade with an army of Cuban refugees.[41] It was an operation that fit into the postwar "rollback" scheme and it was a continuation of the covert and counter-revolutionary use of special forces developed by Gehlen, Dulles, Wisner, and SS advisors. In this particular operation, Richard M. Bissell, the new Deputy Director of Plans and Operations, who continued to rely on Gehlen, was in charge. The top CIA representative that dealt with the Cuban counter-revolutionaries was also a Gehlen agent who went by the name of "Frank Bender" and who, according to Dominican Republic dictator Rafael Trujillo, was a leader of ex-Nazis in Peru.[42]

It is apparent that the planners of the invasion at the Bay of Pigs distrusted both Presidents Eisenhower and Kennedy. According to Fletcher Prouty, members of the secret government, particularly those within the CIA took advantage of period between November 1960 and January 1961, when Kennedy was President-elect to transform the training of Cuban refugees into an invasion plan. Writes Prouty, "The ST [secret government] had strong-armed the early Eisenhower authorization of the training and arming of Cubans into an invasion of a foreign

country, during the 'lame duck' period of his administration." With
regard to Kennedy the distrust was mutual. Kennedy had rejected a
Castro assassination plot that had been part of the original plan. Kennedy also rejected the direct use of U.S. forces and during the early
phase of the operation, when after two days the cover story began to
crumble, he withdrew authorization for air support for the second
phase, thus contributing to invasion's failure. Cuban exile commanders
had been quoted as saying that if Kennedy had called off the operation altogether, they were going to proceed anyway, in order to force
Kennedy to go along. In the end, Kennedy felt that he had been manipulated and after the fiasco he fired several top CIA officials including
Allen Dulles and directed that covert actions be brought under the jurisdiction of the Joint Chiefs of Staff and the Department of Defense.[43]

The tension between the secret government and President Kennedy over the relation of the United States to revolutionary movements
increased during the remainder of his administration. Peter Dale Scott
has argued that the assassination of President Kennedy permitted (what
I have been calling) the secret government to reverse Kennedy's announced troop withdrawal and to escalate U.S. military involvement in
Vietnam. Scott's analysis rests upon policy directives before and after
the assassination as revealed by National Security Action Memoranda
(NSAM). For example, key NSAM before the assassination were the following:

- NSAM 111 (November 22, 1961): This NSAM committed the United
  States to "helping" the South Vietnamese but pointedly avoided language which would commit the United States helping the South Vietnamese "win."
- NSAM 249 (June 25, 1963): This NSAM suspended all covert action
  against North Vietnam pending review of policy. This was the last
  official JFK document on the subject of covert action toward North
  Vietnam.
- NSAM 263 (October 11, 1963): This NSAM provided for a phased
  withdrawal of between 1,000 and 1,300 U.S. troops from Vietnam.

On November 20, 1963 Kennedy publicly announced an "ac-
celerated" troop withdrawal of 1,300 troops. Two days later, on November 22, President Kennedy was assassinated. Two days after that,

November 24 (on Sunday evening, hours after Jack Ruby had executed Lee Harvey Oswald), at a secret meeting of the National Security Council, each of the NSAMs listed above were rescinded. In other words, NSAM 273, which was formally recorded on November 26, 1963, committed the United States to a "win" policy in Vietnam, resumed covert action against the North, authorized increased troop levels and explorations of an expanded war. The Deputy Chief of Staff for Personnel has also stated that it was on November 25, the Monday after the assassination, that a dramatic escalation of "manpower" levels was called for by the Joint Chiefs of Staff.[44]

Scott's research also indicates that while Kennedy may have ordered a halt to covert action in June 1963 pending further study, covert action against the North was continued by the CIA in defiance of the President's directive. The independence of the secret government was clearly evident at this point. States Scott, "President Kennedy had lost control of covert planning and operations." Moreover, Scott shows that the Pentagon Papers, a history of the Vietnam war written by the Pentagon and ordered by Defense Secretary Robert McNamara, covered up the abrupt change in policy and instead suggested that there was a continuity between Kennedy's policy toward Vietnam and his successor Lyndon Johnson by incorrectly stating the contents of the NSAM described above. The implications regarding the Kennedy assassination are all too obvious. Prouty, who "had the unique assignment of being the Focal Point officer for contacts between the CIA and the Department of Defense on matters pertaining to the military support of the Special [covert] Operations of that Agency," has written the following regarding Lyndon Johnson and the Kennedy assassination: "He knew exactly what had happened there in Dallas. He did not need to wait for the findings of the Warren Commission. He already knew that the death of Lee Harvey Oswald would never bring any relief to him or to his successors."[45]

The Secret Government and the Secret Team of Today[46]

The chief political officer of the NSC's Special Group which planned the Bay of Pigs invasion in 1959 was then Vice-President Richard Nixon. Following the precedent set by the Gehlen-Dulles-Wisner secret armies that penetrated the Soviet Union, Nixon and Dulles also established secret military training bases for counter-revolutionary Cubans whose assignment would be to infiltrate back into Cuba, establish centers of guerrilla military resistance (much like Gehlen's Werewolves) and wage terrorist military attacks against the economic infra-structure of Cuba. The code-name for this operation was Operation 40. In addition, Robert Mahue, a key figure in the empire of billionaire Howard Hughes, and Santo Trafficante, a Mafia casino, hotel, and prostitution operator who had been kicked out of Cuba by Fidel Castro, were brought into Operation 40. Their job was to carry out a "private" sub-operation, the assassination of Castro, his brother Raul Castro, Che Guevara and five other revolutionary Cuban government leaders.

The training of these political assassins by Trafficante and his associates, called the Shooter Team,[47] took place in Mexico at a secret Triangular-Fire Training Base. The Shooter Team attempted several assassinations of Castro between 1960 and 1963. Operation 40 (after the Bay of Pigs it was called Operation Mongoose; it is also referred to as JM/Wave, the name of a Miami CIA station), involving up to 6,000 (Cuban) counter-revolutionaries or "freedom fighters," had the support of members within the Kennedy administration. In 1963, members of Operation Mongoose were caught smuggling narcotics to the U.S. from Cuba. For reasons that are unclear, President Kennedy ordered the CIA to halt the raids in 1963.[48] According to the House Select Committee on Assassinations, it was "likely" that Santo Trafficante participated in the assassination of President Kennedy in 1963.

Operation Mongoose continued into 1965 when it was shut down. Theodore Shackley, a young CIA agent who had been brought in directly from Berlin where he had worked with Gehlen, to head Operation

Mongoose along with his deputy, Thomas Clines, were then transferred to Laos where Shackley was made Deputy Chief of Station for the CIA in Laos. While in Laos, Shackley and Clines arranged air support for one Vang Pao in a three-sided war in which Vang Pao was fighting to gain control of the Laotian opium trade. Vang Pao, in turn, helped Shackley and Clines, by financing the training of indigenous Hmong tribesmen in guerrilla war tactics for use in "unconventional warfare" activities which included the art of political assassination. A Special Operations Group, supervised by Shackley and Clines, was created which was a multi-service or Joint Task Force for unconventional warfare. General John K. Singlaub supervised the political assassination program in Laos, Cambodia, and Thailand. One of his deputies was Oliver North, a major in the Marines at the time. The Deputy Air Wing commander for the Special Operations Group was Air Force General Richard Secord. Between 1966 and 1971, this operation, using the secret Hmong tribesmen unit funded by Vang Pao's opium trade, assassinated over 100,000 suspected communists ("non-combatant village mayors, book-keepers, clerks and other civilian bureaucrats") in Laos, Cambodia, and Thailand. In 1969, Vang Pao's opium trade increased substantially as did the money flowing from it to the Special Operations Group as Santo Trafficante, from the initial Operation 40 team, worked with Vang Pao to become the number one importer and distributor of China White heroin in the United States.

In 1971, Shackley was brought back to the U.S. and made the chief of the CIA's Western Hemisphere operations. Clines was made his deputy. And from this post they directed the political assassination of Chilean socialist President Salvador Allende and his Chief of Staff in Chile as well as the military overthrow of the Chilean democratically elected government in 1973. It was during this time that Henry Kissinger declared, "I don't see why we need to stand by and watch a country go Communist due to the irresponsibility of its own people."

In 1973, Shackley and Clines were sent to Vietnam where they directed the Phoenix Project which carried out the assassination of members of the economic and political bureaucracy so that once the U.S. withdrew from Vietnam, its ability to function successfully and validate a communist alternative would be crippled. Within the Phoenix

Project, the CIA, through Shackley, Clines, and others, carried out the assassination of some "60,000 village mayors, treasurers, school teachers and other non-Viet Cong administrators." Vang Pao opium money was also used in the Phoenix Project. In charge of this drug money in Vietnam was Richard Armitage, a member of the Saigon's U.S. office of Naval Operations from 1973 to 1975.

"However, because Theodore Shackley, Thomas Clines and Richard Armitage knew that their secret anti-communist extermination program was going to be shut down in Vietnam, Laos, Cambodia, and Thailand in the very near future, they, in 1973 began a highly secret non-CIA authorized program setting up their own private anti-communist assassination and unconventional warfare program, to operate after the end of the Vietnam campaign." Shackley and Clines, therefore, began taking tons of U.S. weapons, ammunition, and explosives (stored in Thailand) and they began funnelling drug money into a secret Australian bank account.

Following the withdrawal of U.S. forces from Vietnam in 1975, Armitage was sent to Iran by Shackley and Clines in order to arrange for a secret "financial conduit" to be set up in Iran that could receive Vang Pao's drug money. These funds were intended to establish a non-CIA authorized secret team that would "seek out, identify, and assassinate socialist and communist sympathizers, who were viewed by Shackley and his 'secret team' members to be 'potential terrorists' against the Shah of Iran's government in Iran." We find, then, a privately organized secret team, run by government officials, emerging out of a government organized secret team that was privately funded. The point simply is that the linkages between private and government covert operations, by the late 1970s were growing more complex. The purpose of assassinating "communists" remained the same. And the assassination of "communists" represented an efficient way of removing obstacles in the path of market expansion. It was a rational solution.

In 1976, Richard Secord was sent to Tehran, Iran as the Deputy Assistant Secretary of Defense in Iran. He was in charge of military sales of U.S. aircraft, weapons and military equipment to "friendly" nations in the Middle East. But Secord used a middle-man, Albert Hakim. He did this so that he could purchase military equipment from the U.S.

government at a low "manufacturer's cost," turn around and sell the equipment to client states, through Hakim, at a higher "replacement cost." The difference was secretly transferred into Shackley's private secret team and into various secret bank accounts. Secord and Hakim, in other words, had joined Shackley, Clines, and Armitage in their anticommunist assassination project.

Just prior to the triumph of the Sandinistas over U.S. created dictator Anatasio Somoza in Nicaragua, representatives of the Shackley's secret team offered to assassinate the top leadership of the Sandinista movement for $650,000. It is worth noting that veterans of the 1960 Nixon-Trafficante Shooter Team that was brought together for Operation 40 were still being used by Shackley. Meanwhile, as Somoza was negotiating a lower price, it became clear that the military situation of Somoza had deteriorated significantly. The Carter administration, in the final days of Somoza's reign, had cut off the supply of military equipment by the United States. Therefore, the Shackley team arranged to fill the gap and provide Somoza with military supplies. Neither President Carter nor director of the CIA, Stansfield Turner, knew of the operations of Shackley's secret team. In fact, Turner ordered that Shackley and Clines resign from the CIA when he discovered that Shackley and Clines were linked to an illegal weapons delivery to Libya.

When the Sandinistas kicked Somoza and his supporters out of Nicaragua, Shackley, now acting privately, sent his representatives to meet with Somoza (in exile in the Bahamas). They entered into a contract to supply aircraft, weapons, ammunition, and military explosives to Somoza and his National Guard or state police which had fled Nicaragua so that they could execute a war against the Sandinista government. The remnants of the National Guard, now known as the Contras, were "virtually identical to the one(s) which Theodore Shackley and Thomas Clines had supervised against the socialist revolutionary government of Cuba from 1961 to 1965." In 1981, with the election of President Reagan, the CIA officially took over Schackley's operation of funding Somoza's National Guard or Contras. And when Congress cut off funding for the Contras in 1983, Lt. Colonel Oliver North, working with the NSC, turned to Shackley, Clines, Hakim, and Secord and had the secret team reactivate its military supply of the Contras. And when President Reagan, Attorney General Meese, CIA Director William Casey, and NSC members Robert McFarlane, John Poindexter and Oliver North decided in 1985 to secretly send weapons to "friendly" factions in Iran, they turned once again to the secret team.

After 200 years, the political system which was rooted in the desire to serve and insulate private power has been forced to circumvent, entirely, the political process. Jonathan Marshall, Peter Dale Scott, and Jane Hunter write that given general public hostility to "rolling back" socialist states in the Third World, overt pursuit of the "Reagan Doctrine" became "difficult or impossible. Even the CIA was a problematic tool of policy owing to legal requirements that it report covert operations to Congress." The reliance on private citizens to carry out foreign policy was effective because a private citizen, noted a "covert missions planner", "has no obligation to tell anyone." And the Policy Development Group within the NSC "could plan secret operations free from the obligation to report to the intelligence committees of Congress." The use of drug money as a means of covert financing also helps to avoid the messiness of prolonged debate and uncertainty.[49]

The Secret Government and Capitalism

Let us clarify the problem of secret government. First recall Madison's fundamental political concern articulated in *Federalist 10* : "...the most common and durable source of factions has been the...unequal distribution of property. Those who hold and those who are without property have ever formed distinct interests in society." The Constitution, as we have seen, was designed to hold in check those people without property, a majority at the time. It was also designed to permit property owners the freedom to own unlimited amounts of property and to have the freedom (from government) to do with that property as they pleased, to invest anywhere, and to have access to raw materials anywhere. When China sought to block Great Britain's effort to create a market for opium, John Adams said that China was acting contrary to the law of nature and that the Chinese exclusion policy is "an enormous outrage upon the rights of human nature, and upon the first principles of the rights of nations."[50] Such are the rights and freedom granted by the Constitution; they rest upon the belief that government is the source of tyranny and unchecked private power is the source of freedom. The Constitution not only was intended to create a political system that would serve private power (freedom), it was intended to guarantee that private power would remain unaccountable.

When we understand that it was the western European powers, primarily, that created and controlled markets around the globe, set up client states, inhibited the development of popular organizations such as labor unions, we understand that with freedom for property owners came institutionalized racism and militarism. Further, the Constitutional imperative to protect private power and correspondingly the need to check the political impulse of non-elites (primarily people of color) has never been relaxed. Even during the immediate postwar period when the security and wealth of the United States was unparalleled, elites were quite alarmed that the "have nots" might threaten their power and privilege. Note George Kennan's (head of the State Department Planning Staff) icy assessment of the security threat posed to the United States in1948:

> ...we have about 50% of the world's wealth, but only 6.3% of its population....In this situation, we cannot fail to be the object of resentment. Our real task in the coming period is to devise a pattern of relationships which will permit us to maintain this position of disparity without positive detriment to our national security. To do so, we will have to dispense with all the sentimentality and day-dreaming; and our attention will have to be concentrated everywhere on our immediate national objectives. We need not deceive ourselves that we can afford today the luxury of altruism and world-benefaction...We should cease to talk about vague and...unreal objectives such as human rights, the raising of the living standards, and democratization. The day is not far off when we are going to have to deal in straight power concepts. The less we are then hampered by idealistic slogans, the better.[51]

The perceived threat to U.S. security has grown in proportion to the degree that the private economy of the United States has become dependent upon the international economy. Following the rise of a monopoly sector in the United States and the subsequent merger period at the start of the twentieth-century, private elites required massive state involvement in order to manage and coordinate their far-flung empires. But the penetration of the state into economic affairs required new layers of insulation and secrecy, particularly in light of nationalist and revolutionary movements that needed to be suppressed. Thus we find that the Council on Foreign Relations, among other private elite organizations, was created in this period in order to orchestrate public policy and still maintain the separation of public and private affairs as desired by the Framers. In other words, to understand the appearance and function of the secret government we must understand the political economic nature of the Constitution. During the twentieth century, it means that we must understand the global imperatives of advanced capitalism.

Note also Lyndon B. Johnson's lament: "There are 3 billion people in the world and we have only 200 million of them. We are outnumbered 15 to one. If might did make right they would sweep over the United States and take what we have. We have what they want." Again it is the Madisonion fear, the distrust of common people, especially people of color, and the corresponding assumption that a few people, primarily white, deserved to be privileged. But there is an insidious dimension to private power that is also an essential feature of classism and racism. It is the mechanical or impersonal nature of market forces that are assumed to be natural, a given. We have become the society described by Richard Rubenstein "whose prosperity depends upon *virtuosi* capable of applying calculating rationality to large-scale corporate enterprise[s]." In fact, we are the society in which technical experts monitor all aspects of our life. We have become the society that "can ill afford the loss of highly trained managerial personnel." And as Rubenstein points out, "the Nazis…were this century's original efficiency experts." So why shouldn't we have used them? Just as Sir Henry Deterding, Chairman of Royal Dutch Shell, pointed out in 1932, the "Nazis are a great stabilizing force which would come in handy against Soviet Russia." Nazis, technical experts, scientists, and others whose notion of the good life resembles a machine-like society always come in handy when real people, with personal needs, emotions, and moral standards step in and say, "Wait a minute. It might be profitable for some, but it's wrong." After all, if political opposition can be viewed simply as an obstacle to economic growth, to be removed or eliminated, the suppression of insurrections can be easily justified.[52]

The one value which the Framers intended the government to respect was the right of individuals to pursue each of their self-interests in the context of the impersonal forces of market competition. A government which acts to curb individual activity on the basis of ethical or moral concerns is precisely what the Framers feared and sought to prevent. The steady advance of the impersonal forces of our political economy, however, has made it easier for us to think of people as things and political opponents as obstacles. And so we now live in a country that is deeply involved with:

> the existence of an international terror network which is integral to the political superstructure of U.S. client-state economies, where human and political rights are eroded with each improvement of the business climate for U.S. based multinational and transnational corporations. Case studies of the repressive instruments required to create this climate—subversion of national economies, coup d'etat, torture, and the annihilation of the political opposition through systematic disappearances and death squad activity— point to systematic cooperation between global frontier managers, such as the Israeli-U.S. connection, and continent-wide coordination between death squad and intelligence forces.[53]

Similarly, Edward S. Herman argues that, "There is a large body of evidence that U.S. training has given not the slightest nod to democracy and human rights...that as human rights conditions deteriorate, factors affecting the 'climate of investment,' like tax laws and labor repression, improve from the viewpoint of the multinational corporation...There is great deal of evidence of U.S. training in methods of torture and provision of torture technology, which have been diffused throughout the system of U.S. client states."[54]

Our own domestic population, of course, cannot escape the siege of this mentality; the situation of common people within the United States is far more similar to the situation of common people outside its borders than it is to corporate elites. Prisoners in the United States are regularly used for medical experiments that result in the "mutilating effects of disease and/or death." One reputable American scientist was reported to have said that, "Criminals in our penitentiaries are fine experimental material and much cheaper than chimpanzees." By "paying" prisoners one dollar a day, corporations maintain the fiction that such prisoners are volunteers. Bristol-Myers, Squibb, Lederle, Merck, Sharp and Dohme, and Upjohn have conducted such experiments and have had the cooperation and approval of such federal bureaucracies as the Department of Health, Education and Welfare and the Food and Drug Administration.[55] Similarly, environmentalists, organized labor, feminists, and civil rights workers present the same obstacle to corporate control in this country as their counterparts do in Europe or the Third World.

It is in this context that we should assess the desire of corporate elites to control domestic political activity in the interest of capitalist expansion and stability. For example, during the mid-1970s, the Trilateral Commission, a commission created by capitalists to coordinate public policy among the major capitalist nations, stated that there was a "crisis of democracy" because certain citizens had become too politically active. They further stated that the "effective operation of a democratic political system usually requires some measure of apathy and non-involvement on the part of some individuals and groups."[56]

In addition, Trilateralists expressed concern about the erosion of "the legitimacy of hierarchy, coercion, discipline, secrecy, and deception—all of which are, in some measure, inescapable attributes of the process of government...people no longer felt the same compulsion to obey those whom they had previously considered superior to themselves in age, rank, status, expertise, character, or talents." And they were quite specific about which people had become too involved politically: "previously passive or unorganized groups in the population, blacks, Indians, Chicanos, white ethnic groups, students, and women now embarked on concerted efforts to establish their claims to opportunities, positions, rewards, and privileges, which they had not considered themselves entitled before." Their explicit suggestion, finally, was that some groups had to be made "marginal"; "marginality on the part of some groups...has enabled democracy to function effectively."[57]

We have seen this "crisis" before. The crisis of today is the crisis of 1787 when the common people also sought to govern themselves, when they were compelled to try to protect their limited local autonomy by taking up arms during Shays Rebellion. Then the problem was defined by the Framers as the "excess of democracy." Today descendants of the Framers call it the "crisis of democracy." Then, the Framers worried that the House of Representatives, elected directly, might legislate in the interests of people with little property. Similarly, Trilateralists have complained of the "chain of picayune legislative restrictions and prohibitions." Meanwhile, executive elites who assume the hidden positions of power within executive intelligence, military, and security agencies and who constitute the secret government worry that the checks and balances designed by the Framers to control public power are inadequate to protect private power. The protections, regulations, and access to secrets that we have won through struggle are under increasing assault. More secrecy and insulation for private power is needed.

The rise of the secret government and the use of secret teams does present us with a Constitutional crisis. But the crisis is not that the values of the Framers or the purpose of the Constitution are being violated. President Eisenhower "preferred not to know about clandestine operations such as the...overthrow of the democratically elected Arbenz regime in Guatemala..." and left the planning and the execution of the covert action to a secret committee within the NSC.[58] This type of deference to the needs of private capital is quite consistent with the purpose of the Constitution and varies insignificantly from the deference President Madison (Father of the Constitution) showed to General Andrew Jackson when he killed 800 Native Americans at the Battle of Horseshoe Bend in 1814 and then as treaty commissioner took away half the land of the Creek nation. Remember, the Constitution states that only Congress can declare war but it says nothing about who can make war or when it should be declared. The crisis occurs when there is a clash between the secret government and the elected government (as in the case of an independent Kennedy) or when there is a clash between the secret government and the people directly, as in the case of social movements during and after Vietnam or in other periods when common people try to become meaningfully involved in public affairs and are repressed by such programs as COINTELPRO. The fundamental crisis, then, is that the values of the Framers and the political system that they created are clearly undemocratic. And the unaccountable private power which they championed has today become so concentrated and the rich citizens they thought would be so virtuous have instead become so desperate to extend a declining empire that the United States now threatens democracy and decency around the globe.

Part III

A Song Without Knees

One of the gravest obstacles to the achievement of liberation is that oppressive reality absorbs those within it and thereby acts to submerge...[our] consciousness. Functionally, oppression is domesticating. To no longer be prey to its force, one must emerge from it and turn upon it.

—**Paolo Freire**

When Protestors Become Police

We are called upon to raise certain basic questions about the whole society...We must see that the evils of racism, economic exploitation, and militarism are all tied together, and you really can't get rid of one without getting rid of the others...The whole structure of American life must be changed.

—Martin Luther King, Jr.

And that, that is the secret of happiness and virtue—liking what you've *got* to do. All conditioning aims at that: making people like their unescapable social destiny.

—The Director, *Brave New World*

Many of us might agree with Martin Luther King, Jr. that the whole structure of American life must be changed. John Judge, a researcher in California who, after comparing the irrationality of our political economy with Germany in the 1930s, was asked, "But where are the camps?" Judge responded:

There are camps. There's slave labor here in the United States. It's hidden under the corporate fronts, on the privately owned farms, in certain industries. But it's here if people took the time to look at it. It's in the institutions. It's in the prisons, the pyschiatric prisons, the legal prisons that are our Third World, that everyone turns their face and attention away from. It's in the VA [Veterans Administration] where people are used 80,000 a month as human guinea pigs to test the drugs and the new techniques for the medical and psychiatric facilities. It's out in the streets where the homeless are not caged, but left to die, left to be surplus population, left to be useless eaters. People are not picked up and put into ovens, ovens are dropped out of the sky, white phosporous and napalm in Vietnam and El Salvador and in the countries that are attacked. It's still genocide. It's still aimed at the same target and it still comes in the end to the same thing. And should power ever shift on this globe, should this ever not be six percent of the population consuming sixty percent of the energy and thirty percent of the resources of the world. And should we ever be held accountable, ask yourself honestly how different will the testimony be from that of those fascists in Nuremberg at the end of World War II, how different from the testimony of Contragate, that I was only following orders? I did what I was told. I was supporting murder, sabotage, death, in the name of freedom, anything in the name of freedom, someone's freedom, somewhere—certainly not the people under the gun, but for their version of freedom and their version of democracy which means class privilege as opposed to their version of communism which means democracy and democratic control.[1]

Suggestions that something is fundamentally wrong with our political economy and the Constitution are more than difficult to accept; they are difficult even to reflect upon. It is far easier to live in the comfort zone and seek happiness, as The Director would have us do, in liking what we have got to do. Even in our protests we slide away from a direct confrontation of the structure of American life. We tend to avoid the harsh implications of reality and cling to the image of the United States as a basically free and democratic country in the way that one clings to prayer beads or a good luck charm. The axioms of empire have become the axioms of faith. The result is that instead of effective radical politics, our movement tends always to be divided into two main camps. One camp, composed of *Congressional Technocrats,* insists that the problems we face are problems which can be dealt with by working through the system; politics for them is essentially legislative work. In the second camp are *Abstract Spiritualists* who believe that the problems we face are problems that can be solved through individual commitments to spiritual renewal, peace, non-violence, and justice. For them political work consists, essentially, of acknowledging that a life force, or god, exists in every human being and in expressing the kind of respect for others that befits a peace-loving community. In neither camp is the Constitution and the global capitalism it supports pointed to as a feature of our existence that is in need of radical change.

These two categories are somewhat artificial as are most analytical tools. It is possible that there is no real single person that fits neat-

ly into either category and certainly there are groups and ways of thinking that overlap both and then some. *Moreover, I wish to state very clearly that this analysis is not an indictment of the people involved in doing
political work in either camp.* Rather it is an attempt to identify a very
dangerous tendency. Because each group is marked by a failure to confront the system, it carries within it an *implicit endorsement* of the system and a very real tendency to discipline, if not purge, those protestors
who seek to pursue a strategy which does have as its center an indictment of the whole structure of American life. There is a dynamic, then,
which moves protestors to become "police."

Congressional Technocrats

The first responsibility of the federal government, as we have
seen, is to promote economic growth. And those people in the private
sector who own industries in the growth sectors also own the "goose
that lays the golden egg." They set the policy agenda. This has been
the theme so far. The theme which I wish to develop in this section is
this: legislation, of necessity, fits within and becomes part of this overall process of expanding the opportunities for investment and profit,
and of limiting political "opposition" so that it too does not challenge
the assumption that all of this makes for a free and healthy society. The
legislative process is an instrument of conquest and social control.
Therefore when we do legislative work, *without at the same time trying
to expose and challenge its limitations,* we inadvertently become complicit in the act of conquest and our efforts at social change slide into
measures of social control. Before we go further, let us identify some
obvious limitations that need to be challenged.

The Bias of Congressional Activity

Have you ever wondered why certain policies, while opposed by
a majority of U.S. citizens (such as the funding of the Contras or the
production of more nuclear weapons), continue to be promoted,

financed, and implemented year after year? The explanation has to do with what is called *structure* . And as we have seen, the Constitution was designed to permit large property owners to have more power or influence over public policy than the majority of people with little or no property. People of property were thought to be wiser; the political tendencies of common people were distrusted because the "have-nots" tend to challenge the privilege of the "haves". The legislative process was and is, in addition to being a process where laws are made, a mechanism intended to insure that common people not "discover their own strength." Let us see exactly how this happens.

A legislative process governed by simple majority rule would look something like this: there is a single body of representatives. Legislative proposals are introduced, debated, and voted upon. If a majority of members vote for the proposal, it either becomes law or, depending on the kind of constitution, sent on to another branch of government. Our system is not like that. First, there are two legislative chambers, the House of Representatives and the Senate, each with different rules. All legislation must be passed by each chamber in identical form before it can become law. And within each chamber, work is done by committees; that is, bills are routed through a series of committees within each chamber. Therefore, there are numerous places at which bills may be blocked or checked and majorities defeated. In other words, powerful interests opposed to any piece of legislation have multiple opportunities to shoot it down. Only a few bills of the ones introduced ever become law. For example, of the 7,458 bills that were introduced into the House of Representatives in the 97th Congress (1982-83), only 251 actually became law or about 3 percent.[2] To use Madisonian language, the process is one of "refinement" and "filtration."

We could spend quite a bit of time going over the legislative process, but that would be as tedious and as boring as the subject of our study.[3] The conclusion we might draw, however, after having studied the legislative process in detail is that it is not only complex, it is biased. As many students of Congress have noted, "The American system of federal government was designed with the intention of making sweeping, decisive reform difficult to enact...[It has] a bias toward 'doing nothing.'"[4] Doing nothing, of course, maintains the *status quo*. But the bias in question does more than give advantage to those opposed to reform. It gives, as was intended, great advantage to property. For example, a group of gas and oil companies known as the Alaska Natural Gas Consortium wanted to bring gas from Alaska to consumers in the United States. They went before Congress in 1981 and argued that because Alaska gas was expensive compared to Texas and Louisiana gas, tax payers should help pay for the cost of doing business. Congress agreed and a bill was passed stating that if the market price of the gas turned out to be so high that it could not find a market in the lower forty-eight states or if the pipeline was only 70 percent completed, the cost would be paid by the consumers who would have gotten the natural gas had the pipeline been completed. Potential liability? Forty-five billion dollars.[5] I think most would agree that such legislation is controversial. But it passed rather easily because it was consistent with the function of the government to promote economic growth and to protect the freedom and privilege of large property owners. The legislative or filtration process as conceived by the Framers was designed to check the compulsive passions of common people because of the anticipated resentment which common people would feel from being used and which would issue in challenges to the prerogatives of private power.

We can better understand the legislative bias when we note that congressional activity itself is but the most visible aspect of the legislative process. Less visible is the very structure of political-economic power in which it is lodged and in which corporate elites set the legislative agenda. Less visible still is the corruption and *covert legislation* that is required by a system which is committed to both protecting privilege and maintaining the appearance of democracy. It is to the less visible structure of power that we now turn.

Structural Imperatives

Mark Green, in a study exposing the enormous collusion between large corporations and members of Congress, has written, "The point is not that members of Congress are corrupt. Few are. It's the system that's corrupt—a system that provides nearly irresistible temptations to public office holders."[6] Green is referring to the constant need of members of Congress to raise money for re-election campaigns and the constant willingness of corporations to engage in various forms of bribery. The dairy industry's conversion in 1971 of its half-million line of credit with Congress into a half-billion in extra income is pretty common stuff. But tales of corruption only remind us that corporate leaders will cheat even when the deck is stacked in their favor. The primary function of the government has always been to advance the interests of the property owning class against all others. It is a *structural imperative*. Their interest is the national interest. The drafting of major legislation has always been rooted in the need to promote the interests of whatever happens to be the major industries—from shipping, tobacco, and cotton on up to the "defense" related industries of today.

Consequently as the U.S. economy became truly international in character, most major legislative initiatives emerged not from Congress but from the executive branch which is a far more effective representative of multinational corporations than are the 535 members of Congress with their parochial interests. For example, between 1882 and 1909, Congress was responsible for drafting 55 percent of the major laws passed while between 1933 and 1940 that percentage had dropped to 8. Also through the creation of the Bureau of the Budget in 1921 (now the Office of Management and Budget) and its movement to the Executive Office of the President in 1939, revenue raising bills, in effect, no longer originate in the House of Representatives as stipulated by the Constitution. While this violates the letter of the Constitution, it does not violate its spirit: major legislation is still initially drafted by private elites or their representatives. It is just that today, the global nature of corporations has rendered Congress and the interstate industries for which it was created somewhat anachronistic. As Ira Katznelson and Mark Kesselman reaffirm, "Most major bills are drafted in the executive agencies and are put on the president's legislative program, which becomes the basic legislative agenda."[7]

But what are executive agencies? They are the government's host of corporate lobbyists, which in 1983 was estimated by *Fortune* magazine to consist of an army of 92,500 or 6 percent of the entire Washington labor force. In addition to bribes, they provide Congressional staffs and executive agencies with information and analysis necessary to draft legislation. During the "energy crisis" of 1973-74, "the government continued to rely heavily on, of all disinterested observers, the oil companies and their lobbyists for data on oil and gas supplies..."[8] But this is a pluralist system. Anyone is free to organize. Tenants' rights organizations can compete with urban real estate magnates, mortgage bankers, downtown merchants, and developers for the attention of the Department of Housing and Urban Development.

Quite often lobbyists are dispensed with and members of the executive branch, Congressional leaders, and executives meet and bargain directly. In June 1981, when the smaller, more conservative wing of big business was about to succeed in drafting tax "reform" measures that would have hugely slashed personal tax rates for top income brackets, the Business Roundtable (a group of about 200 of chief executive officers of the nation's very largest corporations), worried that personal tax cuts would risk increased budget deficits and jeopardize many corporate tax breaks, called an emergency meeting. The result of the meeting was that "executives of America's top firms descended on Washington in droves, for an orgy of lobbying that became known as the 'Lear Jet Weekend.' " Working directly with White House officials, other business groups (such as the American Council for Capital Formation, the American Business Council, the Chamber of Commerce, and the National Association of Manufacturers), and leaders of the congressional Ways and Means Committee, the Business Roundtable's conception of tax reform prevailed. Normally, such emergency action is not necessary. The different sets of big-business coalitions work very closely together to form what are often quaintly referred to as political parties. And it is through political parties that private elites choose the congressional leaders (the Speaker of the House, Majority Leaders, Minority Leaders, and party whips in both chambers) who are, essentially, corporate gate-keepers positioned strategically along the legislative path.[9]

Today, with the American empire in decline, the projection of force and power abroad and the imposition of economic repression upon workers in the weakest sectors of the economy at home ("sacrifice") have become structural imperatives. Policy options have narrowed. Congressional debate and competition has fallen to unprecedented levels, while most campaign contributions are invested in incumbents, who in 1984 won 96.4 percent of all congressional races. An ominous consensus has emerged and it is within this very structured set of options, called *reindustrialization,* that Congressional Technocrats must, with their meager resources and divergent views, "pressure" Congress.[10]

The basic thrust of reindustrialization is to move away from a liberal approach to state intervention in the economy where the imperial dividends of an expanding empire were once sufficient to pay for a variety of limited social programs. The newer approach, based on the shared understanding that the imperial dividends are drying up and America's economic pie is shrinking, requires that the state "curtail business regulation ('deregulation'), subsidize businesses with a promising future in the international economy, reduce taxes on capital and savings, increase depreciation allowances, decontrol oil and natural gas prices, subsidize a shift from oil to coal, give private management more help in improving worker productivity, and sharply increase military production."[11]

Business Week, in June 1980, spelled out the new reality confronting embattled elites: no longer could they comply with the Foreign Corrupt Practices Act because it "severely limits corporate payments of fees to obtain contracts abroad." In other words, bribery is a necessary part of doing business. Trade embargoes designed to protect human rights must be abandoned; they "limit sales of grain and high technology equipment to the East bloc." The Nuclear Proliferation Treaty needs to be reconsidered because it "limits exports of nuclear reactors and materials to countries that might produce a bomb." An emphasis on human rights is problematic because it "limits trade with certain countries that violate human rights." Antitrust laws need to be revised because they "prohibit U.S. corporations from establishing joint trading companies." Health, safety, and environmental regulations are too costly to comply with at home and they "enforce strict U.S. standards for overseas operation of U.S. companies." What we need, suggests *Busi-*

ness Week, is a "remodeling…of the social contract," one that reflects the "understanding that our common interest in returning the country to a path of strong economic growth overrides other conflicting interests."[12] We need a social contract, in other words, in which we agree to put profits before people.

To keep the system afloat, it is generally agreed, the state must provide the most important corporations with as many resources and with as much military support as is politically feasible. Elites are being quite blunt about it. The state can no longer "support an ever rising standard of living; create endless jobs; provide education, medical care and housing for everyone; abolish poverty; rebuild the cities; restore the environment; satisfy the demands of blacks, Hispanics, women and other groups." But the state can satisfy the demands of capitalists because the political system is *their* system. Here, in so many words, elites have told us that the purpose of the state is to do everything it can to assist capital but it cannot meet the demands of environmentalists, women, blacks, Latinos, and "other groups." I doubt that we shall get clearer signals. *Reindustrialization means discipline.* As Congressional Technocrats, our oppositional stance merely lends legitimacy to a process that needs to be challenged.

Legislative Dirty Tricks

As if the checks built into the legislative process were not enough, there is yet another another undemocratic weapon in the legislative arsenal of elites called covert or "black budget" financing where "billions of dollars in Federal funds remain hidden from public view. They undergo no audit by the General Accounting Office [GAO]. They are concealed even from most Members of Congress." And there are "dark corners of the budget, where congressional knowledge" is "nonexistent."[13]

Covert financing is nothing new. The Framers supported the need for "perfect secrecy" (*Federalist No. 64*) and President Washington was provided a $40,000 fund in 1790 that he could spend secretly. But today there are funds which remain secret at every stage, from appropriation on through to auditing. Often this is done through sleight of hand bookkeeping. Money appropriated for refugee programs, for public health, agriculture, economic and technical projects, and for the Food for Peace program, for example, was once diverted for CIA- directed paramilitary programs in Laos.[14] Also covert activities are sometimes carried out by agencies such as the Drug Enforcement Agency because they do not have to be reported to Congress.[15] Today, budget manipulation has assumed greater regularity and deception. There is a secret budget within the Pentagon, which the Pentagon calls its "black budget," and about which national security laws forbid public congressional debate. It has tripled to $35 billion since President Reagan took office in 1981. Bigger than the entire federal budget for health care, it is used for the research and development of super-secret projects. Moreover, it is the fastest growing of any major sector within the federal government.[16]

Thomas Amlie, a Pentagon missile expert, stated that with regard to the black budget "there is no accountability whatsoever." Representative John D. Dingell (D-Michigan) notes that "the Pentagon keeps these programs of almost unbelievable size secret from Congress, from the General Accounting Office, from its own auditing agencies," and that covert financing "conceals outright illegal activities." The Pentagon can hide what it is doing by simply deleting projects from unclassified budgets and then classify them so that they are beyond the reach of congressional investigators. The Pentagon also uses code names such as "Elegant Lady" or vague classifications such as "special activities," as well as a double ledger system of accounting in which "brooms become computers and computers become bombs" in order to cover its tracks. In other words, it lies. Representative Denny Smith (R-Oregon) has complained, "As a congressman, I can't get information...They don't want us munching around in their budget. There's a real question here. Will the military accept civilian leadership when it comes to choosing weapons?"

The seamy side of U.S. military activity was inadvertently exposed a bit when in March 1983 a retired colonel testifying before a House Foreign Affairs subcommittee acknowledged that he had worked with "the Activity" on a secret mission to find U.S. soldiers that had been missing in Laos. Congress had never heard of anything called "the Activity." Further investigation revealed that "the Activity" was the Intelligence Support Activity, a secret spy squad, with a corps of at least 250 officers, that was created in 1981 without the knowledge of Congress. The unit was intended to be a "permanent, unified, clandestine group to coordinate paramilitary actions and intelligence gathering." It has been active in Nicaragua, Europe, Africa, Southeast Asia, and the Middle East. The Activity appears to be part of what Defense Secretary Caspar Weinberger has told Congress to be "one of this administration's highest priorities," and that is the building up of the U.S. Special Operations Forces, or covert soldiers, to a level of 20,000 by 1989. Special Operations Forces, unlike the CIA, "are not required to report their covert activities to Congress." Senator Jim Sasser (D-Tennessee) has warned that "There is a real danger that these Special Forces could be used by CIA programs and thus skirt congressional review."

More startling has been the Pentagon use of covert financing to fund weapons systems that would be able to operate in a post-nuclear war battlefield and orchestrate space satellites and nuclear weapons during *World War IV*. Since 1981, according to Tim Weiner, "the fundamental U.S. defense strategy has been to be able to fight and win a six-month nuclear conflict—World War III—and remain strong enough afterward to strike again." The strategy is as follows: nuclear war command posts would consist of 747s in the air, lead-lined tractor-trailers positioned on interstate highways, and deep underground command centers in the Catoctin Mountains near Raven, Pennsylvania. Robot soldiers or "hexapods" that move like a tank and "quadrupeds" that gallop and trot, in addition to "walking vehicles," would operate in "an enhanced nuclear environment." Eight satellites (Milstar), placed in orbit 70,000 miles into space—above the electromagnetic pulse generated by nuclear blasts, would become the global nuclear-communications switchboard, transmitting information to the secret command posts. Lest anyone think this is pure fantasy, on December 4, 1986, an Atlas-Centaur rocket blasted off from Cape Canaveral to carry out the first space test of the Milstar system. The projected cost of preparing for World War IV is $40 billion, but it too has become an imperative.

The Policing Effect of Congressional Technocrats

Congressional Technocrats assume that our political system is democratic, that congressional policy options are not structured, that there are no systemic imperatives, and that the good men and women of Congress can write, and implement, policies within a range that is virtually unlimited. If we work hard enough, it is assumed, and carefully enough, and if we educate enough people, we can build a broad enough coalition to pressure congress into writing policies that we want. I have argued that our political system does not work that way. We do not live in a democracy. We live in a capitalist system in which freedom means the individual freedom to own and accumulate property. The function of the government is to help property owners do just that. Policy options are structured, in short, to make the economy grow. At any given stage of development, there are certain growth imperatives—protecting market relations in 1787, acquiring land and subsidizing railroad expansion following the Civil War, and today the consensus among many elites is that reindustrialization must move forward. The function of representatives is to write policies toward that end *and help us to understand that what we need is what the system can provide.* When our perceived needs and systemic imperatives collide, it is the job of representatives to channel our demands into systemic imperatives. Thus, wars of aggression are defined in ways that validate our values: the United States is fighting for democracy. If we refuse to pay higher taxes, that is taken as an opportunity to cut corporate taxes, increase budget deficits, and discipline the poor. Preparation for nuclear war is increasing the inventory of "peace keepers." And so on. Let us examine one example of co-optation in more detail.[17]

In 1982, the Reagan administration's economic policy had failed to reverse the downturn that had begun with Carter. In addition, its huge military buildup and Regan's own "Evil Empire" rhetoric toward the Soviet Union appeared to be destabilizing. These failed policies particularly disturbed a faction of elites within the Democratic party that were linked to multinational corporations that were oriented toward Europe and interested in doing business with the Soviet Union. Among them were Averell Harriman (a prominent investment banker), Thomas J. Watson, Jr. (IBM), Robert McNamara (World Bank, Shell, Ford Foundation), Admiral Bobby Inman (former Deputy Director of the CIA, head of MCC, a computer consortium), Sol Linowitz (Xerox, Time Inc.), Roberto Goizueta (Coca-Cola), Robert Pheiffer (IBM-AFE), Donald Platen (Chemical Bank), Frank Shakespeare (RKO General), Jerome Wiesner (director of Schlumberger, a giant French oil-drilling concern). Also concerned were Richard Lyman, president of the Rockefeller Foundation, the Rockefeller grandchildren (The Rockefeller Family Fund), and leaders of the MacArthur foundation, the Ford Foundation, and the Carnegie Endowment for International Peace. This alliance, of which the above is but a sampling, began funding a host of studies on arms control and nuclear issues, various peace related groups, and meetings. Their objective was to build up conventional land and air forces, especially in Europe, cut back and save on the huge naval build-up, and reduce the reliance on nuclear weapons. This would reduce tensions among First World nations and the Soviet Union and enhance the U.S. capability to militarily penetrate and control strategic areas of the Third World. Their strategy was build a movement among dissident elites. This was necessary to pass legislation. And their strategy was to co-opt the growing grassroots campaign for a "nuclear freeze." This would popularize and legitimize empire building. It was the old liberal strategy revisited.

Forbes 400 contributed to groups like the Council for a Livable World and the Union of Concerned Scientists. Physicians whose salaries were diminished by Reagan's budget cuts now flocked to Physicians for Social Responsibility. They could do good and get rich at the same time. New England anti-nuclear activists suddenly found themselves in meetings in posh urban hotels. But as Ferguson and Rogers note, there was a danger in funding the grassroots part of the movement; "Few of the business groups and foundations that how helped push it along wanted to explore the relations between multinational business, the use of force in American foreign policy and social class. Accordingly, the critical content of the early freeze proposals largely evaporated." At the great anti-nuclear demonstration of June 1982, for example, where 2.5 million people would march in New York and

San Francisco, sponsors of the actions met privately and decided not to protest Israel's invasion of Lebanon that had taken place days before. This is an important point: whenever our work is centered on passing legislation we must build coalitions by appealing to those elements in society for whom the legislative process was designed, is meaningful, and in whom there is no genuine sympathy for fundamental change. We invariably are compelled to discipline and police those whose politics suggest that, in some important ways, the legislative process is a fraud.[18]

With a relatively controlled "popular movement" behind them, the Democrats went on to endorse the "freeze." This meant they could move away from supporting some of the "big-ticket" items (the MX, B-1, Trident II) and escalate the drive for a whole new generation of conventional weapons (precision-guided munitions, battlefield missiles, pilotless drones and robots, supersophisticated tanks). The "movement" also permitted the "freeze-inspired" Reagan administration to push for the scrapping of old nuclear weapons ("build-down") and the modernizing of strategic forces as freeze-inspired.

Toward the end of the 1984 campaign, Walter Mondale, the Democratic nominee, deviated a bit from orthodox elitism and made vague statements about redistributing income from the rich to the poor. When his business supporters complained bitterly, Mondale responded: "Oh my goodness, I'm so sorry. There's nothing wrong with wanting to be rich. I want to be rich." The statement illustrates quite well the real range of policy options within our political system today. The point is that when we work as Congressional Technocrats, not only are political questions transformed into technical considerations regarding the legislative and electoral strategy, not only is our ability to think reflectively and critically diminished, but our assumptions to start with are wrong. Consider the role of doing "educational" work. Focusing on education implies that the irrationality of contemporary public policy is due to the fact that citizens are uninformed. It may be that we are not as informed as we should be. But the argument I have developed so far suggests that having more information will not translate into having more power. American political institutions were not intended to ensure that those people who were best informed or who had the best argument would write public policy. Our political structure was designed to ensure that those people who own significant property and who have power will write policy whether or not they are informed, wise, or rational.

Because Congressional Technocrats assume that our system of electoral politics permits the decency of most Americans to find expression in public policy, it is unlikely that they will examine the possibility that our political system was designed to help the few who have economic power keep it to themselves. Educational strategies that teach people to believe that their lives would be noticeably improved if everyone "kept informed," voted, assembled quietly, signed petitions, and wrote letters to their representatives *is a strategy for purging those who believe that a system which holds them in contempt must be confronted.* For when political opposition is defined in such a way as to fit within the space provided by the Constitution for political opposition, then those who work outside that space must appear to be irresponsible and deserve to have rationality imposed upon them. Confrontational acts which disrupt then must be viewed as mocking perseverance and patience. And radicals who engineer such confrontations, it must seem, carelessly alienate the very constituencies that have influence and that must be enlisted in order to effect social change. Regrettably, perhaps, but necessarily, such radicals must be contained.

Abstract Spiritualists

[A]mong some humanistic and transpersonal psychologists...[it is assumed] that at the core of every person is a fundamental spiritual harmony that links him or her not only to every other person but to the cosmos as a whole. Here, too, external authority, cultural tradition, and social institutions are all eschewed. The self in all its pristine purity is affirmed. But somehow that self, once discovered, turns out to be at one with the universe....But such romantic individualism is remarkably thin when it comes to any but the vaguest prescription about how to live in an actual society.

—**Bellah, Madsen, Sullivan, Swidler, and Tipton,**
Habits of the Heart

Protest of modern life has always been, in various ways, an attempt to overcome its expressive deadness. In this respect protest may be generally thought of as embodying a spiritual dimension. And as protestors, we are all spiritualists to varying degrees. Indeed, spiritualism allows our souls to be nourished. It permits us to dream. It is the source of our poetry.

Many dissidents today are attempting to bring forward spiritual rhythms and a sensitivity to the hidden poetry of everyday life. Many identify with the New Age movement which is centered, according to Harvey Wasserman, upon an "overriding commitment to health, both individual and planetary," and to "holism," or the interrelationship of mind, body, emotions, relationships, plants, and animals as a whole organism. The roots of the New Age movement make contact with earlier peace and environmental movements, self-treatment and back-to-the-earth tendencies of previous decades, the influx of Asian gurus in the 1960s, and the revival of interest in Native American culture. Many have been drawn into the practices of Zen, Sufism, Vipassana Buddhism, Sikhism and eastern religious philosophies which unlike mainstream western ways of living call attention to the value of opening ourselves to the rewards of direct experience and discovering the "god within."[19]

Spiritualism has also spread rapidly within certain branches of the women's movement, particularly among radical feminists (increasingly referred to as cultural or spiritual feminists) who emphasize the power relations emerging not out of class but out of the sex/gender system. According to Joan Cocks, radical feminists today pay a good deal of attention to mutuality and their organic connection with other women "as well as with the good, beleagured earth." Their work has shifted away from politics as such and into the domain of culture and "to the introspective domain of the psyche."[20] Among more traditional spiritualists have been Jewish and Christian groups. In the 1980s, particularly within the solidarity and peace movements, traditional spiritualists such as the Unitarians and the Quakers have frequently provided the leadership. This in part is due to the broad acceptance of their stress upon Gandhian principles of non-violence and pacifism and the value in moral witness, the strength of their organizations, and their steady, hard work.

Although quite varied, efforts to open ourselves to spiritual life seem to express a longing for elements of a world gone by. We can glimpse that world by putting ourselves in the place of Crollius who looked out at the world in 1624 and understood the following:

> The stars are the matrix of all the plants and every star in the sky is only the spiritual prefiguration of a plant, such that it represents that plant, and just as each herb or plant is a terrestrial star looking up at the sky, so also each star is a celestial plant in spiritual form, which differs from the terrestrial plants in matter alone...The celestial plants and herbs are turned toward the earth and look directly upon the plants they have procreated, imbuing them with some particular virtue.[21]

The relationship between the stars and the plants in Crollius's world may seem odd to us until we understand *his way* of understanding. It is a world in which nature, sacred texts, and even words are "alive with God's signature and purpose."[22] Joan Cocks adds that "...the medieval Christians understood the world as the manifestation of...divine reason that in turn justified—indeed, required—specific emotional attitudes on the part of humans toward the various things in the world, from floods to hazelnuts, from magnanimity to war." Crollius's interpretation of his world was his attempt to understand "something of the purposeful order given to us by God." Knowledge assumed "the form of commentary on meanings and affinities inscribed in the text of the world by God." To know, as Cocks points out, was also to know a feeling; reason and emotion were unified. The world was enchanted, full of spiritual life. Today our knowledge is based upon "laws of nature" which have been established experimentally and upon the collection of "facts" which in themselves have no meaning. Reason and emotion are separate. The world is disenchanted, emptied of spiritual life.[23]

The great advance in the shift away from the spiritual world toward modern institutions had to do with how we thought of our-selves as a subject. Whereas in previous ages each of us was defined in relation to a larger divine or cosmic order, today we are self-defining, conscious of ourselves, and therefore self-creating. Consequently we understand ourselves to be responsible for the way we live. We have a bicameral legislature, for example, not because it is the signature of God but because a group of men in Philadelphia in 1787 decided that that is what we should have. The disenchantment of our world, in other words, permitted us to see ourselves, not God, as the creators of our world. We became subjects. We became citizens. Legitimacy became an issue. And protest, political change, reform, and revolution became possibilities.

But at what a cost! What a high price we have payed for subjectivity. We have been divided into mind and body, body and soul. Emotion has been separated from reason. Passion and spontaneity have been devalued. Nature has become inert, dead, an object for scientific and industrial manipulation. Society has become bureaucratic organization. Our everyday life has become routinized and predictable as we strap clocks to our bodies. Our lives are measured in terms of production, utility, and profit. In short, we have gained a mind and have acquired the ability to create but little that we do expresses what it means to be human. We have gained minds and lost our souls.

Protest that arises both out of clear critical thought and deep sensitivity to spiritual life promises a great deal. It promises to recover the lost expressive unity in order that the personality of the modern subject may be made full. It promises, in other words, to give bureaucrats back their soul. *But spiritualism itself, however, can also be expressively dead.* As some Nicaraguans pointed out prior to their revolution, the trouble with many priests was that they spent most of their time praying in the church. A priest who spends nearly all his time praying would be someone whose spiritualism is expressively dead. It is pure, to be sure. But it finds no expression on the public stage. Its principles do not directly challenge any principles of this world about which the priest prays. Spiritualism of this nature is without situation. It becomes abstract. And Abstract Spiritualism, rather than becoming a source of liberation, becomes an *escape from politics,* and ultimately a source of discipline. But it is the escape from politics that makes Abstract Spiritualism so attractive.

For those of us who cherish the hidden poetry of a simple life but who avoid the pain and difficulty of confronting our responsibility for the orgy of grotesque inhumanity that flows from empire, Abstract Spiritualism seems to provide a way out. We can retreat to the edge of conflict where our purity and our outrage can be maintained without jeopardizing our identity as a free and innocent people. But while we live on the edge of conflict, we live on the edge of history. Our spiritualism must become private and directed inward. The celebration of peace and the artificial construction of harmony displaces political struggle. In order to keep the peace, Abstract Spiritualists must dampen the struggle.

A Case Study: The Pledge of Resistance

Founded by "major peace, justice, and anti-interventionist groups" in October 1984 and led by religious activists, the "Pledge of Resistance" is a national campaign to mobilize opposition to U.S. military intervention in Central America. The organizing vehicle for the campaign is a pledge. Already signed by tens of thousands of U.S. citizens, the pledge is a commitment to "engage in acts of nonviolent civil disobedience and/or legal protest in the wake of significant U.S. military escalation in Central America."[24] The Pledge of Resistance, or simply the Pledge, has come to dominate the mode of response by activists working within the solidarity movement; and given the importance of Central America within the Reagan administration's foreign policy agenda as well as its linkage to broader questions of militarism, budgetary concerns, and global peace, the influence of Pledge organizers extends well beyond the issues of Central America. Moreover, much of what the Pledge is about—the marriage of resistance and spiritualism, a strict obedience to nonviolence, the practice of consensus, the use of small, "autonomous" groups, the emphasis on respecting all people, and the development of orderly and disciplined protest is an amalgamation of principles derived from previous campaigns directed against weapons production and nuclear power. Pledge activists, as most unhappily agree, are white and middle-class. The thinking of Pledge organizers represents the thinking, perhaps, of the "better educated," better organized, more privileged elements within "the movement" today. In any case, among resistance-minded activists it is a major, if not dominant, force. I shall argue that in spite of their decency and honorable intentions, the thinking of Pledge organizers compels them, in the end, to work with elites in isolating and purging dissidents whose vision of community challenges the political-economy of the United States.[25]

Given the analysis presented in the *Pledge of Resistance Handbook,* the position of Pledge organizers may be briefly characterized as follows: It is urgent that we begin to live our lives in a way that implies love, respect, and human dignity. Many of the pledge signers are like the pastor who, by signing the pledge, believes s\he is living out "what's called the good news, that is the good news of God's peace and justice." The general threat to peace and justice is violence. Specifically the threat is war and repressive economic and social structures. Living out the "good news" or simply living a life which expresses respect for others inevitably brings one into confrontation with repressive structures and with those who carry out war.

But how does one confront these things? The traditional answer, namely that war can be stopped by more decisive violence, must be rejected; "the means by which we come together and act determine and affect our ends." The "guiding vision" of the Pledge suggests an alternative approach: "war can be repudiated before it fully erupts...by the nonviolent withdrawal of support for it." Indeed, Pledge organizers emphasize, "This campaign is rooted in the simple intuition that wars happen because people cooperate with them—and wars end when that collaboration also ends." Each of us has power, therefore. And the power to wage war depends upon our continuing obedience, "so when we refuse to obey our rulers, their power begins to crumble." Moreover, by resisting in a nonviolent way, we reveal "another model of human nature," one which encourages love, respect, and human dignity within the broader community.

There can be no question but that the ends of the Pledge organizers are noble. Their general effort to empower people by encouraging resistance to the corruption of public policy needs to be kept as the first item on every citizen's agenda. Moreover, the Pledge appears to offer an opportunity to link spiritual principles to effective, practical action. But there are serious, if not dangerous, defects within this approach as well. The source of these defects lies in the failure of the Pledge analysis to attend to the complexities of the relation between the structural features of the U.S. political economy and the subversion of peace and justice. Reference is made to such maladies as "corporate lies" and we learn that Gandhi "bade his followers to focus their anger and hatred on their true enemy—repressive economic and social structures"—not people, but nowhere is there the suggestion that the very structure in which we are implicated (the U.S. political economy) begets violence and repression. Of course this is a tremendous advantage. *It means that signers of the Pledge are able to link spiritual principles with a practical course of action without having to develop a general critique of our political economy, without, in other words, having to be placed outside the mainstream of American political thought.* Or to put it quite bluntly, it means that as protestors they are able to stake out a position whicih avoids official pronouncement as a deviant, troublemaker, or radical. The Pledge looks like protest but it does not really challenge our political-economic institutions and therefore contributes to their legitimation. The appearance of political freedom within the United States, for example, tends to be reinforced by their example. By working within the Pledge framework, we risk becoming Hegel's beautiful soul who "lives in dread of besmirching the splendour of its inner being by action...in order to preserve the purity of its heart...it flees from contact with the actual world and persists in its self-willed impotence to give itself a substantial existence or to translate its thought into being."[26]

The danger in preserving the purity of our heart in the face of the national security state is not simply one of living with the illusion of effectiveness, it is, ironically, becoming complicit in repression. We are moving in this dangerous direction in several ways. Although these tendencies are not confined to the Pledge movement, Pledge organizers are far more explicit about their politics; therefore their writings and actions serve as useful illustrations. Let us probe, then, these tendencies.

Nonviolence and Peace: A Dangerous Focus

Pledge organizers make it very clear that all those who choose to participate in civil disobedience are required to take a "day-long introduction to the philosophy and methods of nonviolence" or nonviolence training. Participation is conditional on the acceptance of a particular philosophy, codified into a set of "nonviolence guidelines" (listed below). The *Handbook* does not reveal who determined what the guidelines would be, but it does state that all who sign the pledge "will abide by the following guidelines of nonviolence." Given the organizational strength of the Pledge, smaller independent groups or unaffiliated individuals who do not share the political philosophy of Pledge organizers frequently find themselves, at demonstrations, confronted with the dilemma of either going along with a strategy which they do not endorse and sometimes oppose or directly challenging Pledge "monitors," which not only undermines the possibility of a unified front but also makes smaller, isolated groups more vulnerable to state repression. Although Pledge organizers say that they are a "leaderless" organization committed to a "feminist process" and "small autonomous groups," decisionmaking and analysis is strictly top-down, with the organizational relationship between the national decisionmakers (the "analyst group" and "signal group") and grassroots "affinity groups" appearing much like a "chain of command." The range of action available to the smallest of local groups is set ahead of time by the official leadership. The Pledge organization, in short, is hierarchical, highly centralized, and distrustful of non-Pledge affiliated solidarity activists within the general population. One cannot help but notice that its structure is not much different than the political structure of the United States.

Why the rigidity and elitism? The answer may lie in the fact that the nonviolence guidelines, which serve to protect property and censor all expressions of anger toward those who hold power, are an affirmation of republican and capitalist values. The guidelines are less a mode of resistance than they are a guide for protestors to earn the respect of mainstream society, the privileged white middle class. At a time in our history when many of our cherished ideals appear hollow, Pledge organizers, unwittingly, are attempting to keep the movement from crossing that historical threshold whereby we become "the other"—the troublemaker, the deviant, the leftist fringe, the communist, or whatever the term is that stigmatizes and disciplines the revolutionary thinker. The guidelines, independent of the intentions of Pledge organizers, become are *disciplinary measures to control and contain protest.*

Nonviolence Guidelines

1. Our attitude will be one of openness, friendliness, and respect toward all whom we encounter as we engage in our witness against U.S. intervention in Central America.
2. We will use no violence, verbal or physical, toward any person.
3. We will not damage property.
4. We will not bring or use any drugs or alcohol other than for medicinal purposes.
5. We will not run—it creates panic.

The need to resist *and* be a respected member of society on the part of Pledge organizers leaves them no room to be other than the gentle and the good protestor. What emerges from their writings is a conception of a person that is one-dimensional, abstract, and perverse. For example, we may assume that to be a person is to be capable of acting in accordance with a socially accepted set of rules such as understanding the implications of one's personal actions on the life chances of others, and of exercising self-restraint in the interest of the health of the community and environment. It is because we understand that a *fully capable* human being may act in accordance with a given set of rules *and may not* that we express such attitudes as love, resentment, trust, hate, and respect for one another. Whether I love someone or hate someone, I am respecting that person *as a human being who is capable of acting in accord with a set of rules* and who may therefore be held accountable to those rules. I may hate President Reagan when I believe that he favors policies knowing that they inflict pain and injury on the poor while they assist the rich in obtaining even greater privilege. Implicitly I am invoking shared standards of fairness, equality, and justice which I endorse and to which I believe, the President, as a fully capable human being, ought to be held accountable. Now if I learn that President Reagan were truly ignorant of the effects of his policies—that he is poorly educated and uninformed, my feelings of hate would diminish. But my feelings would still be based on my respect for him as a fully capable person. On the other hand, if I were to learn that President Reagan had suffered brain damage as a child and had never been capable of acting in accordance with a socially prescribed set of rules, I would not be able to consider him a fully capable person and my feelings of hate would be inappropriate. We do not hate trees or bicycles because we cannot hold them responsible; we only hate, resent, trust, respect, and love people for their actions and we do that in the context of what we believe their capabilities are. It is in light of our respect for a person's capabilities that we distrust, resent, or hate (among other attitudes) that person. *The point is that the expression of negative attitudes towards someone and the expression of respect for someone as a person is not contradictory; they are not contrary essences.* Similarly, if we were to act unfriendly toward a bank president during a civil disobedience at a bank, it would be because we consider that person a *subject,* capable of acting in accordance with social standards that we endorse. It would be one very small way of holding that person responsible for him or herself. Acting unfriendly toward someone could quite possibly be the most appropriate way of expressing respect toward that person.[27]

By denying us the opportunity to express negative attitudes towards those whom we encounter, Pledge organizers limit our opportunity to judge the actions of powerful elites against our own values and our own standards. They are, in effect, letting responsible people off the hook. Outside the federal building in San Francisco during a symbolic blockade, Pledge monitors scolded one demonstrator for calling a police officer (who was arresting a non-Pledge protestor quite roughly) a fascist.[28] Presumably, real fascists could not be so identified. Murderers cannot be called murderers. States the *Handbook,* "The truly nonviolent will not have 'enemies'...the true enemies of our human family...[are] manmade structures..." But with U.S. political and economic structures never specified and critically evaluated and with no enemies to confront, our outrage, finding no direct expression toward accountable human beings, melts into resignation. *For without responsible people to confront, there is no responsibility. There is only crisis.*

One effect of this abstraction is the drift, like the beautiful soul, toward an apolitical purity. Spiritualism in this setting tends to become personal and private only. It seeps into institutions separated from centers of power, such as the church, the synagogue, or ashram. Our principles of unity and wholeness are not pushed toward the center of the community and held. Instead, our life-giving principles are expressed in the deepest recesses possible, in the darkest rooms, in the most private and isolated chambers, quietly, silently, in meditation, in prayer, and in the unconscious mind. And it is there that they are nurtured and visited. And ironically, we become split and dichotomized as we go into the public world, disguised as mainstream citizens blending into the mainstream deadness, only to reappear at night and on weekends to pray and chant, to eat organic foods, to talk of peace perhaps, or to set up literature tables in parks and on street corners. Rallies become solemn, downbeat affairs sprinkled with prayer, moments of silence, dreary singing ("all we are saying, is give peace a chance") and where in hushed tones we are reminded that we have no enemies, that we are whole, and one with the earth.

Winning the approval of responsible middle-class professionals is costly. Positions which might invite their sharp rebuke tend to be avoided. Prior to a radio interview, Pledge activists in Santa Barbara, California cautioned a young woman who had returned from a visit to El Salvador not to use the phrase "U.S.-sponsored terror." We tend to shift our focus, particularly as New Agers, from the political to the cultural. We tend to think of the health of our political economy in terms of our own personal health and well-being. This is not to say that the cultural is separate from the political *but it is ominous when we substitute the body for the body politic.* It may be of little consequence that we know more about which herbs ease constipation than we do about which corporate interests explain a given set of public policies. But it is terribly significant when as spiritualists we become far more concerned with physical injury than with spiritual death, the suffocation of our ability to express ourselves critically, imaginatively, artistically in ways not yet clearly comprehended—of our ability to become revolutionary. It is significant that the term nonviolence has become the watchword of our movement and not the term used throughout most of the world, the term which signifies the creation of space for the expressive unity of both body and soul in the modern era, the term *liberation*.

But the issue is greater than falling short of a liberation movement. The issue is one of unintended complicity. First note the shift within the nonviolence movement itself. Martin Luther King, Jr., by the time of the Birmingham campaign (1963), which was called Project Confrontation, had decided not to depend upon the value of moral appeal. "Instead of submitting to surreptitious cruelty in thousands of dark jail cells and on countless shadowed street corners," King said, the nonviolent resister "would force his oppressor to commit his brutality openly—in the light of day—with the rest of the world looking on." Adds, Stephen Oates, his biographer, "provocation was now a crucial aspect of King's nonviolent strategy." The point, King emphasized, was "to dramatize the gulf between promise and fulfillment...to make the invisible visible." The point was to create a situation in which political and economic elites, through their agents such as the police, would commit their crimes in broad daylight so that the reality of political economic structures and the responsibility of human beings within them could be made clear. In the campaign that King never lived to complete, his advisors recalled they "were going to confront the economic foundations of the system and *demand* reforms" (emphasis added).

King's philosophy of nonviolence stands in marked contrast to the nonviolent strategy of Pledge organizers. Today, the pretense that situations are unstructured and that friendliness and openness (moral appeal) is the basis of social change is made a unifying principle. Relationships of power and responsibility remain mystified and unclear. Conflict or what King sometimes referred to as "creative tension" (but not violence) was once thought to have been necessary to expose the hidden structural realities of racism, militarism, and poverty. "We merely bring to the surface the hidden tension that is already alive...injustice must be exposed, with all the tension its exposure creates…" "Non-violence is effective," King summarized, "if it's militant enough, if it's really doing something." The nonviolence guidelines of the Pledge, intended to avoid conflict, are at odds with King's nonviolence which was often designed to provoke conflict, to create tension, and to identify human beings who treat others contemptibly. So, strangely, the confrontational dimension of King's strategy, his direct criticisms of capitalism, or his suggestion that the United States is on the wrong side of a world revolution are elements of a critical analysis that are often dropped by many today who are fond of invoking his name. Instead, those who identify with King today are more likely to bring forward his emphasis on nonviolence, his love for his enemy, his perseverance, and the religious backdrop that seemed to nourish his politics. King, the revolutionary, has been exorcised. King, the spiritual leader, has been embraced. And the dichotomy, dreadfully, has been protected.[29]

Thus, if there is one tendency that weds Pledge activists with other spiritual activists today, it is the rejection of conflict and tension as a political strategy. Instead there is the complete embrace of the concept peace. Indeed, the term "peace" is somewhat ubiquitous. There are marches for peace, dances for peace, veterans for peace, peace resource centers, peace days, peace bumper stickers, and so on. It is the political equivalent of the happy face logo, which is not so bad if that is all that is meant. After all, who is not in favor of a more relaxed, open community? But the danger is that our unreflective, unqualified quest for peace may become a movement to eliminate all conflict. And here we come to the crux of the matter.

The vision of peace which guides us, which everyone seemingly endorses, is nowhere, to my knowledge, spelled out. *Conveniently, it is not situated and remains abstract;* that is, there is no discussion or attempt to identify what forms of tension, anxiety, opacity, indirectness, and conflict are inescapable and ineliminable features of the human condition and which tend to suffocate the human spirit or, if you prefer, are forms of violence. The concept of peace bandied about is sterile and empty; it is situation-less. One must presume that it is an extension of the terribly unrealistic model of human activity which animates the Pledge movement, a world in which there are no enemies, no hate, no resentment—just the truth of love and human dignity.

The use of the consensus process by Pledge members, and many other activists as well, illustrates the dangers in assuming that real world conflict is due alone to aggressive desires, uncontrolled anger, or some other form of wrong thinking. According to the *Handbook*, consensus is "a process for group decisionmaking...by which an entire group of people can come to an agreement. The input and ideas of all participants are gathered and synthesized to arrive at a final decision acceptable to all." As opposed to voting, which "is a means by which we choose one alternative from several," consensus "is a process of synthesizing many diverse elements together." The goal, to give everyone an opportunity to express him- or herself is laudable. But the situation in which fundamentally competing political perspectives are introduced—the situation in which there is a great deal of anxiety and conflict and *potential growth*—has been pushed aside. Suppose someone like myself were to participate in a Pledge meeting and suppose that person in the interest of contributing to the movement were to (carefully and respectfully) introduce some of the critical ideas thus far delineated. According to consensus rules, any individual who objects to a proposal on "moral grounds" (I trust that includes strong political objections) may "*block*" the consensus, thus forcing more discussion and synthesis. Anyone who has been at a meeting of twenty-five or more people that stretches late into the night because of the strong convictions of a "blocker" knows how difficult it is for anyone to sustain an unfavorable position. The consensus process, while it may provide more space for those who share the assumptions which underlie a given position, tends to isolate, derogate (the term blocker is pejorative), and eventually grind down the position that enlightens and inevitably disturbs.

What is missing? The concept peace is itself in tension with the process of change. Whites who were personally confronted by blacks in the 1960s and held accountable for the subtle expressions of racism (for using the term colored for example), men confronted by women in the early 1970s for their sexism within the context of personal relationships, or students who challenge their parents (and vice-versa) on political grounds will recall that the introduction of competing perspectives and the subsequent modification of assumptions requires *prolonged* and, at times, quite anguishing discussions, perhaps even over years. The challenging of one's identity involves a great deal of anxiety because the movement to new relationships and understanding are not without loss and not without pain. *Change, fundamental change, is not peaceful; it is conflictual because it requires the persistent and rigorous advance of competing ideas which initially appear wholly untenable.* A proposal to fundamentally modify the consensus process could not be adopted when using the consensus process. ("We alienate some by acting, just as we perhaps exclude some who don't 'believe' in consensus process," note Pledge organizers.) The option reserved for those who challenge the Pledge framework is the same: exclusion. Much like the New Ager who, when pressed to clarify his or her assumptions, cuts short the discussion because of "bad energy," Pledge organizers will suppress serious intellectual confrontation and debate in the interest of preserving a conflict-free mode of decision making.

The suppression of conflict within an organization may serve only to diminish the ability of members of that organization to think critically and act boldly. But when abstract notions of peace are used by self-appointed monitors to dampen conflict at points of protest across America, Abstract Spiritualists risk working in complicity with authorities in the repression of protest. Let us outline the steps:

1. In order to avoid conflict and to act in an open and friendly manner, Pledge organizers cooperate fully with the police and local officials when organizing demonstrations. (In Concord, California, one groups states explicitly in their Covenant of Non-violence, "We will show respect for the police.") Police are notified in advance of the time, place, and number of people wishing to be arrested. The police, at the demonstration site, typically cordon off a specific area with yellow ribbons in order to identify an area in which demonstrators are not permitted to go. Those wishing to be arrested then cross the yellow line and are arrested. While this scenario does not hold in every instance, it is the orderly, disciplined, and nonviolent situation aimed for.

2. This cooperation with authorities by the authorities themselves is encouraged. Symbolic blockades are much less likely to disrupt "business as usual." In a recent civil disobedience, for example, nine busloads of peace activists "blocked" the gates of the Rocky Flats unclear weapons plant in Boulder, Colorado between 5:30 and 10:30 am. Yet "no cars or trucks were prevented from entering the plant...[although] two trucks had to wait a half hour to enter and two other drivers decided not to cross the blockade."[30] In Oakland, California officials at the Oakland Airport asked leaders of the Contragate Action Committee, a group seeking to remove the CIA airline Southern Air Transport from Oakland by means of disruptive but nonviolent direct action, if they would forgo their plans in favor of "doing arrests."

3. Many who believe that "doing arrests" is less disobedience than it is accommodation and who seek to raise the political costs of low intensity warfare through confrontation and disruption are viewed by Pledge organizers either as "aggressors," or as an extension of the "heavy-handed authority" found in everyday life, or as "masculine oppressors" or other terms which tend to invalidate militancy. The violation of peace can never be valid. For Pledge organizers and many peace activists, therefore, the concept of peace as a conflictless society serves as a license to intervene and stop actions which they believe are potentially violent. In Northampton, Massachusetts, following the invasion of Grenada, demonstrators turned up in unexpectedly large numbers to protest the appearance of a local Congressperson who had expressed support of the invasion. The large crowd of demonstrators had achieved an unusual degree of militancy and sense of empowerment. Non-pledge organizers were planning to attempt to penetrate police lines (a quite feasible goal given the disproportionate number of demonstrators) and enter into the building in which the Congressperson was being received. At that moment, Pledge activists who had been notified by the police and who identified themselves as "peacekeepers" interceded. Linking arms they sided with police against the demonstrators. Unwilling to break through a line of Pledge activists who had

been, until that time, their allies, the demonstrators receded. Peace was preserved. And property was protected, which according to the "peacekeepers," was the reason they were called. Activists in the 1980s know this to be a common situation.

Perhaps we do believe that the nonviolent person has no enemies and that repressive structures, not people, are responsible for the crimes we witness. Perhaps we will go to great lengths to cooperate with authorities in order to avoid conflict. It may be the case that many of us want to treat everyone with friendliness and respect all the while knowing that if authorities treat us violently, we shall not resist and if they treat other demonstrators violently we shall bear nonviolent witness. And perhaps, in spite of the violence perpetrated on people, we do promise not to damage property. Okay. Fine. We are nonviolent peace activists. But when we intercede as "peacekeepers" and stop the action of protestors because it is confrontational while at the same time we fail to do the same to agents of the state whom with our own eyes we watch commit violence, then we are peacekeepers of a particular species. We are peace officers, we are police.

To a more disinterested observer, might it not appear a bit Orwellian for us to make it a practice to consult with the authorities, to cooperate with the police in curbing militancy, to permit violence to be done to our own bodies while we promise not to damage property, all the while we present ourselves to disaffected citizens as the pledge of resistance?

An Alternative Approach: Politics Without Knees

I have charged that Congressional Technocrats and Abstract Spiritualists are escaping politics; that is, while having superbly trained our critical sights on a number of important areas (such as environmental degradation, military intervention abroad, patriarchy, and nuclear proliferation), they have failed to train their critical sights on the fundamental assumptions undergirding our political and economic institutions. We tend to believe that we live in a free country that is governed by consent, which means of course, that we have freely endorsed or consented to our laws. Therefore, we move in two directions when we are greatly outraged by what our country is doing. We attempt to use the democratic institutions available to us (Congressional Technocrats) or we call attention to policies which we feel are unjust (even though they may have the consent of the governed) by, as respectfully as possible, violating laws generally related to the implementation of those policies (Abstract Spiritualists). We tend, therefore, to identify with and respect the work of members of Congress and the police more than we do confrontational demonstrators. We believe that it makes sense to work within the rules to which we have freely consented and that if one chooses to deviate from those rules, then that person deserves to be punished.

The purpose of this book, essentially, is to encourage you, the reader, to reflect upon and critically assess your political beliefs. The implication is that many of our beliefs, such as the one which suggests that we are governed by consent, are not justified. Why then do we hold them? People, generally, are neither dupes nor dopes, but we do need to *believe in what we have got to do.* That is what ideology helps us to do. It provides a reasonable set of beliefs that match up with the limited job opportunities within a given set of power relationships. During the feudal era, serfs believed that their station in life was God's will. It would have been quite difficult for serfs to accept our beliefs concerning individual freedom even if they were "liberating" because to do so would have made it exceedingly difficult for them to carry out the tasks of a serf, to perform the only role available to them given the set of power relations at that time. We face the same predicament today. It is much easier and painless for us to be critics of our way of life so long as we do not do anything that would make it difficult for the army of workers to perform their assigned tasks. Once we do cross that threshold, however, we are no longer escaping politics, we are becoming *political.* Let us probe this line of reasoning a bit more.

Robert Henri in 1918 wrote, "I have no sympathy with the belief that art is the restricted province of those who paint, sculpt, and make music and verse. I hope we will come to an understanding that the material used is only incidental, that there is an artist in every man; and that to him the possibility of development and of expression and the happiness of creation is as much a right and as much a duty to himself, as to any of those who work in the especially ticketed ways."[31] That all men and women are essentially creative and that it is our duty to ourselves to express ourselves creatively is an idea which I think most of us share. Virtually everyone dances, sings, writes poetry, paints, or draws. We are a veritable army of artists busily creating in our *off* time. It is strange that we do not consider the time and space to be creative a need that must be satisfied. But then again, we live in a world according to John Locke and Adam Smith, not Robert Henri. While each of us has the capacity to create, we cannot satisfy our creative need as workers unless we have control over our worklives and to do that we must own, perhaps with others, our tools of production. But we live in a society where the private ownership of productive property is called freedom and where a few people own most of the productive property; "In a nation of 236 million people, the means of production are owned by a group no larger than the population of Denver, Colorado."[32] Therefore, *most of us have little choice particularly given the Constitution's protection of private property and our endorsement of the Constitution* but to sell our creative capacity to those who own productive property in order to live. Our unreflective acceptance of *their* notion of freedom compels us to accept the prevailing conditions of work. Our creative need becomes a curse.

This obviously gives owners great power over our creative capacities and great power over how we express ourselves and over who we are. Many "radicals" have noted this power relationship and have based a critical assessment of capitalism upon it. But it is difficult for the radical, as a worker to sustain his or her beliefs. As William Connolly points out, "The worker must be punctual, obey the commands of the boss, adjust work rhythms to the pace of the machinery, accept wages as the incentive to work, live up to the terms of the wage contract, and adjust overt attitudes and behavior in a thousand ways to established rules, norms and expectations." One can try to be a dissident and a worker at the same time but "if there is no chance of finding a role consistent with one's real beliefs" then one's political commitment is always at odds with what one does, thus eroding one's own sense of integrity. Friends and co-workers tend to feel resentment and betrayal if what they do is implicitly repudiated by frequent political commentary.[33]

Under these structural pressures we tend either to let our radical critique slip into private memory and gradually adopt the beliefs appropriate to our work lives: "the relation between owner and worker is one of free exchange." Or we may hold on to critical insights in those areas where we have support at the same time that we affirm the basic soundness of our institutions by adopting beliefs appropriate to the roles we play within them. Congressional Technocrats may, for example, deplore U.S. intervention in Central America, and at the same time adopt the belief that economic growth is in the interest of all without seriously exploring the notion that expansion of the private economy *requires* state support of economic and military aggression in Central America. Abstract Spiritualists may, for example, deplore the violence carried out by the state and at the same time adopt the belief that production in advanced industrial societies must necessarily be organized in authoritarian and routinized ways without seriously exploring the notion that the relatively privileged, middle-class standard of living within the United States requires the violent extraction of workers' labor on a daily basis.

One virtue of doing political work through the building of a movement is that it is sometimes possible to clarify these rather complicated relationships of power in a way that reaffirms, publicly, what many people already knew but were afraid to say. At times, dramatic and public forms of resistance empower and liberate in ways that essays simply cannot do. When our grievances go unexpressed or remain unclear because they cannot be linked to their structural source, we often withdraw from political activity and become resigned to accepting the system as it is. Often when ordinary practices are challenged and confronted, debate and conflict over the appropriateness of such disruptions helps us to connect our grievances to their sources simply because we are compelled on such occasions to probe more deeply the assumptions and understandings that we share. This is not to suggest that all confrontation is healthy. It is, rather, to suggest that to be political is to become strategist. It is in this context that I would like to advance the following proposal. I believe it makes contact with the Congressional Technocrat's interest in electoral politics, the concern of Abstract Spiritualists with nonviolence, and the belief of many other critics of our way of life that we need to contest the way the average citizen is treated with contempt.

An Example

Prior to the 1984 presidential election, Frances Fox Piven and Richard Cloward, in their effort to register the millions of unregistered "clients of the welfare state," said that they hoped to "increase the electoral participation of people at the bottom, and to politicize the terms of their participation." We can anticipate once again that similar serious efforts will be made to encourage voter registration of the people at the bottom. But it may be worth considering that the most effective way of increasing the electoral participation of these citizens is to politicize the terms of participation by *challenging* voter registration.

It is important for those who would focus their energy on registration campaigns to recall James Madison's understanding (in Federalist No. 10), noted earlier, that the problem confronting the Framers in designing the Constitution was how to "secure...private rights against the danger of...faction, and at the same time...the spirit and form of popular government." The solution arrived at, you will recall, was a design which so fragmented political power that it would be difficult for the majority to "discover their own strength and act in unison with each other." The Framers' lack of confidence in the ability of the "people at the bottom" to think or act as citizens is the source of contempt that is felt by the tens of millions of Americans who today are altogether outside the voting universe and whose "active alienation," according to Walter Dean Burnham, is "on a scale quite unknown anywhere else in the Western world."[34]

Personal registration legislation, ostensibly intended to prevent ballot box stuffing, was introduced in urban areas at the turn of the century and was erected as a barrier to impede the ethnic and working-class voter. It represented just one of several changes in the rules governing electoral activity. The poll tax, the literacy test, "white primaries," and a variety of municipal reforms were others. At a time when cities were becoming vital centers of economic life and in some instances when city officials were siding with workers by refusing to use police to protect strikebreakers, elites were busily using these kinds of reforms to weaken the political influence of blacks, agrarian populists, and immigrant workers and to eliminate the partisan possibilities of political parties and urban machines.

Comparison studies, as is noted below, suggest that our form of voter registration obligations may be uniquely undemocratic. Moreover, research developed by Kevin Phillips and Paul Blackman reveals that voter registration does not prevent fraud. Therefore, without calling into question the contempt for the underclasses which is expressed by voter registration, organizers of registration campaigns unwittingly construct the pathology of the "apathetic voter."

Much like the Freedom Rides of the 1960s which challenged the legitimacy of specific laws, we need a form of resistance which directly challenges the legitimacy of personal registration requirements. I have called the strategy outlined below *Freedom Voting*.

The purpose of Freedom Voting is to alter or abolish the practice, as we now know it, of voter registration. The process would consist of the mobilization of those people for whom voter registration is a clear barrier to voting. The homeless, for example, who find it very difficult to vote given registration requirements and whose political needs are great, would become ideal Freedom Voters. Freedom Voters, after legal consultation and resistance training, would attempt to vote *without first having registered to vote*. Undoubtedly the effectiveness of Freedom Voting would be enhanced if it were used in the context of a program with several components such as proposals for twenty-four hour voting or weekend voting and a slate of candidates (within the Rainbow coalition perhaps) pushing at the boundaries of electoral politics by endorsing a host of redistributional programs.[35]

The resulting arrests would politicize the terms of their political participation in a particular way. Arrest of this nature in sufficient numbers could reveal the contradiction of our democratic system, namely that it works when certain constituencies are disenfranchised (recall Trilateralist arguments to this effect in Chapter 5). Much in the way that Martin Luther King, Jr. sought to make the invisible visible, Freedom Voting could make our electoral process' contempt for people without property quite visible. For all the world to see, police would be dragging away the poorest of our society for attempting to vote.

The process could also be initiated in the context of presidential primaries so that 1) the actions could be linked to a progressive party coalition (such as the Rainbow Coalition) and candidate (such as Jesse Jackson); 2) the issue could be politicized in several states over a prolonged period; 3) others would be encouraged to participate in succeeding primaries as the process was repeated and as momentum built; and 4) the presidential candidates, and citizens generally, would be compelled to come to grips with the bias internal to our electoral process.

It would be important for the participants, and especially candidates that headed the movement, to clarify the reasons behind the action. Points similar to the following could be made:

1. The United States is alone in placing the onus of registering on the individual citizen. All other developed countries produce voting lists and do not leave it to the individual to register as elector.

2. Our system of voter registration does not prevent voter fraud. If fraud is the reason for voter registration we would do well to follow the example of other countries. Accurate registers are considered so important in "Canada, for example, that the length of Canadian election campaigns is determined by the time deemed necessary to enroll the electorate.

3. While foreign systems differ from one another greatly, they all share a vital willingness to accept responsibility to initiate voter registration, usually registering 90 to 99 percent of the voting-age population and have fairly high voter participation rates.

4. Several nations, such as Australia, have compulsory registration. It is similar to our own compulsory military registration for
males eighteen years of age. The point here is to illustrate how
as a nation we are capable of accepting compulsory registration
and that our government is capable of administering such a
program.

5. The simplest way to register voters and not obstruct voter participation is the process of registering as one votes.[36]

The repeated (within the context of a presidential primary) arrests
of thousands of the poorest citizens attempting to vote would not only
make clear that the U.S. government does not permit the enfranchise-
ment of all it citizens, it might broaden the range of debate to include
such critiques as Walter Dean Burnham's that, "the American political
system is...significantly less democratic today than is any other Western
political system which conducts free elections."[37] Hopefully, the national self-awareness that actions of this sort might help to generate would
channel the political alienation of many citizens into the creation of
more political space that would parallel the political mobilization of the
early 1950s' Civil Rights movement. The important point regarding confrontational strategies is this: our political system was designed with
distrust and fear of common people in mind. When we participate in
electoral politics or established politics generally we must act in a dozen
subtle ways (registering to vote for example) that show deference to
ruling elites. Agreeing to participate in the current political process does
not empower us. Rather, it reminds us of how politically impotent we
are, drains our confidence and self-respect and, consequently, dis-
courages us from future attempts to engage in politics. Therefore, before
we participate in the system, we must challenge the beliefs that underlie it—the beliefs that say we, the "common people" should not have
an active, powerful voice in the structuring of our lives.

In August of 1987, the FBI fired John Ryan, a twenty-one year
veteran of the Bureau, because he refused to begin a "domestic
security/terrorism investigation of the Veterans Fast For life." Stated Special Agent Ryan, "I believe that in the past members of our government
have used the FBI to quell dissent, sometimes where the dissent was

warranted. I feel history will judge this to be another such instance." Ryan's refusal was a confrontation to and a sort of emancipation from a system of which he had been an integral part for a long time. We need to do make that challenge more often. And we need to do it together. It sounds strange to our political ear because we do our politics in a spiritually dead society where our involvement is scorned. But we must struggle, nonetheless, to acquire a clear conception of our creative freedom and our responsibility to exercise it.[38]

The Need for Revolutionaries

The figure of a labourer—some furrows in a ploughed field—a bit
of sand, sea and sky—are serious subjects, so diffucult, but at the
same time so beautiful, that it is indeed worthwile to devote one's
life to the task of expressing the poetry hidden in them.

—Vincent Van Gogh

The people, sir, are a great beast.

—Alexander Hamilton

Prior to his resignation, Richard Nixon had been warned by his
legal counsel John Dean, that there was a cancer growing on the
presidency. During the recent celebration of our Constitution's bicentennial, again the term cancer has again been used to characterize the
health of our political institutions. Both Daniel Sheehan, chief counsel
for the Christic Institute, and I.F. Stone have said, in reference to the
Iran-Contra Affair (see Chapter 5), that a cancer lies deep within the
bowels of our constitutional government. Sheehan argues that that cancer needs to be removed so that we can return to the principles set out
in the Constitution and so that we can restore the health of the body-
politic.[1]

My argument is fundamentally different: private property and
production for profit, which is protected by the Constitution, is the
source of the cancer. The problems which so trouble Sheehan and
others emerge in part out of a Constitution which enables relatively few
people to control of our worklives and our resources, which tends to
insulate private power from public pressure, which compels us to act
in narrowly self-interested ways, and which strips away the bonds of
community and sets in its place the impersonal relations of the market.
The Constitution, in this period of decline, invites the private control

of public policy and given the corporate domination of public policy
it should hardly surprise anyone that the largest corporate owners apply
the most efficient and impersonal methods in their effort to protect their
privilege and power.

One may counter that in spite of its defects, the Constitution
remains the last best defense against all the repressive tendencies outlined in this study thus far. No one disagrees that the Bill of Rights
protects some people from the federal government some of the time.
However, the Constitution, given its protection of property rights and
its deference to private power, cannot live up to its own standards. We
cannot realistically expect, for example, the federal government to live
up to the 14th Amendment and guarantee equal protection before the
law for both corporate owners and people whose daily subordination
contributes to greater opportunities for corporate expansion and enhanced revenues upon which the federal government itself depends.
The shield against state repression which the Constitution provides individuals has never been large enough to protect the victims of
capitalism in their attempt to organize an alternative political economy,
particularly abroad where from a Constitutional viewpoint only resources, not people, exist. If we seek to expand the kind of protection which
the Bill of Rights affords some people then we need to talk more about
the oppression which our political economy requires and the repression the Constitution permits.

Furthermore, we need to understand that a defense of Constitutional protection without a clear and strong indictment of the way in
which Constitutional provisions protect corporate interests abroad, particularly death squad activity, is also a defense of the very narrow definition of the self which capitalism is based upon. We should keep in
mind that it is an obligation under international law, as articulated
within the Nuremberg Protocols, to restrain one's government from en-
gaging in criminal conduct. It is in this spirit that we must expose the
contradiction within the Bill of Rights. I don't think we can be reminded
too often of the simple truth, as stated by progressive activist Brian Wilson, that "the lives of people in the Third World are worth no less than
our own." We need, in other words, to talk about moving beyond the

present Constitution and its definition of what deserves protection, and toward a new social order.

The point is this: we must accept our humanity, but to accept our humanity means that we must work to regain control our worklives, to build communities that are not structured by market considerations, to establish a harmonious relationship with nature, and to live our lives in a way that is in solidarity with the oppressed. To accept one's humanity, then, means that we must let the world know and feel who we are. And there is precious little space in the United States today for the many progressive thinkers and caring people to live a life that they can genuinely endorse upon reflection. Sheldon Wolin writes,

> It is naive to expect the initiative for reform of the state to issue from the political process that serves the interests of political capitalism. This structure can only be reduced if citizens withdraw and direct their energies and civic commitment to finding new life forms. Toward these ends, our whole mode of thinking must be turned upside-down. Instead of imitating most other political theories and adopting the state as the primary structure and then adapting the activity of the citizen to the state, democratic thinking should renounce the state paradigm and, along with it, the liberal-legal corruption of the citizen. The old citizenship must be replaced by a fuller and wider notion of being whose politicalness will be expressed not in one or two modes of activity—voting or protesting—but in many.[2]

In short, to accept one's humanity means to openly reject many of the values and principles of the Constitution. And that is a revolutionary act. As has been suggested throughout, the struggle that surrounded the establishment of the Constitution is still on-going. We have yet to have *our* revolution.

Taking Back the Concept of Revolution

Walk through the shopping malls which have in many ways taken the place of neighborhood communities and you will see what makes up the so-called "good life" in America. You will see the massive attempt to avoid the pain, complexity, and conflict of life that cannot be avoided. And you will see the equally massive attempt to control pleasure, attempts that become mindless stimulation once packaged. If you have brown hair and want to be blond, no problem. If you have blue eyes and want purple eyes, it's easy. If you have crooked teeth, tiny breasts, a bald head, droopy eyes, or a big nose, you need not suffer the shame and undeserved ridicule any longer. Dyes, pills, creams, pads, straps, powders, sprays, paste and an army of surgeons can do the trick. No one needs to be the wrong shape or the wrong size. This is America: You can buy your image. Just produce the cash and sign your name here. Happiness is comfort and comfort is at your fingertips. You can make hot days cool, cool days warm, and you can take care of all of your entertainment needs with one flip of the remote control switch. If you want those things which will make your life a little easier, get a credit card. Yes, indeed, a full shopping bag is a full life.

But turn this artificial existence over and you will see the reality of domination and control. Consider that richly colored shawl woven by the Quiche Indians of Guatemala, or the Texas Instrument calculator manufactured in the barrios of El Salvador, or the grapes you bought last week that were harvested by farmworkers in the valleys of California. Stop and think how these goods were produced, who owned the loom, the factory, the land? Who determined what time the workers began, what time they ate and under what conditions they worked? Who died of PCB and pesticide poisoning? Who got rich from this exchange and who was made poor? And let us ask ourselves, is the right which entitles us to own and become rich also the right to exploit those who must sell their lives in order to live? Is this right to transform nature into things the right also to separate ourselves from nature and from each other and from all that is spiritually alive? Whether at high school football games or at the Superbowl, whether at play in a back alley or in the Olympics, whether in private industry or in the Oval Office, our relations to one another are organized around competition and conquest. Our fantasy is to stand out from the rest, to shout in spastic frenzy, in some appropriate place of triumph, "We are Number 1." The need to see ourselves as better than others or as less than what we are betrays a thinness of generosity and a self-awareness that mocks imagination.

What happens to our integrity as citizens when our government is compelled to lie, assassinate its political opposition abroad, condemn the World Court after it unanimously asserted that our war against Nicaragua is a violation of the Geneva Conventions? What happens to our bond to the international community when the United States sends weapons to over twenty countries which practice torture and covertly attempts to destabilize several dozen more? Are we not citizens separated from the teachings of the world community just as we are separated from ourselves and from each other and from the discomfort, anxiety, pain, conflict, and struggle that is an inescapable feature of simple life? Separated from the natural rhythms of pleasure and pain have we not constructed an artificial existence organized around the technical rhythms of the machine? Images of being awakened by the birds or the rooster or the sun seem relatively quaint and unreal. More genuine for us is the morning that begins with alarms, caffeine, traffic lights, and rush hours. Each day becomes an agenda dictated by the clock; each week a unit of production; each year a measure of accumulation. Even our language reflects the erosion of our humanity. We are increasingly machines that are "turned-off," "cooled-out," "charged-up," "burned-out", "turned-on," and "programmed" or given "feedback," "input," or which send out and receive different kinds of "energy."

What does this tell us about our sensitivity to unhealthy social relations? We live amidst massive inequality. We don't really care that most people have little power to alter the conditions of their lives. We refuse to acknowledge that the earth is dying and that we are killing it. We play games with the most horrible weapons imaginable and actually seem to take pride in our ability to end life as we know it. Our unthinking celebration of individual achievement and upward mobility works to damage the life-giving ties of kinship and the bonds of community. Whether with regard to women or workers or people of color, we, as a nation, accept the systematic subordination of human beings. We pretend not to understand the linkages between our comfortable standard of living and the dictatorships we impose and protect through an international military presence.

Signs that something is terribly wrong are everywhere but the struggle to see ourselves as a free people and as superior people forces us to look away, to deny our experience and to repress what our experience means. And so with righteous indignation public officials admonish the Supreme Court nominee who smoked marijuana while they keep information from the public that would expose U.S.-sponsored terror and the criminal history of the Secret Team. The U.S. orchestration of the heaviest aerial war ever seen in the Americas, directed against the civilian population of El Salvador, is ignored while the assassination of Marines in that same country is held aloft as a banner of our innocence.

But the struggle to see ourselves as free and innocent is one that is self-defeating. For to deny and repress what we see and hear and know is to live in a purely invented world, a world where reason must die and where stupidity must reign. As Nietzsche warned, restlessly, violently, headlong like a river that wants to reach the end, we move toward catastrophe.

It is against this backdrop of illusion and ill-fated destiny that the perception of the life-giving aspects of resistance, struggle, and change is most striking. Consider the Nicaraguan revolution. The Sandinistas, following the overthrow the U.S.-backed Somoza regime in 1979 and the ending of forty years of dictatorship "embarked almost immediately on a program aimed at changing the basic social structure..." The data on the accomplishments of the revolution as well as the destructive effects of the U.S.-backed Contra attacks have been well documented elsewhere. I shall provide you with but a glimpse of the picture. In health care, the Sandinistas reduced the infant mortality rate from 121 per 1,000 births in 1979 to 75 per 1,000 births in 1984. They eliminated polio by 1982 and sharply increased the number of health facilities, such as hospitals, health centers, and health posts. In 1982 Nicaragua received the UNICEF/World Health Organization prize for the Third World country that had made the greatest improvement in health. By 1984, however, the Contras had killed sixty-nine health care providers and had destroyed fifty-nine rural health outposts, three health centers, and one hospital. The economic costs of the war in 1984 alone could have built 8,000 rural health outposts, 196 health centers, or twenty-five hospitals of 200-bed capacity.[3]

President Reagan, when initiating the U.S. embargo against Nicaragua in 1985, stated that the "policies and actions of...Nicaragua constitute an unusual and extraordinary threat to the national security and foreign policy of the United States..." To be sure, the accomplishments of the Nicaraguan revolution marked the inception of a new age in Central America for they provide new bearings for political and moral life. But what is really provocative about Nicaragua and what most stirs the imagination is the sense one gets from the place that it is a country and a people transformed. Nicaraguans seem to be in touch with a spirit which we repress, with a fascination for ideas and discovery which we deny, and with the excitement of self-transformation which we filter out. It is the sensuality that is youth and the pride that marks an honest life. It is, in a word, a simple lust.

We, of course, cannot put all of this on Nicaragua. The sensuality, pride, honesty, and lust of which I speak are particularly dramatic and striking to North Americans who experience them in sharp contrast to the deadening repression that defines their native culture and politics. Nicaraguans resisted and won; it is not surprising that their country stimulates and excites those who are needful of self-discovery. It happens in the United States as well. The interviews of activists in the 1950s and 1960s by Sara Evans remind us that it is possible here as well. Statements such as "...the work so far has been far more gratifying than anything I ever anticipated," leaving the movement "would be like living death," or "I go home at night completely exhausted but very happy" are statements which acknowledge that it is possible to be buried alive in the United States by the sterile rituals we call freedom and democracy and electoral politics.[4] I picked cotton on a "harvest brigade" for a short time in Nicaragua and I found myself counting the days and mumbling from time to time, "This has to be hell on earth." But the good news of the Nicaraguan revolution doesn't mean good times. Good news often means difficult times, hard work, and intense challenge. But when one person stands up for what he or she believes, and is joined by another, and another, then risks are taken and things begin to change: That's good news.

In Nicaragua, I was able to experience for a moment what it feels like to participate in and win a liberation struggle. I walked through the barrios of Managua and down dusty, impassable rural roads and saw barefoot children as they began work with the rising sun. I spoke with a woman in her 70s who shared with me what it meant to have finally learned to read. I noted with humility the graffiti that declares, "We will never be slaves again." I listened to the personal testimonies of insurrection and of courage and of accomplishment. I sensed the expectancy of a peasant who explained, "Christ did not die for your sins, he died for his beliefs and we are inspired by his example." I studied the expression of a dirty-faced child, who is fourteen but looks nine, and who responds when asked if he goes to school, "No, but someday I hope to." I felt the massive patience of an old man who when asked by a hostile questioner if he had been brainwashed by the Sandinistas replied, "I don't know if my brain has yet been washed clean after fifty years of Somoza, but I hope that my childrens' brains will be washed clean and that you will help us in that struggle."

All of this helped me begin to understand the meaning of U.S.-imposed dictatorship and of the dream called revolution. What I saw when I looked into the dark eyes of Nicaraguans were the eyes of people who once were made the wretched of the earth, who have now stood up. With stubbornness of will that was indestructible, the slaves have arisen. That spirit of an ongoing, magnificent struggle is thick in Nicaragua. It hangs in the air. You feel it everywhere. You see it in their eyes. You feel it in their patience. It grips your soul and takes hold of you.

Stated one *brigadista* upon her return, "I learned love and hope, which are hard to sustain now that I'm 'home' in the U.S. I want to go back home—to Nicaragua."

The barefoot revolutionaries of the world are teaching us that change is possible and that our beliefs are real. Perhaps the single greatest failure of our Constitution and the political-economic system erected upon it is that it accepts Hamilton's notion of people as beasts while it rejects the understanding, articulated by Van Gogh and others, that there is a hidden poetry within all people that is worthy of discovery. The failure of the Constitution is its rejection of human beauty, its rejection of life.

Let us pursue the thinking of Vincent Van Gogh a step further. I believe it has political relevance. Van Gogh said: "I want to do drawings that touch people, so that people will say of my work, 'He feels deeply, he feels tenderly.' What am I in people's eyes? A non-entity or an eccentric and disagreeable man? Somebody who has no position in society? The lowest of the low? I want my work to show what's in the heart of such an eccentric, of such a nobody. This is my ambition." As alive and imaginative political people, it could be our ambition as well. But then we would be revolutionaries.

Remember Which Side They Were On

Two hundred years after the writing of the Constitution, the terms "the power-structure" and "political activist" are in wide usage. They refer to camps of politically engaged citizens that are often opposed philosophically. If the "Founding Fathers" were alive today, which side would they be on? To help us answer that question, let us look at someone who might typify each group.

Lee Iacocca, head of the Chrysler Corporation, is someone who is a member of the power structure. He is, presumably, good at running a corporation, at making it efficient, at getting it to produce many things which can be sold for a profit. His skills are highly valued in this society. In fact, in 1986, he received $20.6 million in salary, bonuses, stock grants, and stock options. And he has stated that such extraordinary privilege is justified, even useful as a motivational incentive in a free society: "That's the American way. If the kids don't aspire to make money like I did what the hell good is this country? You gotta give them a role model, right?"[5] Many "experts" believed that Iacocca would make a good presidential candidate and encouraged him to run for the office in 1988.

Benjamin Linder was someone who might have been considered a political activist. We came to know Ben not for his accomplishments, but from the unusual circumstances of his death. He was a North American engineer who did not want to be like most engineers and work for the military-industrial complex. Instead he was a volunteer worker in Nicaragua who helped bring electricity to remote rural villages there. He lived at a subsistence level. His salary was paid by contributions from other U.S. citizens like himself who were disturbed by U.S. policy toward the people of Central America. Although his engineering skills may have been valued in the United States, his political attitude was not and neither, therefore, was his work, at least within the context of establishment values. "Why do the Contras kill those who bring light to the city and drinking water for the children?" he asked. "These are Ronald Reagan's freedom fighters." Ben was targeted and then murdered by the Contras, who in the bicentennial year of the Constitution, were trained, supplied, and directed by the government of the United States.

It is important to understand that the Framers were the political ancestors, not of people like Ben Linder, but of people like Lee Iacocca. The Framers struggled with and defeated the Ben Linders of 1787. The Framers, contrary to popular myth, came from a very narrow and elite strata of society which feared and distrusted common people. It is not coincidental that Lee Iacocca is thought of as a presidential candidate while Ben Linder is tracked down and murdered by agents of the government of the United States. The life of Iacocca gives expression to the vision of empire and privilege expressed by most of the Framers. Linder's life gave expression to a kind of love and generosity which threatens and subverts the way of life the Framers established. The tension between the visions expressed by the life work of Iacocca and of Linder frames the conflicts of our age and is a tension that is made necessary by the Constitution.

David Viscott has written that because our energy is limited, "it's wasteful to use it in any way except in the pursuit of the truth," otherwise "we end up trying to justify what's simply not true." And when we work to support a lie, especially if we are unaware of doing it, "it becomes increasingly difficult to tell what's real" and that "to give up the lie seems like losing a part of ourselves."[6] Are we capable of confronting the reality of who we are, of not avoiding the pain of that con-

frontation, and of speaking the truth of that pain in order to get free
from the myths and half-truths which make us prisoners of a distorted
reality?

Confronting the Beast

Not long ago I saw a sign on the wall of a natural food store that
said, "Stop Reagan's War." At first I felt good about it. Perhaps because
any political sign in a depoliticized society, particularly in a grocery
store, was welcomed. Yet the more I thought about it the more I began
to realize that that sign represented where we are as a movement. It
seemed to capture the essence of our political awareness. It seemed to
be suggesting that the latest military intervention was the fault of a particular president, or administration, or party. But as Donald Pfost notes,
the United States has "forcibly intervened in the sovereign affairs of the
nations of Latin America on at least 120 different occasions...[in order
to] establish and protect a system of economic dependency beneficial
to U.S. economic interests, particularly corporate interests."[7] Might it not
be useful to think in terms not of individual presidents or administra-
tions but in terms of what "our" political-economic system requires?

Consider an indictment of U.S. foreign policy that goes beyond
thinking in terms of individual presidents. Edward Herman, for example, in reference to "the sponsorship of terrorist armies to invade
Guatemala in 1954 (successful), Cuba in 1961 (unsuccessful), and
Nicaragua 1981-1988 (unsuccessful)" were responses by the United
States to "cases of revolutions from below, with governments coming
into power that addressed the basic needs of a formerly depressed and
repressed majority." Newly unleashed ideas of democracy and opportunity, says Herman, "have been consistently horrifying and intolerable
to the U.S. elite. That elite is happy only with elite rule and amenable
clients...What if the masses in other countries of the empire were to
get the idea that they were not necessarily born to serve their masters?"[8]

Herman and others are suggesting that we can better explain the
120 military interventions in Latin America as well as the scores of in-

terventions in other parts of the world when we understand that the U.S. political-economic system is not a democratic system, that its power and wealth depends upon rule by a few and the subordination of the many, and that the people who run it are horrified by genuine democratic movements which aim to give majorities political and economic power. Therefore, it is not Reagan or Carter or Kennedy or Eisenhower, necessarily, that is responsible for a given intervention. Rather it is a system—the ideas, values, beliefs, and practices within it, that require such intervention for its preservation. Presidents simply help manage the system and try to maintain its political and economic stability.

Moreover, as we argued in Chapters 4 and 5, genuine democratic movements in this country are also defined by elites as crises. We need to begin to explore the idea that the threads of injustice and corruption and repression within U.S. client states run throughout our institutions here. We need to emphasize that many of the people within the United States and within U.S. client states face a common power structure and experience similar forms of oppression. We have a common interest and we need to work together. Therefore, when we speak of the torture and mass murder that takes place within U.S. client states let us also speak of the situation of dependent populations here. For example, the percentage of blacks in our overall prison population has doubled since 1962 to 46 percent. Blacks in this country go to prison more often than blacks in South Africa. The Public Health Service estimates that every year prolonged exposure to toxic chemicals, dusts, noise, heat, cold, and radiation kills nearly 200,000 workers. The leading cause of death of teenagers is suicide. Twenty-five percent of all children will be sexually molested before they are eighteen. Two out of three poor adults are women. Twenty-five million adults can't read poison labels. An additional 35 million are functionally illiterate, all of which means that the United States ranks 49th among the 158 United Nation members in literacy. With regard to infant mortality, the United States ranks 18th. Nine thousand Americans are killed yearly by commercial reactor emissions.[9] The National Academy of Sciences reports that "The average consumer is exposed to pesticide residues...in nearly every food, including meat, dairy products, fruits, vegetables, sugar, coffee, oils, dried goods and most processed foods."[10] Information such as this leads us to conclude that in some respects we are all dependent upon the decisions made by corporate elites. It leads us to the understanding that Santiago and the South Bronx are all part of the same corporate empire. And so while unions are being busted and social programs are being slashed, the right women have to their bodies is being challenged, affirmative action is being denied, "voting rights" are being circumvented, and while we are all being monitored, F-16 fighters and M-1 tanks are being built, and a 600 ship navy is being assembled so that intervention, penetration, forcible entry, assault, and rape can be as easily carried out in Libya, Grenada, and Nicaragua as it can in Detroit, Oakland, and East L.A. The the low intensity warfare that is being waged abroad to protect the system of production for private profit is being waged at home as well.

Acquiring a More Real Identity

I can think of no greater task for activists today than to study the reasons why so many common people, surely a majority, objected to the ratification of the Constitution. We must understand the design and structure of our national institutions before we can begin to understand what our government is up to at home and around the world.

The Constitution was designed to ensure that the majority of citizens (without property) would not have a real voice in political affairs and it is no coincidence that that is the case today. And the Constitution was designed to ensure that real political power in this country would always be held by the handful of very large property owners and it is no coincidence that that is the case today. Simply stated, the Constitution was designed to protect the privilege and power of large property owners and shatter the logic of the majority in Nicaragua, South Africa, Guatemala, Chile, Newark, Detroit, most of the South, most of California where soon the majority will be of Third World origins, and so many other places. The merchants, bankers, and plantation slaveowners of 1787 have become a global corporate clan of

1987. And I am asking you how many more plucked eyes and wrenched throats must we pay for in the villages of the poor before we figure out that Congress does the dirty work of corporations and that respectfully petitioning those men and women can only be the work of imperial citizens who are slowly dying.

The interpretation presented on these pages, for many, will be one that is hard to accept. Criticism of the ideas, beliefs, and values with which we identify generally are. But it may be helpful to ponder the validity of a Soviet citizen's remark that the essential difference between the Soviets and Americans is that while Soviet citizens often disbelieve their propaganda, we seem to fully accept ours. Take the war in Southeast Asia. It was just a little over ten years ago that the armed forces of the United States ended its killing of over *four million people.* Yet government officials within the Reagan administration tell us it was one of "our" finest hours.[11] Or take Lincoln, probably our greatest president. His contribution was preserving the union. But as we know, he was going to preserve it with or without slavery. Now, do you believe that the preservation of any country is worth more than the freedom of four million slaves? The Emancipation Proclamation was signed primarily out of military necessity. Stated Lincoln near the end of the Emancipation Proclamation: "I further declare and make known that such persons, of suitable condition, will be received into the armed service of the United States to garrison forts, positions, stations, and other places, and to man vessels of all sorts in said service." As Vincent Harding concludes, "The heart of the matter was this: while the concrete historical realities of the time testified to the costly, daring, courageous activities of hundreds of thousands of black people breaking loose from slavery and setting themselves free, the myth [that Lincoln freed the slaves] gave the credit for this freedom to a white Republican president. In those same times when black men and women saw visions of a new society of equals, and heard voices pressing them against the American Union of white supremacy, Abraham Lincoln was unable to see beyond the limits of his own race, class, and time, and dreamed of a Haitian island and of Central American colonies to rid the country of the constantly accusing, constantly challenging black presence."[12] For whom is he the "great emancipator?"

Or consider Andrew Jackson, the "Father of Democracy." We know that the Father of Democracy enslaved human beings and was the first U.S. president to use troops to break a strike. In addition, much like George Washington, his early fame came about because of his aggressiveness with regard to killing Native Americans and his cunning in stealing their land. Also, Jackson as a military leader had developed an effective way of dealing with the high rate of desertion. He suggested " whipping for the first two attempts, and the third time, execution." As Howard Zinn points out, "If you look through high school textbooks and elementary school textbooks in American history you will find Jackson the frontiersman, soldier, democrat, man of the people—not Jackson, the slaveholder, land speculator, executioner of dissident soldiers, and exterminator of Indians." For whom is he the Father of Democracy?[13]

The question is one of moving beyond a political economy that rests upon the assumption that massive inequality is natural and functional. Early in the 19th century when China resisted Great Britain's "free trade" policy of having opium shipped from India to China, John Quincy Adams argued that China's resistance was "an enormous outrage upon the rights of human nature, and upon the first principles of the rights of nations."[14] The same arrogance disguised as natural law underscores much of U.S. foreign policy today. I think it is important that we let go of these sorts of myths so that we can be free from the lie, from the need to distort reality, and from the need to identify with a set of assumptions and values simply because we inherited them. It would do us well, I believe, to identify with the slaves, not the slavemasters. For we work in the tradition of and are inspired not by Washington, Jefferson, and Lincoln, but by Denmark Vessey, Frederick Douglass, and Harriet Tubman, slaves who by virtue of their resistance and their solidarity with the oppressed expressed what it meant to be human.

We Are In Danger

> The American Constitution of 1787 was explicitly designed to prevent the emergence of an internally sovereign and accountable political power structure. James Madison quite properly referred to it as "our feudal constitution."
>
> **—Walter Dean Burnham**[15]

We the people have control over neither political nor economic power. We are a dependent population. Let us have no illusions about the government of the United States. Following World War II, when the military, economic, and political strength of this country knew no historical parallel, the government quite explicitly, and one could say feverishly, struggled to maintain its relationships of disparity with most of the rest of the world. Efforts by indigenous people to move in the direction of modest reform and democratization were, without sentimentality, crushed.[16] Now the American Empire is in decline. The government of the United States, particularly in light of liberation movements both at home and abroad, has revealed a kind of desperation. The suggestion, for example, that the embattled and impoverished little nation of Nicaragua (whose population is equal to that of greater Boston) poses a security threat to the United States compares to Hitler's suggestion that Czechoslovakia was "a dagger pointed at the heart of Germany" and that the "aggressiveness" of the Poles threatened the Third Reich. Domestically there have been a variety of recent attempts to strengthen the ability of the U.S. government to repress dissent. Gregory Shank has identified the following expressions of what he calls the "criminalization of dissent":

- Reagan's 1980 blueprint for conservative government recommended the abolition of restrictions on domestic intelligence work and the renewal of congressional panels on internal security. The blueprint also urged that national security requirements and the quelling of internal disorder take precedence over individual liberties.
- The term "street crime" has been developed as the code word for domestic law and order. In 1981 for example, Chief Justice of the Supreme Court, Warren Burger, referred to "street crime" as "day-by-day terrorism." Law violators were called domestic terrorists. "Burger

explicitly called for a law and order campaign to combat the internal and external problems which were reducing the United States to 'the status of an impotent society.' What was needed was a War on Crime that raised it to the status of the War on terrorism."

- Along with the massive cuts in social programs which has the effect of pushing many within the activist communities of the 1960s and 1970s (blacks, students, women, Hispanics and working people generally) to the margin of society, the Reagan administration has proposed limiting constitutional protection of individuals from the federal government. These proposals included the weakening of "rules excluding use of illegally seized evidence, the right to counsel of individual defendants, the right to trial by jury, and the precept of 'innocent until proven guilty' " and the advocacy of preventive detention.

- Efforts are underway to widen the definition of criminal conduct to include "potential disrupters of the economic, political, and ideological rule of global capital." Attempts have been made to "vastly enlarge the countersubversive and counterterrorist roles of intelligence agencies."

- There are campaigns to "build more prisons, lengthen and maximize the severity of prison sentences, destroy social service alternatives to imprisonment, enlarge and better equip police forces, and vigorously reintroduce the death penalty."

- Senate Bill 1762 signed into law October 12, 1984 permits "preventive detention" for federal defendants considered "dangerous" and legalized unwarranted search and seizure of people and vehicles by customs officials suspecting violations of currency transaction laws.

- H.R. 6311 redefined terrorism as a "violent act" (including violence against property and persons) which "appears to be intended...to influence the policy of the government by intimidation or coercion." Shank notes that by this definition demonstrators that push down a chain fence in order to hold a sit-in at a nuclear power plant could be prosecuted as terrorists. And rewards up to $500,000 could be paid to informers.

- Senate Bill 2626 (introduced but not yet passed as of this writing) could "imprison Americans for up to ten years for supporting or acting 'in concert with' international 'terrorist' groups or nations designated by the Secretary of State." Moreover the defendant would not be able to challenge the Secretary's designation of the group as "terrorist" in court.[17]

Not unlike other periods of protest in U.S. history, citizens working in solidarity with the peoples of Central America have come under attack by the federal government. C. J. Grossman notes that "U.S. citizens have been denied the right to hear ideas, express differences, travel freely anywhere in the world, be safe in their homes, and remain free of harassment." One legal vehicle the federal government has used to repress dissent has been the McCarran-Walter Act (passed in 1952) which allows the government to prevent "aliens" who are "communists, anarchists, gays, affiliates of communists or those who 'advocate international or governmental doctrines of world communism' " from living in the United States. More recently we find that El Salvador's notorious security forces or "death squads" have been terrorizing civilians in the United States. Most troubling is the fact that the FBI has shared intelligence about Salvadoran activists in the United States with the death squads. Investigators of the death squad attacks in the Los Angeles area note that the evidence "raises the disturbing question of whether the death squads are using FBI intelligence to terrorize residents of the United States."[18] The point is this: when we understand the attitude of the Framers toward common people, when we understand that the power of elites can be legitimized by our ignorance of what is really going on, and when we know that the rest of the world knows what our secret government and their secret teams are doing and that the secrets are kept only from us, then we may conclude that the real enemy of the corporate power structure is the American people because the day is coming you and I will say, "Enough."

In many ways we are like the proverbial frog which is capable of jumping out of boiling water if suddenly dropped into it, but which boils to death if the temperature of the water is slowly and steadily increased. We need to act resolutely and in new directions: We have to let go of our own self-conception (that is nurtured by our everyday involvement in political and economic life) which tells us that we are not capable of really governing ourselves, that each of us is just some human aparatus put here to serve others, to work for others, to be used, whose own ideas are of no value, and who ultimately is incapable of participating meaningfully in a system of self-government. To act resolutely and to move in new directions means that we have to declare that our ideas and our wisdom are as good as that of the rich and powerful. It means that we have to declare that we know what our needs are and that we cannot and will not be involved in relationships any longer in which we are held in contempt. The self that secretly hates going to work because the job is mindless or resents being lied to by government officials or poisoned by our air and water and food or is offended by what the government does in our name with our money is the self that needs to be rewarded and allowed to step forward and speak in a critical voice. It is the self of self-respect. It is the self of liberation. It is the self which constitutional values have put down for 200 years and it is the self that must emerge before political analysis and political organizing can begin.

But constitutional values run through us in ways that are unclear and in ways that we shall discover and struggle with for the rest of our lives. And so we have a need to believe that resolute and radical action is premature, certainly unnecessary, and perhaps even wrong. Moreover, for each of us to declare that we are not the contemptible being embedded in the mind of the Framers is to confront in a thousand different ways the shared values and institutional practices of the broader social order. To move in a direction which frees us from the lie that common people are contemptible is necessarily conflictual and painful. And so there is a great deal of pressure on us to avoid pain, to scramble back to our old identities, and to doubt ourselves. The concept of peace, so central to so many movements, helps us to do this. It is a political concept which projects an abstract vision of a better world at the same time that it gives space to our fears, the fear of leaving our confinement and of discovering that perhaps the Framers were right. The concept of peace permits us to hold back and to accept the Framers' values in the name of respect for other people.

Let us keep in mind the following: to say that we are for peace in the abstract means that we might unthinkingly align ourselves with elites who will scream "bloody murder" the moment the repressive peace is disrupted by people getting off their knees. If we are to identify with the 17,000 auto-workers laid off this year, poor kids who had their milk money cut from the federal budget, black teenagers who face 50 percent unemployment, battered women, Vets dying of agent orange poisoning, or gays confronting the AIDS epidemic, we would not be asking for peace. We would be asking for change, radical change. The peace which harbors situations of oppression—"drug addiction, alcoholism, mental illness, crimes of violence, and all those thousands of instances of despair which will never be entered in the hospital records or the police blotter because they have been safely contained by society's instruments of control" is a peace which must be disturbed. As Howard Zinn has stated, to the extent that a government remains unjust, "it should have trouble governing." Our elitist government should have trouble governing not because we simply become rebellious but because we see the system for what it is, refuse to collaborate, and declare through acts of confrontation, which lead to rigorous organizing and long-term planning, that we believe in ourselves and our vision, and are capable of taking charge of our lives.[19]

Beginning It Now

Whatever you can do or dream you can, begin it. Boldness has genius, power, and magic in it. Begin it now.

—Goethe

The purpose of this book is to make the point that saving this country does not mean going back to the values of the Framers. Rather it means expressing our values. It means letting the world know and feel who we are. Developing confidence in ourselves is not easy. We live in a country where we are taught that only a few people are gifted or talented or are special in some important way. We are taught to think in a way which permits, for example, the richest 1 percent of the population to hold greater wealth than the bottom 90 percent of the population.[20] So the doubts about what we can accomplish are reinforced, perhaps, by acute structures of inequality. One of the greatest creative forces that ever lived was Ludwig Van Beethoven. On one occasion, in a very angry moment, Beethoven refusing to play his music for a prince, wrote the following message: "Dear Prince, what you are, you are through chance and birth. What I am, I am through myself. There have been and there will be thousands of princes. But there is only one Beethoven." And yet on his deathbed, Beethoven turned to a friend and asked, "I did have a certain talent, didn't I?" For Beethoven and for us, the doubt is false. The belief is real.

So here we are. Watched over. Infiltrated at meetings. Monitored at work. Spied on when we come back from Nicaragua or Cuba. Legislated at instead of self-governed. Indoctrinated in not so subtle ways. Poisoned and experimented on. Assessed and ordered about by rich white men who are corrupt and really not very much alive. And at each turn, on just about each day, we are exploited, lied to, ripped-off, pressed to work harder, extorted, and generally held in contempt. And when we resist, when we organize, or when we stand up and say no, we are repressed, fined, assaulted and battered, followed, censored, photographed, wire-tapped, lie-detected, drug-tested, ridiculed, insulted, stigmatized, harassed, left unemployed or underpaid, and increasingly made to speak English.

But you know, things are going to change.[21] We are going to stand up because we know who we are. We are the enlightened souls of history who disturb, upset, and open ways for a better understanding. The Doubt is false. We are restlessness, hunger, and lust. We are a great furnace of resolve. The doubt is false.

We state the bare facts and let them sing. We are the perfection of sensuality and we dream of celebrating the fierce joy of victory and that dream is real. We are luxuriant play; we are sin; we are god; we are transcendent humanity. And we shall turn the page of history. The doubt is false.

We ride on some undiscovered spirit. We are unarmed warriors, we reverberate with shattering force. We are the stars and nothing can stop us. The doubt is false.

We have the capacity to ennoble. We are voices strong and steady. We are defiant, rebellious. The doubt is false.

We have been told all our lives that we can't change anything, that you can't fight city hall. At every meeting there is someone who always makes a case why we should not be radical—it will alienate someone, we are not ready, we need to educate a little more, read a little more, get more numbers. Well, you can always make the case not to be radical. But don't. It's a lie. The doubt is false.

We are activists. We are liberators. We are revolutionaries. We are here on earth in this hour of danger and we must move beyond the vision of the Framers to express our own. And that belief is real.

Appendix

The Constitution of the United States of America

We the people of the United States, in order to form a more perfect union, establish justice, insure domestic tranquility, provide for the common defense, promote the general welfare, and secure the blessings of liberty to ourselves and our posterity, do ordain and establish this Constitution for the United States of America.

ARTICLE I

SECTION 1. All legislative powers herein granted shall be vested in a Congress of the United States, which shall consist of a Senate and House of Representatives.

SECTION 2. The House of Representatives shall be composed of members chosen every second year by the people of the several states, and the electors in each state shall have the qualifications requisite for electors of the most numerous branch of the state legislature.

No person shall be a representative who shall not have attained to the age of 25 years, and been seven years a citizens of the United

States, and who shall not, when elected, be an inhabitant of that state in which he shall be chosen.

Representatives and direct taxes shall be apportioned among the several states which may be included within this union, according to their respective numbers, which shall be determined by adding to the whole number of free persons, including those taxed, three-fifths of all other persons. The actual enumeration shall be made within three years after the first meeting of the Congress of the United States, and within every subsequent term of ten years, in such manner as they shall by law direct. The number of representatives shall not exceed one for every 30,000, but each state shall have at least one representative; and until such enumeration shall be made, the state of New Hampshire shall be entitled to choose three, Massachusetts eight, Rhode Island and Providence Plantations one, Connecticut five, New York six, New Jersey four, Pennsylvania eight, Delaware one, Maryland six, Virginia ten, North Carolina five, South Carolina five, and Georgia three.

When vacancies happen in the representation from any state, the executive authority thereof shall issue writs of election to fill such vacancies.

The House of Representatives shall choose their speaker and other officers; and shall have the sole power of impeachment.

SECTION 3. The Senate of the United States shall be composed of two senators from each state, chosen by the legislature thereof, for six years; and each senator shall have one vote.

Immediately after they shall be assembled in consequence of the first election, they shall be divided as equally as may be into three classes. The seats of the senators of the first class shall be vacated at the expiration of the second year, of the second class at the expiration of the fourth year, and of the third class at the expiration of the sixth year, so that one-third may be chosen every second year; and if vacancies happen by resignation, or otherwise, during the recess of the legislature of any state, the executive thereof may make temporary appointments until the next meeting of the legislature, which shall then fill such vacancies.

No person shall be a senator who shall not have attained to the age of 30 years, and been nine years a citizen of the United States, and who shall not, when elected, be an inhabitant of that state for which he shall be chosen.

The vice president of the United States shall be president of the Senate, but shall have no vote, unless they be equally divided.

The Senate shall choose their other officers, and also a president *pro tempore*, in the absence of the vice president, or when he shall exercise the office of president of the United States.

The Senate shall have the sole power to try all impeachments. When sitting for that purpose, they shall be on oath or affirmation. When the president of the United States is tried, the chief justice shall preside: And no person shall be convicted without the concurrence of two-thirds of the members present.

Judgment in cases of impeachment shall not extend further than to removal from office, and disqualification to hold and enjoy any office of honour, trust or profit under the United States; but the party convicted shall nevertheless be liable and subject to indictment, trial, judgment and punishment, according to law.

SECTION 4. The times, places and manner of holding elections, for senators and representatives, shall be prescribed in each state by the legislature thereof; but Congress may at any time by law make or alter such regulations, except as to the places of choosing senators.

The Congress shall assemble at least once in every year, and such meeting shall be on the first Monday in December, unless they shall by law appoint a different day.

SECTION 5. Each house shall be the judge of the elections, returns and qualifications of its own members, and a majority of each shall constitute a quorum to do business; but a smaller number may adjourn from day to day, and may be authorized to compel the attendance of absent members, in such manner, and under such penalties as each house may provide.

Each house may determine the rules of its proceedings, punish its members for disorderly behaviour, and, with the concurrence of two-thirds, expel a member.

Each house shall keep a journal of its proceedings, and from time to time publish the same, excepting such parts as may in their judgment require secrecy; and the yeas and nays of the members of either house on any question shall, at the desire of one-fifth of those present, be entered on the journal.

Neither house, during the session of Congress, shall, without the consent of the other, adjourn for more than three days, nor to any other place than that in which the two houses shall be sitting.

SECTION 6. The senators and representatives shall receive a compensation for their services, to be ascertained by law, and paid out of the treasury of the United States. They shall in all cases, except treason, felony and breach of the peace, be privileged from arrest during their attendance at the session of their respective houses, and in going to and returning from the same; and for any speech or debate in either house, they shall not be questioned in any other place.

No senator or representative shall, during the time for which he was elected, be appointed to any civil office under the authority of the United States, which shall have been created, or the emoluments whereof shall have been increased during such time; and no person holding any office under the United States, shall be a member of either house during this continuance in office.

SECTION 7. All bills for raising revenue shall originate in the House of Representatives; but the Senate may propose or concur with amendments as on other bills.

Every bill which shall have passed the House of Representatives and the Senate, shall, before it becomes a law, be presented to the president of the United States; if he approve, he shall sign it, but if not, he shall return it, with his objections, to that house in which it shall have originated, who shall enter the objections at large on their journal, and proceed to reconsider it. After the bill is reconsidered, it shall be sent together with the objections, to the other house, by which it shall likewise be reconsidered, and if approved by two-thirds of that house, it shall become a law. But in all cases the votes of both houses shall be determined by yeas and nays, and the names of the persons voting for and against the bill shall be entered on the journal of each house respectively. If any bill shall not be returned by the president within ten days, (Sundays excepted) after it shall have been presented to him, the same shall be a law, in like manner as if he had signed it, unless the Congress by their adjournment prevent its return, in which case it shall not be a law.

Every order, resolution, or vote to which the concurrence of the Senate and House of Representatives, according to the rules and limitations prescribed in the case of a bill.

SECTION 8. The Congress shall have the power to lay and collect taxes, duties, imposts and excises, to pay the debts and provide for the common defence and general welfare of the United States; but all duties, imposts and excises shall be uniform throughout the United States:

To borrow money on the credit of the United States:

To regulate commerce with foreign nations, and among the several states, and with the Indian tribes:

To establish an uniform rule of naturalization, and uniform laws on the subject of bankruptcies throughout the Untied States:

To coin money, regulate the value thereof, and of foreign coin, and fix the standard of weights and measures:

To provide for the punishment of counterfeiting the securities and current coin of the Untied States:

To establish post-offices and post-roads:

To promote the progress of science and useful arts, by securing for limited times to authors and inventors the exclusive rights to their respective writings and discoveries:

To constitute tribunals inferior to the supreme court:

To define and punish piracies and felonies committed on the high seas, and offences against the law of nations:

To declare war, grant letters of marque and reprisal, and make rules concerning captures on land and water:

To raise and support armies, but no appropriation of money to that use shall be for a longer term than two years:

To provide and maintain a navy:

To make rules for the government and regulation of the land and naval offices:

To provide for calling forth the militia to execute the laws of the union, suppress insurrections and repel invasions:

To provide for organizing, arming and disciplining the militia, and for governing such part of them as may be employed in the service of the United States, reserving to the states respectively, the appointment of the officers, and the authority of training the militia according to the discipline prescribed by Congress:

To exercise exclusive legislation in all cases whatsoever, over such district (not exceeding ten miles square) as may, by cession of particular states, and the acceptance of Congress, become the seat of the government of the United states, and to exercise like authority over all places purchased by the consent of the legislature of the state in which the same shall be, for the erection of forts, magazines, arsenals, dock-yards, and other needful buildings:

And,

To make all laws which shall be necessary and proper for carrying into execution the foregoing powers, and all other powers vested by this constitution in the government of the United States, or in any department or officer thereof.

SECTION 9. The migration or importation of such persons as any of the states now existing shall think proper to admit, shall not be prohibited by the Congress prior to the year 1808, but a tax or duty may be imposed on such importation, not exceeding 10 dollars for each person.

The privilege of the writ of *habeas corpus* shall not be suspended, unless when in cases of rebellion or invasion of the public safety may require it.

No bill of attainder or *ex post facto* law shall be passed.

No capitation, or other direct tax shall be laid unless in proportion to the census or enumeration herein before directed to be taken.

No tax or duty shall be laid on articles exported from any state.

No preference shall be given by any regulation of commerce or revenue to the ports of one state over those of another; nor shall vessels bound to, or from, one state, be obliged to enter, clear, or pay duties in another.

No money shall be drawn from the treasury, but in consequence of appropriations made by law; and a regular statement and account of the receipts and expenditures of all public money shall be published from time to time.

No title of nobility shall be granted by the United States: And no person holding any office of profit or trust under them, shall, without the consent of Congress, accept of any present, emolument, office, or title, of any kind whatever, from any king, prince or foreign state.

SECTION 10. No state shall enter into any treaty, alliance, or confederation; grant letters of marque and reprisal; coin money; emit bills of credit; make any thing but gold and silver coin a tender in payment of debts; pass any bill of attainder, *ex post facto* law, or law impairing the obligation of contracts, or grant any title of nobility.

No state shall, without the consent of Congress, lay any impost or duties on imports or exports, except what may be absolutely necessary for executing its inspection laws; and the net produce of all duties and imposts, laid by any state on imports or exports, shall be for the use of the treasury of the United States; and all such laws shall be subject to the revision and control of the Congress.

No state shall, without the consent of Congress, lay any duty on tonnage, keep troops, or ships of war in time of peace, enter into any agreement or compact with another state, or with a foreign power, or engage in war, unless actually invaded, or in such imminent danger as will not admit of delay.

ARTICLE II.

SECTION 1. The executive power shall be vested in a president of the United States of America. He shall hold his office during the term of four years, and, together with the vice-president chosen for the same term, be elected as follows:

Each state shall appoint, in such manner as the legislature thereof may direct, a number of electors, equal to the whole number of senators and representatives to which the state may be entitled in the Congress; but no senator or representative, or person holding an office of trust or profit under the United States, shall be appointed an elector.

The electors shall meet in their respective states, and vote by ballot for two persons, of whom one at least shall not be an inhabitant of the same state with themselves. And they shall make a list of all the persons voted for, and of the number of votes for each; which list they shall sign and certify, and transmit sealed to the seat of the government of the United States, directed to the president of the Senate. The president of the Senate shall, in the presence of the Senate and House of Representatives, open all the certificates and the votes shall then be counted. The person having the greatest number of votes shall be president, if such number be a majority of the whole number of electors appointed; and if there be more than one who have such majority, and have an equal number of votes, then the House of Representatives shall immediately choose by ballot one of them for president; and if no person has a majority, then from the five highest on the list, the said House shall, in like manner, choose the president. But in choosing the president, the votes shall be taken by states, the representation from each state having one vote; a quorum for this purpose shall consist of a member or members from two-thirds of the states, and a majority of all the states shall be necessary to a choice. In every case, after the choice of the president, the person having the greatest number of votes of the electors shall be the vice president. But if there should remain two or more who have equal votes, the Senate shall choose from them by ballot the vice-president.

The Congress may determine the time of choosing the electors, and the day on which they shall give their votes; which day shall be the same throughout the United States.

No person except a natural born citizen, or a citizen of the United States, at the time of the adoption of this constitution, shall be eligible to the office of president; neither shall any person be eligible to that office, who shall not have attained to the age of 35 years, and been 14 years a resident within the United States.

In case of the removal of the president from office, or of his death, resignation or inability to discharge the powers and duties of the said office, the same shall devolve on the vice president, death, resignation, or inability, both of the president and vice president, declaring what officer shall then act as president, and such officer shall act according-ly, until the disability be removed, or a president shall be elected.

The president shall, at stated times, receive for his services a com-pensation, which shall neither be increased nor diminished during the period for which he shall have been elected, and he shall not receive within that period any other emolument from the United States, or any of them.

Before he enter on the execution of his office, he shall take the following oath or affirmation:

"I do solemnly swear (or affirm) that I will faithfully execute the office of president of the United States, and will to the best of my ability, preserve, protect and defend the constitution of the United States."

SECTION 2. The president shall be commander in chief of the army and navy of the United States, and of the militia of the several states, when called into actual service of the United States; he may re-quire the opinion, in writing, or the principal officer in each of the ex-ecutive departments, upon any subject relating to the duties of their respective offices, and he shall have power to grant reprieves and par-dons for offences against the United States, except in cases of impeach-ment.

He shall have power, by and with the advice and consent of the Senate, to make treaties, provided two-thirds of the senators present concur; and he shall nominate, and by and with the advice and con-sent of the Senate, shall appoint ambassadors, and all other officers of the United States, whose appointments are not herein otherwise provided for, and which shall be established by law. But the Congress may by law vest the appointment of such inferior officers, as they think proper, in the president alone, in the courts of law, or in the heads of departments.

The president shall have power to fill up all vacancies that may happen during the recess of the Senate, by granting commissions, which shall expire at the end of their next session.

SECTION 3. He shall, from time to time, give to the Congress in-formation of the state of the union, and recommend to their considera-tion, such measures as he shall judge necessary and expedient; he may, on extraordinary occasions, convene both houses, or either of them, and in case of disagreement between them, with respect to the time of adjournment, he may adjourn them to such time as he shall think proper; he shall receive ambassadors and other public ministers; he shall take care that the laws be faithfully executed, and shall commission all the officers of the United States.

SECTION 4. The president, vice president, and all civil officers of the United States shall be removed from office on impeachment for, and conviction of, treason, bribery, or other high crimes and misdemeanors.

ARTICLE III.

SECTION 1. The judicial power of the United States, shall be vested in one supreme court, and in such inferior courts as the Congress may, from time to time, ordain and establish. The judges, both of the supreme and inferior courts, shall hold their offices during good behavior, and shall, at stated times, receive for their services a compensation, which shall not be diminished during their continuance in office.

SECTION 2. The judicial power shall extend to all cases, in law and equity, arising under this constitution, the laws of the United States, and treaties made, or which shall be made under their authority; to all cases affecting ambassadors, other public ministers and consuls; to all cases of admiralty and maritime jurisdiction; to controversies to which the United States shall be a party: to controversies between two or more states, between a state and citizens of another state, between citizens of different states, between citizens of the same state, claiming lands under grants of different states, and between a state, or citizens thereof, and foreign states, citizens or subjects.

In all cases affecting ambassadors, other public ministers and consuls, and those in which a state shall be party, the supreme court shall have original jurisdiction. In all the other cases before-mentioned, the supreme court shall have appellate jurisdiction, both as to law and fact, with such exceptions, and under such regulations as the Congress shall make.

The trial of all crimes, except in cases of impeachment, shall be by jury; and such trial shall be held in the state where the said crimes shall have been committed; but when not committed within any state, the trial shall be at such place or places as the Congress may by law have directed.

SECTION 3. Treason against the United States shall consist only in levying war against them, or in adhering to their enemies, giving them aid and comfort. No person shall be convicted of treason unless on the testimony of two witnesses to the same overt act, or on confession in open court.

The Congress shall have power to declare the punishment of treason, but no attainder of treason shall work corruption of blood, or forfeiture, except during the life of the person attained.

ARTICLE IV.

SECTION 1. Full faith and credit shall be given in each state to the public acts, records and judicial proceedings of every other state. And the Congress may by general laws prescribe the manner in which such acts, records, and proceedings shall be proved, and the effect thereof.

SECTION 2. The citizens of each state shall be entitled to all privileges and immunities of citizens in the several states.

A person charged in any state with treason, felony, or other crime, who shall flee from justice, and be found in another state, shall, on demand of the executive authority of the state from which he fled, be delivered up, to be removed to the state having jurisdiction of the crime.

No person held to service or labour in one state, under the laws thereof, escaping into another, shall, in consequence of any law or regulation therein, be discharged from such service or labour, but shall be delivered upon claim of the party to whom such service or labour may be due.

SECTION 3. New states may be admitted by Congress into this union; but no new state shall be formed or erected within the jurisdiction of any other state, nor any state be formed by the junction of two or more states, or parts of states, without the consent of the legislatures of the states concerned, as well as of the Congress.

The Congress shall have power to dispose of and make all needful rules and regulations respecting the territory or other property belonging to the United States; and nothing in this constitution shall be so construed as to prejudice any claims of the United States, or of any particular state.

SECTION 4. The United States shall guarantee to every state in this union, a republican form of government, and shall protect each of them against invasion; and on application of the legislature, or of the executive (when the legislature cannot be convened), against domestic violence.

ARTICLE V.

The Congress, whenever two-thirds of both houses shall deem it necessary, shall propose amendments to this constitution, or on the application of the legislatures of two-thirds of the several states, shall call a convention for proposing amendments, which, in either case, shall be valid to all intents and purposes, as part of this constitution, when ratified by the legislatures of three-fourths of the several states, or by conventions in three-fourths thereof, as the one or the other mode of ratification may be proposed by the congress: Provided, that no amendment which may be made prior to the year 1808, shall in any manner affect the first and fourth clauses in the ninth section of the first article; and that no state, without its consent, shall be deprived of its equal suffrage in the Senate.

ARTICLE VI.

All debts contracted and engagements entered into, before the adoption of this constitution, shall be as valid against the United States under this constitution, as under the confederation.

This constitution, and the laws of the United States which shall be made in pursuance thereof: and all treaties made, or which shall be made, under the authority of the United States shall be the supreme law of the land; and the judges in every state shall be bound thereby, anything in the constitution or laws of any state to the contrary not-withstanding.

The senators and representatives before-mentioned, and the member of the several state legislatures, and all executive and judicial officers, both of the United States and of the several states, shall be bound by oath or affirmation, to support this constitution; but no religious test shall ever be required as a qualification to any office or public trust under the United States.

Ratification of the conventions of nine states, shall be sufficient for the establishment of this constitution between the states so ratify-ing the same.

Done in convention, by the unanimous consent of the States present, the 17th day of September, in the year of our Lord 1787, and of the independence of the United States of America the 12th. In wit-ness whereof we have hereunto subscribed our names.

[Names omitted]

Articles of Amendment

AMENDMENT 1.

Congress shall make no law respecting an establishment of religion, or prohibiting the free exercise thereof; or abridging the freedom of speech or of the press; or the right of the people peaceably to assemble, and to petition the government for a redress of grievances.

AMENDMENT 2.

A well-regulated militia being necessary to the security of a free state, the right of the people to keep and bear arms shall not be infringed.

AMENDMENT 3.

No soldier shall, in time of peace, be quartered in any house without the consent of the owner, nor in time of war but in a manner to be prescribed by law.

AMENDMENT 4.

The right of the people to be secure in their persons, houses, papers, and effects, against unreasonable searches and seizures, shall not be violated, and no warrants shall issue but upon probable cause, supported by oath or affirmation, and particularly describing the place to be searched, and the persons or things to be seized.

AMENDMENT 5.

No person shall be held to answer for a capital or other infamous crime unless on a presentment or indictment of a grand jury, except in cases arising in the land or naval forces, or in the militia, when in actual service, in time of war or public danger; nor shall any person be subject for the same offence to be twice put in jeopardy of life or limb; nor shall be compelled in any criminal case to be witness against himself, nor be deprived of life, liberty, or property, without due process of law; nor shall private property be taken for public use without just compensation.

AMENDMENT 6.

In all criminal prosecutions, the accused shall enjoy the right to a speedy and public trial, by an impartial jury of the state and district wherein the crime shall have been committed, which district shall have been previously ascertained by law, and to be informed of the nature and cause of the accusation; to be confronted with the witnesses against him; to have compulsory process for obtaining witnesses in his favor, and to have the assistance of counsel for his defense.

AMENDMENT 7.

In suits at common law, where the value in controversy shall exceed twenty dollars, the right of trial by jury shall be preserved, and no fact tried by a jury shall be otherwise re-examined in any court of the United States than according to the rules of the common law.

AMENDMENT 8.

Excessive bail shall not be required, nor excessive fines imposed, nor cruel and unusual punishments inflicted.

AMENDMENT 9.

The enumeration in the constitution of certain rights shall not be construed to deny or disparage others retained by the people.

AMENDMENT 10.

The powers not delegated to the United States by the constitution, nor prohibited by it to the states, are reserved to the states respectively, or to the people.

AMENDMENT 11 (1798).

The judicial power of the United States shall not be construed to extend to any suit in law or equity, commenced or prosecuted against one of the United States, by citizens of another state, or by citizens or subjects of any foreign state.

AMENDMENT 12 (1804).

The electors shall meet in their respective states, and vote by ballot for President and vice president, one of whom at least shall not be an inhabitant of the same state with themselves; they shall name in their ballots the person voted for as President, and in distinct ballots the person voted for as vice president; and they shall make distinct lists of all persons voted for as President, and of all persons voted for as vice president, and of the number of votes for each, which lists they shall sign and certify, and transmit, sealed, to the seat of the government of the United States directed to the president of the Senate; the president of the Senate shall, in the presence of the Senate and House of

Representatives, open all the certificates, and the votes shall then be counted; the person having the greatest number of votes for President shall be the president, if such number be a majority of the whole number of electors appointed; and if no person have such majority, then from the persons having the highest numbers no exceeding three, on the list of those voted for as President, the House of Representatives shall choose immediately, by ballot, the President. But in choosing the President, the votes shall be taken by states, the representation from each state having one vote; a quorum for this purpose shall consist of a member or members from two-thirds of the states, and a majority of all the states shall be necessary to a choice. And if the House of Representatives shall not choose a President, whenever the right of choice shall devolve upon them, before the fourth day of March next following, then the vice president shall act as President, as in the case of the death or other constitutional disability as vice president shall be the vice president, if such number be a majority of the whole number of electors appointed, and if no person have a majority, then from the two highest numbers on the list the Senate shall choose the vice president; a quorum for the purpose shall consist of two-thirds of the whole number of senators, and a majority of the whole number shall be necessary to a choice. But no person constitutionally ineligible to the office of President shall be eligible to that of vice president of the United States.

AMENDMENT 13 (1865).

SECTION 1. Neither slavery nor involuntary servitude, except as a punishment for crime whereof the party shall have been duly convicted, shall exist within the United States, or any place subject to their jurisdiction.

SECTION 2. Congress shall have power to enforce this article by appropriate legislation.

AMENDMENT 14 (1868).

SECTION 1. All persons born or naturalized in the United States, and subject to the jurisdiction thereof, are citizens of the United States and of the state wherein they reside. No state shall make or enforce any law which shall abridge the privileges or immunities of citizens of the United States; nor shall any state deprive any person of life, liberty, or property without due process of law; nor deny to any person within its jurisdiction the equal protection of the law.

SECTION 2. Representatives shall be apportioned among the several States according to their respective numbers, counting the whole number of persons in each state, excluding Indians not taxed. But when the right to vote at any election for the choice of electors for president and vice president of the United States, representatives in Congress, the executive and judicial officers of a State, or the members of the legislature thereof, is denied to any of the male members of such state being of twenty-one years of age, and citizens of the United States, or in any way abridged, except for participation in rebellion or other crime, the basis of representation therein shall be reduced in the proportion which the number of such male citizens shall bear to the whole number of male citizens twenty-one years of age in such state.

SECTION 3. No person shall be a senator or representative in Congress, or elector of President and Vice-President, or hold any office, civil or military, under the United States, or under any state, who, having previously taken an oath, as a member of Congress, or as an officer of the United States, or as a member of any state legislature, or as an executive or judicial officer of any state, to support the Constitution of the United States, shall have engaged in insurrection or rebellion against the same, or given aid and comfort to the enemies thereof. But Congress may, by a vote of two-thirds of each House, remove such disability.

SECTION 4. The validity of the public debt of the United States, authorized by law, including debts incurred for payment of pensions and bounties for services in suppressing insurrection or rebellion, shall not be questioned. But neither the United States nor any state shall assume or pay any debt or obligation incurred in aid of insurrection or rebellion against the United States, or any claim for the loss or emancipation of any slave; but all such debts, obligations, and claims shall be held illegal and void.

SECTION 5. The Congress shall have power to enforce, by appropriate legislation, the provisions of this article.

AMENDMENT 15 (1870).

SECTION 1. The right of citizens of the United States to vote shall not be denied or abridged by the United States or by any state, on account of race, color, or previous condition of servitude.

SECTION 2. The Congress shall have power to enforce this article by appropriate legislation.

AMENDMENT 16 (1913).

The Congress shall have power to lay and collect taxes on income, from whatever source derived, without apportionment among the several states, and without regard to any census or enumeration.

AMENDMENT 17 (1913).

The Senate of the United States shall be composed of two senators from each state, elected by the people thereof for six years; and each senator shall have one vote. The electors in each state shall have the qualifications requisite for electors of the most numerous branch of the state legislatures.

When vacancies happen in the representation of any state in the Senate, the executive authority of such state shall issue writs of election to fill such vacancies; provided, that the legislature of any state may empower the executive thereof to make temporary appointments until the people fill the vacancies by election as the legislature may direct.

This amendment shall not be so construed as to affect the election or term of any senator chosen before it becomes valid as part of the Constitution.

AMENDMENT 18 (1919).

SECTION 1. After one year from the ratification of this article the manufacture, sale, or transportation of intoxicating liquors with, the importation thereof into, or exportation thereof from the United States and all territory subject to the jurisdiction thereof, for beverage purposes is hereby prohibited.

SECTION 2. The Congress and the several states shall have concurrent power to enforce this article by appropriate legislation.

SECTION 3. This article shall be inoperative unless it shall have been ratified as an amendment to the Constitution by the legislatures of the several states, as provided in the Constitution, within seven years from the date of submission hereof to the states by the Congress.

AMENDMENT 19 (1920).

The right of the citizens of the United States to vote shall not be denied or abridged by the United States or by any state on account of sex.

Congress shall have power to enforce this article by appropriate legislation.

AMENDMENT 20 (1933)

SECTION 1. The terms of the president and Vice-President shall end at noon on the 20th day of January, and the terms of senators and representatives at noon on the 3rd day of January, of the year in which such terms would have ended if this article had not been ratified; and the terms of their successors shall then begin.

SECTION 2. The Congress shall assemble at least once in every year, and such meeting shall begin at noon on the 3rd day of January, unless they shall by law appoint a different day.

SECTION 3. If, at the time fixed for the beginning of the term of President, the President elect shall have died, the Vice-President elect shall become President. If a President shall not have been chosen before the time fixed for the beginning of his term, or it the President elect shall have failed to qualify, then the Vice-President elect shall act as President until a President shall have qualified; and the Congress may by law provide for the case wherein neither a President elect nor a Vice-President elect shall have qualified, declaring who shall then act as President, or the manner in which one who is to act shall be selected, and such person shall act accordingly until a president or Vice-President shall have qualified.

SECTION 4. The Congress may by law provide for the case of the death of any of the persons from whom the House of Representatives may choose a President, whenever the right of choice shall have devolved upon them, and for the case of the death of any of the persons from whom the Senate may choose a Vice-President, whenever the right of choice shall have devolved upon them.

SECTION 5. Sections 1 and 2 shall take effect on the 15th day of October following the ratification of this article.

SECTION 6. This article shall be inoperative unless it shall have been ratified as an amendment to the Constitution by the legislatures of three-fourths of the several sates within seven years from the date of its submission.

AMENDMENT 21 (1933).

SECTION 1. The eighteenth article of amendment to the Constitution of the United States is hereby repealed.

SECTION 2. The transportation or importation into any state, territory, or possession of the United States, for delivery or use therein of intoxicating liquors, in violation of the laws thereof, is hereby prohibited.

SECTION 3. This article shall be inoperative unless it shall have been ratified as an amendment to the Constitution by conventions in the several states, as provided in the Constitution, within seven years from the date of the submission hereof to the states by the Congress.

AMENDMENT 22 (1951).

No person shall be elected to the office of the President more than twice, and no person who has held the office of President, or acted as President, for more than two years of a term to which some other person was elected President shall be elected to the office of the President more than once. But this Article shall not apply to any person holding the office fo President when this Article was proposed by the Congress, and shall not prevent any person who may be holding the office of President, or acting as President, during the term within which this Article becomes operative from holding the office of President or acting as President during the remainder of such term.

AMENDMENT 23 (1961).

SECTION 1. The District constituting the seat of Government of the United States shall appoint in such manner as the Congress may direct:

A number of electors of President and Vice-President equal to the whole number of Senators and Representatives in Congress to which the District would be entitled if it were a State, but in no event more than the least populous State; they shall be in addition to those appointed by the States, but they shall be considered, for the purpose of the election of President and Vice-President, to be electors appointed by a State; and they shall meet in the District and perform such duties as provided by the twelfth article of amendment.

SECTION 2. The Congress shall have power to enforce this article by appropriate legislation.

AMENDMENT 24 (1964).

SECTION 1. The right of citizens of the United States to vote in any primary or other election for President or Vice-President, for electors for President or Vice-President, or for Senator or Representative in Congress, shall not be denied or abridged by the United States or any State by reason of failure to pay any poll tax or other tax.

SECTION 2. The Congress shall have power to enforce this article by appropriate legislation.

AMENDMENT 25 (1967).

SECTION 1. In case of the removal of the President from office or of his death or resignation, the Vice-President shall become President.

SECTION 2. Whenever there is a vacancy in the office of the Vice-President, the president shall nominate a Vice-President who shall take office upon confirmation by a majority of vote of both Houses of Congress.

SECTION 3. Whenever the President transmits to the President *pro tempore* of the Senate and the Speaker of the House of Representatives his written declaration that he is unable to discharged the powers and duties of his office, and until he transmits to them a written declaration to the contrary, such powers and duties shall be discharge by the Vice-President as Acting President.

SECTION 4. Whenever the Vice-President and a majority of either the principal officers of the executive departments or of either the principal officers of the executive departments or of such other body as Congress may by law provide, transmit to the President *pro tempore* of the Senate and the Speaker of the House of Representatives their written declaration that the President is unable to discharge the powers and duties of his office, the Vice-President shall immediately assume the powers and duties of the office as Acting President.

Thereafter, when the President transmits to the President pro tempore of the Senate and the Speaker of the House of Representatives his written declaration that no inability exists, he shall resume the powers and duties of his office unless the Vice-President and a majority of either the principal officers of the executive departments or of such other body as Congress may by law provide, transmit within four days to the President pro tempore of the Senate and the Speaker of the House of Representatives their written declaration that the President is unable to discharge the powers and duties of his office. Thereupon Congress shall decide the issue, assembling within forty-eight hours for that purpose if not in session. If the Congress, within twenty-one days after receipt of the latter written declaration, or, if Congress is not in session, within twenty-one days after Congress is required to assemble, determines by two-thirds vote of both Houses that the President is unable to discharge the powers and duties of his office, the Vice-President shall continue to discharge the same as Acting President; otherwise, the President shall resume the powers and duties of his office.

AMENDMENT 26 (1971).

SECTION 1. The right of citizens of the United States, who are eighteen years or older, to vote shall not be denied or abridged by the United States or any State on account of age.

SECTION 2. The Congress shall have the power to enforce this article by appropriate legislation.

Federalist Paper No. 10:

James Madison

Among the numerous advantages promised by a well constructed Union, none deserves to be more accurately developed than its tendency to break and control the violence of faction. The friend of popular governments never finds himself so much alarmed for their character and fate as when he contemplates their propensity to this dangerous vice. He will not fail, therefore, to set a due value on any plan which, without violating the principles to which he is attached, provides a proper cure for it. The instability, injustice, and confusion introduced into the public councils have, in truth, been the mortal diseases under which popular governments have everywhere perished, as they continue to be the favorite and fruitful topics from which the adversaries to liberty derive their most specious declamations. The valuable improvements made by the American constitutions on the popular modes, both ancient and modern, cannot certainly be too much admired; but it would be an unwarrantable partiality to contend that they have as effectually obviated the danger on this side, as was wished and expected. Complaints are everywhere heard from our most considerate and virtuous citizens, equally the friends of public and private faith and of public and personal liberty, that our governments are too unstable, that the public good is disregarded in the conflicts of rival parties, and that measures are too often decided, not according to the rules of justice and the rights of the minor party, but by the superior force of an interested and overbearing majority. However anxiously we may wish that these complaints had no foundation, the evidence of known facts will not permit us to deny that they are in some degree true. It will be found, indeed, on a candid review of our situation, that some of the distresses under which we labor have been erroneously charged on the operation of our governments; but it will be found, at the same time, that other causes will not alone account for many of our heaviest misfortunes; and, particularly, for that prevailing and increasing distrust of public engagements and alarm for private rights which are echoed from one end of the continent to the other. These must be chiefly, if not wholly, effects of the unsteadiness and injustice with which a factious spirit has tainted our public administration.

By a faction I understand a number of citizens, whether amounting to a majority or minority of the whole, who are united and actuated by some common impulse of passion, or of interest, adverse to the rights of other citizens, or to the permanent and aggregate interests of the community.

There are two methods of curing the mischiefs of faction: the one, by removing its causes; the other, by controlling its effects.

There are again two methods of removing the causes of faction; the one, by destroying the liberty which is essential to its existence; the other, by giving to every citizen the same opinions, the same passions, and the same interests.

It could never be more truly said than of the first remedy that it was worse than the disease. Liberty is to faction what air is to fire, an aliment without which it instantly expires. But it could not be a less folly to abolish liberty, which is essential to political life, because it nourishes faction than it would be to wish the annihilation of air, which is essential to animal life, because it imparts to fire its destructive agency.

The second expedient is as impracticable as the first would be unwise. As long as the reason of man continues fallible, and he is at liberty to exercise it, different opinions will be formed. As long as the connection subsists between his reason and his self-love, his opinions and his passions will have a reciprocal influence on each other; and the former will be objects to which the latter will attach themselves. The diversity in the faculties of men, from which the rights of property originate, is not less an insuperable obstacle to a uniformity of interests. The protection of these faculties is the first object of government. From the protection of different and unequal faculties of acquiring property, the possession of different degrees and kinds of property immediately results; and from the influence of these on the sentiments and views of the respective property immediately results; and from the influence of these on the sentiments and views of the respective proprietors ensues a division of the society into different interests and parties.

The latent causes of faction are thus sown in the nature of man; and we have them everywhere brought into different degrees of activity, according to the different circumstances of civil society. A zeal for different opinions concerning religion, concerning government, and many other points, as well of speculation as of practice; an attachment to different leaders ambitiously contending for pre-eminence and power; or to persons of other descriptions whose fortunes have been interesting to the human passion, have, in turn, divided mankind into parties, inflamed them with mutual animosity, and rendered them much more disposed to vex and oppress each other than to co-operate for their common good. So strong is this propensity of mankind to fall into mutual animosities that where no substantial occasion presents itself the most frivolous and fanciful distinctions have been sufficient to kindle their unfriendly passions and excite their most violent conflicts. But the most common and durable source of factions has been the various and unequal distribution of property. Those who hold and those who are without property have ever formed distinct interests in society. Those who are creditors, and those who are debtors, fall under a like discrimination. A landed interest, a manufacturing interest, a mercantile interest, a moneyed interest, with many lesser interests, grow up of necessity in civilized nations, and divide them into different classes, actuated by different sentiments and views. The regulation of these various and interfering interests forms the principal task of modern legislation and involves the spirit of party and faction in the necessary and ordinary operations of government.

No man is allowed to be a judge in his own cause, because his interest would certainly bias his judgment, and, not improbably, corrupt his integrity. With equal, nay with greater reason, a body of men are unfit to be both judges and parties at the same time; yet what are many of the most important acts of legislation but so many judicial determinations, not indeed concerning the rights of single persons, but concerning the rights of large bodies of citizens? And what are the different causes which they determine? Is a law proposed concerning private debts? It is a question to which the creditors are parties on one side and the debtors on the other. Justice ought to hold the balance between them. Yet the parties are, and must be, themselves the judges; and the most numerous party, or in other words, the most powerful faction must be expected to prevail. Shall domestic manufacturers be encouraged, and in what degree, by restrictions on foreign manufacturers? These are questions which would be differently decided by the landed and the manufacturing classes, and probably by neither with a sole regard to justice and the public good. The apportionment of taxes on the various descriptions of property is an act which seems to require the most exact impartiality; yet there is, perhaps, no legislative act in which greater opportunity and temptation are given to a predominant party to trample on the rules of justice. Every shilling with which they overburden the inferior number is a shilling saved to their own pockets.

It is in vain to say that enlightened statesmen will be able to adjust these clashing interests and render them all subservient to the public good. Enlightened statesmen will not always be at the helm. Nor, in many cases, can such an adjustment be made at all without taking into view indirect and remote considerations, which will rarely prevail over the immediate interest which one party may find in disregarding the rights of another or the good of the whole.

The inference to which we are brought is that the *causes* of faction cannot be removed and that relief is only to be sought in the means of controlling its *effects*.

If a faction consists of less then a majority, relief is supplied by the republican principle, which enables the majority to defeat its sinister views by regular vote. It may clog the administration, it may convulse the society; but it will be unable to execute and mask its violence under the forms of the Constitution. When a majority is included in a faction, the form of popular government, on the other hand, enables it to sacrifice to its ruling passion or interest both the public good and the rights of other citizens. To secure the public good and private rights against the danger of such a faction, and at the same time to preserve the spirit and the form of popular government, is then the great object to which our inquiries are directed. Let me add that it is the great desideratum by which alone this form of government can be rescued from the opprobrium under which it has so long labored and be recommended to the esteem and adoption of mankind.

By what means is this object attainable? Evidently by one of two only. Either the existence of the same passion or interest in a majority at the same time must be prevented, or the majority, having such coexistent passion or interest, must be rendered, by their number and local situation, unable to concert and carry into effect schemes of oppression. If the impulse and the opportunity be suffered to coincide, we well know that neither moral nor religious motives can be relied on as an adequate control. They are not found to be such on the injustice and violence of individuals, and lose their efficacy in proportion to the number combined together, that is, in proportion as their efficacy becomes needful.

From this view of the subject it may be concluded that a pure democracy, by which I mean a society consisting of a small number of citizens, who assemble and administer the government in person, can admit of no cure for the mischiefs of faction. A common passion or interest will, in almost every case, be felt by a majority of the whole; a communication and concert results from the form of government itself; and there is nothing to check the inducements to sacrifice the weaker party or an obnoxious individual. Hence it is that such democracies have ever been spectacles of turbulence and contention; have ever been found incompatible with personal security or the rights of property; and have in general been as short in their lives as they have been violent in their deaths. Theoretic politicians, who have patronized this species of government, have erroneously supposed that by reducing mankind to a perfect equality in their political rights, they would at the same time be perfectly equalized and assimilated in their possessions, their opinons, and their passions.

A republic, by which I mean a government in which the scheme of representation takes place, opens a different prospect and promises the cure for which we are seeking. Let us examine the points in which it varies from pure democracy, and we shall comprehend both the nature of the cure and the efficacy which it must derive from the Union. The two great points of difference between a democracy and a republic are: first, the delegation of the government, in the latter, to a small number of citizens elected by the rest; secondly, the greater number of citizens and greater sphere of country over which the latter may be extended.

The effect of the first difference is, on the one hand, to refine and enlarge the public views by passing them through the medium of a chosen body of citizens, whose wisdom may best discern the true interest of their country and whose patriotism and love of justice will be lease likely to sacrifice it to temporary or partial consideration. Under such a regulation it may well happen that the public voice, pronounced by the representatives of the people, will be more consonant to the public good than if pronounced by the representatives of the people, will be more consonant to the public good than if pronounced by the people themselves, convened for the purpose. On the other hand, the effect may be inverted. Men of factious tempers, of local prejudices, or of sinister designs, may, by intrigue, by corruption, or by other means, first obtain the suffrages, and then betray the interests of the people. The question resulting is, whether small or extensive republics are most favorable to the election of proper guardians of the public weal; and it is clearly decided in favor of the latter by two obvious considerations.

In the first place it is to be remarked that however small the republic may be the representatives must be raised to a certain number in order to guard against the cabals of a few; and that however large it may be they must be limited to a certain number in order to guard against the confusion of a multitude. Hence, the number of representatives in the two cases not being in proportion to that of the constituents, and being proportionally greatest in the small republic, it follows that if the proportion of fit characters be not less in the large than in the small republic, the former will present a greater option, and consequently a greater probability of a fit choice.

In the next place, as each representative will be chosen by a greater number of citizens in the large than in the small republic, it will be more difficult for unworthy candidates to practise with success the vicious arts by which elections are too often carried; and the suffrages of the people being more free, will be more likely to center on men who possess the most attractive merit and the most diffusive and established characters.

It must be confessed that in this, as in most other cases, there is a mean, on both sides of which inconveniences will be found to lie. By enlarging too much the number of electors, you render the representative too little acquainted with all their local circumstances and lesser interests; as by reducing it too much, you render him unduly attached to these, and too little fit to comprehend and pursue great and national objects. The federal Constitution forms a happy combination in this respect; the great and aggregate interests being referred to the national, the local and particular to the State legislatures.

The other point of difference is the greater number of citizens and extent of territory which may be brought within the compass of republican than of democratic government; and it is this circumstance principally which renders factious combinations less to be dreaded in the former than in the latter. The smaller the society, the fewer probably will be the distinct parties and interests composing it; the fewer the distinct parties and interests, the more frequently will a majority be found of the same party; and the smaller the number of individuals composing a majority, and the smaller the compass within which they are placed, the more easily will they concert and execute their plans of oppression. Extend the sphere and you take in a greater variety of parties and interests; you make it less probable that a majority of the whole will have a common motive to invade the rights of other citizens; or if such a common motive exists, it will be more difficult for all who feel it to discover their own strength and to act in unison with each other. Besides other impediments, it may be remarked that, where there is a consciousness of unjust or dishonorable purposes, communication is always checked by distrust in proportion to the number whose concurrence is necessary.

Hence, it clearly appears that the same advantage which a republic has over a democracy in controlling the effects of faction is enjoyed by a large over a small republic—is enjoyed by the Union over the States composing it. Does this advantage consist in the substitution of representatives whose enlightened views and virtuous sentiments render them superior to local prejudices and to schemes of injustice? It will not be denied that the representation of the Union will be most likely to possess these requisite endowments. Does it consist in the greater security afforded by a greater variety of parties, against the event of any one party being able to outnumber and oppress the rest? In an equal degree does the increased variety of parties comprised within the Union increase this security? Does it consist in the greater obstacles opposed to the concert and accomplishment of the secret wishes of the Union gives it the most palpable advantage.

The influence of factious leaders may kindle a flame within their particular States but will be unable to spread a general conflagration through the other States. A religious sect may degenerate into a political faction in a part of the Confederacy; but the variety of sects dispersed over the entire fact of it must secure the national councils against any danger from that source. A rage for paper money, for an abolition of debts, for an equal division of property, or for any other improper or wicked project, will be less apt to pervade the whole body of the Union than a particular member of it, in the same proportion as such a malady is more likely to taint a particular county or district than an entire State.

In the extent and proper structure of the Union, therefore, we behold a republican remedy for the diseases most incident to republican government. And according to the degree of pleasure and pride we feel in being republicans ought to be our zeal in cherishing the spirit and supporting the character of federalists.

Notes

Chapter 1

1. Frederick Nietzsche, *The Will to Power* (ed.) Walter Kaufman and (tr.) Walter Kaufman and R.J. Hollingdale (New York: Random House, 1967), 4.

2. Charles A. Beard, *An Economic Interpretation of the Constitution of the United States* (New York: The Macmillian Company, 1948), 144, 145.

3. Howard Zinn, *A Framers History of the United States* (New York: Harper & Row, 1980), 67.

4. Fawn M. Brodie, *Thomas Jefferson* (New York: W.W. Norton & Co., 1974).

5. This statement was made in a lecture at the Evergreen State College, Olympia, Washington, in October 1987.

6. Eric Foner, *Tom Paine and Revolutionary America* (New York: Oxford University Press, 1976), 190. Here I am using the term Framers broadly. It refers not only to those who wrote the Constitution but to others such as John Adams, Thomas Jefferson, Benjamin Rush, Robert Morris and others who played leading roles in shaping our political and economic institutions.

7. *Newsweek*, May 25, 1987, 47.

8. *Time*, July 6, 1987, 35.

9. John F. Kasson, *Civilizing the Machine* (New York: Penguin Books, 1976), 31,32.

10. Foner, 123.

11. Foner, 90.

12. Thomas Ferguson and Joel Rogers, *Right Turn: The Decline of the Democrats and the Future of American Politics* (New York: Hill and Wang, 1986).

13. Stephen B. Oates, *Let the Trumpet Sound* (New York: Harper & Row, 1982), 361.

232   TOWARD AN AMERICAN REVOLUTION

14. Starhawk, *Dreaming the Dark* (Boston: Beacon Press, 1982), 101.

15. Wilfred E. Binkley, *American Political Parties* (New York: Alfred A. Knopf, 1943), 40.

16. Max Farrand, ed., *The Records of the Federal Convention of 1787* (New Haven: Yale University Press, 1966), 288.

Chapter 2

1. Francis Jennings, "The Indians' Revolution," in Alfred F. Young, ed., *The American Revolution (DeKalb, IL: Northern Illinois University Press, 1976), 322.*

2. John C. Miller, "The American Revolution as a Democratic Movement," in Earl Latham, ed., *The Declaration of Independence and the Constitution* (Boston: D.C. Heath, 1956), 9.

3. Philip Foner, *History of the Labor Movement in the United States,* Vol. 1, (New York: International Publishers,1975), 13-18.

4. The data on wealth distribution come from Gar B. Nash, "Social Change and the Growth of Prerevolutionary Urban Radicalism," in Young, 3-37. The voting information comes from P. Foner, 28.

5. See Howard Zinn, *A People's History of the United States* (New York: Harper Colophon Books, 1980), 39,59; Alce S. Rossi, ed., *The Feminist Papers: From Adams to de Beauvoir* (New York: Columbia University Press,1973); and Barbara Leslie Epstein, *The Politics of Domesticity* (Middletown, Connecticut: Wesleyan University Press, 1981).

6. P. Foner, 33.

7. See Dirk Hoerder, "Boston Leaders and Boston Crowds, 1765-1776," in Young, 232-271; and Zinn, Chapter 4.

8. Hoerder, 243,244.

9. See Marvin L. Michael Kay, "The North Carolina Regulation, 1774-1776: A Class Conflict" in Young, 71-124; and P. Foner, 34.

10. P. Foner, 8,39.

11. Nash, 31; Eric Foner, *Tom Paine and Revolutionary America* (New York: Oxford University Press, 1976), 61.

12. Kenneth M. Dolbeare, *Democracy at Risk: The Politics of Economic Renewal* (Chatham, New Jersey: Chatham House Publishers, Inc., 1984), 2, 4.

13. E. Foner, 135-138.

14. Zinn, 74. For a discussion of Locke's treatment of the laboring class, see C.B. Macpherson, *The Political Theory of Possessive Individualism* (New York: Oxford University Press, 1962).

15. P. Foner, 84.

16. Zinn, 81

17. Zinn, 76-101.

18. The data on slavery is from Zinn, 87; the information on subsistence farming is from David P. Szatmary, *Shays' Rebellion: The Making of an Agrarian Insurrection* (Amherst, MA: University of Massachusetts Press, 1980), 1; unless otherwise specified, the account of period surrounding Shays Rebellion is drawn from Szatmary's work.

19. Szatmary, 7-8.

20. Szatmary, 11.

21. Zinn, 99.

22. Szatmary, 34.

23. Szatmary, 35.

24. Szatmary, 40.

25. Szatmary, 41.

26. Szatmary, 47.

27. Szatmary, 45.

28. Szatmary, 53.

29. See Szatmary, Chapter 7.

30. Szatmary, 124-129.

31. Zinn, 94.

32. Szatmary, 129.

33. This discussion is drawn from Szatmary, Chapter. 7.

34. Thomas P. Slaughter, *The Whiskey Rebellion* (New York: Oxford University Press, 1986), 224; the action also had the effect of raising the value of Washington's property by about 50 percent.

35. Ralph Ketcham, *The Anti-Federalist Papers and the Constitutional Convention Debates* (New York: New American Library, 1986), 17,18.

36. Merrill Jensen, "The Articles of Confederation," in Earl Latham, 17, 19.

Chapter 3

1. William Appleman Williams, *Empire As A Way of Life* (New York: Oxford University Press, 1980), viii, 43.

2. Charles L. Mee, Jr., *The Genius of the People* (NY: Harper & Row, 1987), 284.

3. See Merrill Jensen, "The Articles of Confederation," in Earl Latham, *The Declaration of Independence and the Constitution* (Boston: D.C. Heath, 1956), 15-19.

4. Gordon S. Wood, "Democracy and the Constitution," *How Democratic Is the Constitution?* Robert A. Goldwin and William A Schambra, eds. (Washington, D.C.: American Enterprise Institute for Public Policy Research, 1980), 12.

5. Jackson Turner Main, *The Antifederalists* (New York: W. W. Norton & Co., 1961), 105.

6. See Andrew C. McLaughlin, "The Confederate Period and the Federal Convention," in Latham.

7. Margit Mayer and Margaret A. Fay, "The Formation of the American Nation-State," *Kapitalistate*, No.6. Fall 1977, 72.

8. Kenneth M. Dolbeare and Linda Medcalf, "The Dark Side of the Constitution," in John F. Manley and Kenneth M. Dolbeare, *The Case Against the Constitution* (New York: M.E. Sharpe, Inc., 1987), 128-130. Dolbeare and Medcalf are making these claims in the context of the translation which Hamilton made of the Constitution into financial and legal institutions.

9. David Smith, *The Convention and the Constitution* (New York: St. Martin's Press, 1965), 13.

10. Vernon L. Parrington, "The Great Debate," in Latham, 63.

11. Quoted by Mee, 111-112.

12. This and the Madison quote are from Parrington, 63,64.

13. The issue of judicial review was not settled until Marbury v. Madison in 1803.

14. Parrington, 66, 61.

15. Quoted by Dolbeare and Medcalf, 124.

16. Amendments 15 and 19 to the Constitution broadened the franchise considerably. They stated that "the right of citizens of the United States to vote shall not be denied or abridged...on account of race" (Amendment 15) and "on account of sex." (Amendment 19) This appears to significantly alter the racism and sexism of the Constitution and certainly these amendments are steps in that direction. But notice the language, "shall not be denied...on account of." Nowhere does it say that blacks or women or even whites shall be guaranteed the right to vote, just that whatever requirements the state decides that one must meet in order to vote cannot be explicitly based upon race or sex. Therefore, voting is still a privilege granted by the state for which we must qualify and because the language of the amendments are negatively ("shall not be denied") instead of positively ("women and people of color shall be guaran-

teed the right"), there is ample opportunity for discrimination based upon race and sex. For example, the poll tax and the literacy test (abolished because of the Civil Rights movement) while they did not explicitly prohibit any specific group from voting and therefore did not directly violate Amendment 15, was used intentionally to prevent many blacks and poor people from voting throughout most of this century. Racism, sexism, and classism is still at the heart of the Constitution and will be until democratic participation is specifically guaranteed.

17 Michael J. Cozier, Samuel P. Huntington, Joji Watanuki, *The Crisis of Democracy* (New York: New York University Press, 1975), 75, 113, 114.

18. Kenneth M. Dolbeare and Murray J. Edelman, *American Politics* (Boston: D.C. Heath, 1974), 253, 254.

19. Main, 147.

20. All quotes from anti-federalists unless otherwise specified are drawn from Main, Chapters V-VII.

21. In addition to Main, a good source on anti-federalist sentiment is Ralph Ketcham, *The Anti-Federalist Papers and the Constitutional Convention Debates* (New York: New American Library, 1986).

22. See Mee's account of the ratification process.

23. Mee, 288, 289.

24. Many of the less radical amendments advanced under these circumstances did contribute to the mounting pressure for a Bill of Rights. See Chapter 4.

25. See Charles A. Beard, *An Economic Interpretation of the Constitution of the United States* (New York: The Macmillan Company, 1948), Chapter IX

26. Sheldon S. Wolin, "The People's Two Bodies," *Democracy*, January, 1981, p. 22.

27. Smith, 46.

Chapter 4

1. The literature, fortunately, is voluminous in this area. For those who are new to the subject I would suggest going to the nearest good library and looking under the heading "United States. Federal Bureau of Investigation." A good general overview is provided by David Wise, *The American Police State* (New York: Random House, 1976).

2. Clinton Rossiter, in *1787: The Grand Convention* (New York: Macmillan Company, 1966), 138, notes that several newspapers at the time expressed great praise of the Framers for their forward thinking such as they were the "collective wisdom of the Continent." The French *charge d'affaires* stated that

they were "the most enlightened men of the continent." Charles M. Lee, Jr. in his *Genius of the People* (New York: Harper & Row, 1987), 4, provides us with an example of a contemporary tribute: the Framers were "representative of what they themselves often referred to as the genius of the people—that cumulative body of knowledge and intuition formed by living for centuries under the legacy of the Magna Carta and the rule of common law."

3. For a discussion of the Iroquois and their relation to the Framers see Bruce E. Johansen, *Forgotten Founders* (Ipswich, Massachusetts: Bambit Incorporated, 1982).

4. Staughton Lynd, "The Constitution and Union Rights," *In These Times*, Sept. 30-Oct. 6, 1987, 13; Lynd goes on to say that such rights are also critical for workers but they are not all the rights that workers need given their dependency in the workplace.

5. Edward Dumbauld, *The Bill of Rights* (Norman, Oklahoma: University of Oklahoma Press, 1957), 8,9.

6. Dumbauld, 14-16.

7. *The Philip Morris Magazine* recently sponsored an essay contest (first prize, $15,000) that asked for essays which explored "First Amendment's application to American business...and questions the ramifications of a tobacco advertising ban."

8. Sheldon S. Wolin, "What Revolutionary Action Means Today," in *Democracy*, Fall 1982, 21.

9. For a discussion of the concept of citizen as it relates to the intention of the Framers see Sheldon S. Wolin, "The People's Two Bodies," *Democracy*, January 1981; Madison, Federalist No. 10; Hamilton, Federalist No. 27.

10. Philip S. Foner, *History of the Labor Movement in the United States*, Vol. I, New York: International Publishers, 1975), 88, 89.

11. David Kairys, "The Tortured History of Free Speech," *In These Times*, Aug. 5-18, 1987, 12.

12. Howard Zinn, *Disobedience and Democracy* (New York: Vintage Books, 1968), 77; Kairys, 12.

13. Kairys, 12.

14. The example is used by Noam Chomsky, *Turning the Tide* (Boston: South End Press, 1985), 50.

15. Delivered in a talk at the University of Colorado at Bolder, December 1986.

16. Kairys, 13.

17. I shall present a very rough overview, but I encourage you to explore two rather comprehensive studies, one by Frank Donner and the other by Robert

Justin Goldstein, upon which this, admittedly thin, overview is based: see Frank J. Donner, *The Age of Surveillance* (New York: Vintage Books, 1980); Robert Justin Goldstein, *Political Repression in Modern America* (New York: Schenkman Publishing Co., 1978).

18. Goldstein, 548.

19. Goldstein, 548.

20. Goldstein, 547-551.

21. Goldstein, 553-555.

22. Cathy Perkus, ed., *COINTELPRO: The FBI's Secret War on Political Freedom* (New York: Monad Press, 1975).

23. Joshua Cohen and Joel Rogers, *On Democracy* (New York: Penguin Books Ltd, 1984), 41.

24. See Lawrence Goodwyn, *The Populist Moment* (New York: Oxford University Press, 1978).

25. Goldstein, 556-557.

26. Joshua Cohen and Joel Rogers, *Rules of the Game: American Politics and the Central America Movement* (Boston: South End Press, 1986), 12; Richard L. Rubenstein, *The Cunning of History: The Holocaust and the American Future* (New York: William Styron, 1978), 54.

27. Donner, 231. Also see, Arnold Rogow, *The Dying of the Light* (New York: Putnam, 1975); and Assata Shakur, *Assata,* (Westport, Conn.: Lawrence Hill and Co., 1987).

28. Fred Hampton, a leader of the BPP, was assassinated by police on 4 December 1969 when a fusillade of between eighty-three and ninety-nine shots were fired into his Chicago apartment at 4:00 AM; see Donner, 226-230.

29. Cohen and Rogers, 42. The rest of Sullivan's is interesting in that it reveals the degree to which the federal government attempts to manipulate movement leadership. It continues: "For some months I have been thinking about this matter. One day I had an opportunity to explore this from a philosophical and sociological standpoint with [name deleted] whom I have known for some years...I asked him...if he knew any Negro of outstanding intelligence or ability...[He] has submitted to me the name of the above-captioned person. Enclosed with this memorandum is an outline [deleted] biography, which is truly remarkable...On scanning this biography, it will be seen that [deleted] does have all the qualifications of the kind of a Negro leader to overshadow Martin Luther King. If this thing can be involved, I think it would be not only a great help to the FBI, but would be a fine thing for the country at large." See David Wise, *The American Police State* (New York: Random House, 1976), 303.

238 TOWARD AN AMERICAN REVOLUTION

30. Donner, 226-230; Cohen and Rogers, 42, 43; Perkus, 22.

31. Cohen and Rogers, 41,42.

32. Kenneth M. Dolbeare and Linda Medcalf, "The Dark Side of the Constitution," in John F. Manley and Kenneth M. Dolbeare, eds., *The Case Against the Constitution* (New York: M.E. Sharpe, Inc.,1987), 128.

33. Dolbeare and Medcalf, 138.

34. Donner, 55.

35. In his televised debate with Walter Mondale, President Reagan acknowledged the "Assassination Manual" and attributed it to the CIA station chief in Tegucigalpa, Honduras. One of the best sources for documentation of U.S.-sponsored assassinations abroad is the Hearings Before The Select Committee to Study Government Operations With Respect to Intelligence Activities of the United States Senate, 94th Congress, First Session, 1975, Volumes I-VII. Perhaps the most infamous involvement of the U.S. government in domestic assassinations was in the murder of JFK. I refer you to The Final Assassination Report of the Select Committee on Intelligence, U.S. House of Representatives, 1979 and to an unpublished work, "Nomenclature of an Assassination Cabal," by Torbitt, available at Tom Davis Books, P.O. Box 1107, Aptos, CA 95001-1107.

36. Chomsky, 235.

37. Donner, 49, 269, 270.

38. John Stockwell, in a talk delivered at the University of California, at Santa Barbara, 8 April, 1986. The tape is available through The Other Americas, UCSB, Santa Barbara, CA.

39. For a complete discussion of the MK Ultra Program see John Marks, *In Search of the Manchurian Candidate* (New York: New York Times Books, 1979). Also see the documents in the appendix of George Katsiaficas, *The Imagination of the New Left* (Boston: South End Press, 1987).

40. Because Congress forbids the use of military personnel for domestic law enforcement purposes, FEMA planned to deputize military personnel. This information was drawn from several sources: an affidavit prepared by the Christic Institute which was filed for a federal civil lawsuit (available from The Christic Institute, 1324 North Capitol Street, Washington, DC 20002); *Miami Herald*, July 5, Alexander Cockburn, "Ashes & Diamonds," *In These Times*, July 22-August 4, 1987, 17; Stockwell.

41. Donner, 17-20.

Chapter 5

1. Charles Higham, *Trading with the Enemy* (New York: Dell, 1984), 184, 185.

2. One important and early study was L. Fletcher Prouty, *The Secret Team* (New Jersey, Prentice-Hall, Inc., 1973). As we shall note, the "secret team" referred to by the Christic Institute is different than Prouty's. While it has its roots in the same corporate-intelligence community, the Christic Institute's secret team tends to carry out policy; Prouty's secret team sets it. For Prouty's secret team I shall use "secret government." When I shall use the term "secret team" I shall use it in the sense that the Christic Institute does.

3. The best recent study on these matters is Johnathan Marshall, Peter Dale Scott, and Jane Hunter, *The Iran Contra Connection* (Boston: South End Press, 1987).

4. Both Daniel Sheehan, Chief Counsel of the Christic Institution and Saul Landau of the Institute for Policy Studies, for example, have emphasized in public talks that the covert activities violate the letter and spirit of the Constitution.

5. Harry Magdoff, *Imperialism: From the Colonial Age to the Present* (New York: Monthly Review Press, 1978), 202.

6. A study by Lawrence Dennis quoted by Magdoff, 199; considering covert activities, the Untied States has been at war continuously since 1941.

7. Prouty, 2.

8. Robert M. Johnstone, Jr., *Jefferson and the Presidency* (Ithaca, New York: Cornell University Press, 1978), 64, 65.

9. See Chapter 3.

10. For a more complete account see Marshall, Scott, and Hunter.

11. Paul Jacobs and Saul Landau, *To Serve the Devil*, Vol. 2, (New York: Random House, 1971), 338-355.

12. Victor Marchetti and John D. Marks, *The CIA and the Cult of Intelligence* (New York: Alfred A. Knopf, 1974), 323, 324, 344; for the Madison quote see Chapter 3.

13. For information on Hoover and the post-war attack on Russia see Albert E. Kahn and Michael Sayers, *The Great Conspiracy: The Secret War Against Soviet Russia* (Boston: Little, Brown Books, 1946); also I have profited very much from the research of Dave Emory and Nip Tuck whose work in this area can be obtained on audio cassettes from Davkore Co., 1300-D Space Park Way, Mountain View, CA 94043.

14. Leonard Mosley, *Dulles* (New York: Dial Press, 1978).

15. Henry Ford received the Grand Cross of the German Eagle from Hitler, the highest award that the Nazis could give a foreigner. Ford had also written anti-Semitic texts, such as *The International Jew* which reportedly influenced Hitler.

16. Higham, *Trading*.

17. Higham, 62; the last quote is taken from an interview conducted with Charles Higham by Louise Belloti, November 1982, broadcast on KPFA, Berkeley, CA

18. See Charles Higham, *American Swastika* (Garden City, New York: Doubleday & Company, 1985), Chapter 16.

19. See for example the description of Lieutenant Commander Canaris, an American intelligence source working with the Germans; Anthony Cave Brown, *Wild Bill Donovan: The Last Hero* (New York: Times Books, 1982), 128.

20. Higham, *Swastika*, 184-186.

21. Higham, *Swastika*, 198; Peter Dale Scott, "How Allen Dulles and the SS Preserved Each Other," *Covert Action* , Number 25 (Winter 1986), 6, 12.

22. Higham, *Swastika*, 190-199.

23. For detailed examinations of this type of collaboration in Europe see T. H. Tetens, *The New Germany and the Old Nazis* (New York: Random House, 1961); Howard Ambruster, *Treason's Peace* (Beechhurst Press, 1947); Kurt Riess, *The Nazis Go Underground* (Garden City, New York: Doubleday, Duran & Co., 1944); Heinz Hohne, *The Order of the Death's Head: The Story of Hitler's SS* (London: Secker & Warburg, 1969), translated by Richard Barry; Ladislas Farago, *Aftermath: Martin Bormann and the Fourth Reich* (New York: Simon and Schuster, 1974); and in Japan, see James Hougan, *Spooks* (New York: William Morrow & Co. Inc., 1978).

24. James S. Martin, *All Honorable Men* (Boston: Little, Brown, and Co., 1950).

25. See Laurence H. Shoup & William Minter, "Shaping a New World Order: The Council on Foreign Relations' Blueprint for World Hegemony," in Holly Sklar, ed., *Trilateralism* (Boston: South End Press, 1980)135-156; Noam Chomsky, *Turning the Tide* (Boston: South End Press, 1985), 65.

26. See Riess and note that publication date is prior to the end of the war.

27. Charles R. Allen, Jr., *Heusinger of the Fourth Reich* (Manzoni and Monzel, 1963).

28. Gehlen's organization was first within the Office of Policy Coordination before it became part of the CIA. The sources for Eichmann and Barbie are Higham, *Swastika*, 252, Chapter 26, and Cookridge, and Scott. Also see Scott, 5, 14.

29. It is interesting to note also that the phrase "iron curtain" was used first not by Churchill but by Hitler's last finance minister Count Von Krosigk.

30. Not surprisingly it was Allen Dulles who saw to it that the legislation which defined the power of the CIA contained the clause enabling the CIA to carry out "such other functions and duties related to intelligence as the National Security Council may from time to time direct."

31. For a discussion of Gehlen and the Green Berets, see Cookridge, Chapter 17.

32. See Noam Chomsky and Edward S. Herman, *The Washington Connection and Third World Fascism* (Boston: South End Press, 1979), 361 and Joshua Cohen and Joel Rogers, *On Democracy* (New York: Penguin Books, 1983), 199.

33. Torture victims, for example, have recently identified CIA personnel as being present during interrogations in Honduras; see *The New York Times*, January 19, 1988, 1, 4.

34. This particular instance of torture was first reported in the January issue of *Alert*, a publication produced by the Committee in Solidarity With the People of El Salvador; it was also reported by Ray Bonner in *The New York Times*, January 11, 1982. The transcript of the interview may be found in "Salvadoran Deserter Discloses Green Beret Torture Role," *Covert Action Information Bulletin*, No. 16, March 1982.

35. Jim Naureckas, "Death Squad Strategy Was Made in U.S.A.," *In These Times*, Jan. 13-19, 1988, 9.

36. John Stockwell, in a speech at the University of California, Santa Barbara, April 8, 1986.

37. David Wise and Thomas B. Ross, *The Invisible Government* (New York: Vintage Books, 1974), 95; for information on Forrestal see Higham, Trading.

38. John Loftus, *The Belarus Secret* (New York: Alfred A. Knopf, inc., 1982), 69.

39. Loftus, 70, 73, 76, 78, 89, 106, 107, 130, 132; Victor Marchetti, who spent 14 years working in the CIA writes that "If one looks back at the CIA's predecessor, the wartime Office of Strategic Service, one finds that its primary activities were...concentrated on trying to create guerrilla movements in occupied territory. When the CIA was formed in 1947, the operatives—most of whom had served in OSS [Allen Dulles, Richard Helms, William Colby, and William Casey]—quickly got control of the Agency, and they have held on ever since." Victor Marchetti, "An Introductory Overview," in Robert L. Borosage and John Marks (ed.), *The CIA File* (New York: Grossman Publishers, 1976), xii. It should be pointed out that Allen Dulles, Richard Helms, William Colby, and William Casey were CIA directors that served in the OSS.

40. Jerry W. Sanders, *Peddlers of Crisis* (Boston: South End Press, 1983), 14, 24, 25.

41. Victor Marchetti and John D. Marks, *The Cult of Intelligence* (New York: Alfred A. Knopf, 1974), 305.

42. Henrik Kruger, *The Great Heroin Coup* (Boston: South End Press, 1976), 144, 205; Cookridge, 218;

43. Carl Oglesby, *The Yankee and Cowboy War* (Kansas City: Sheed Andrews and McMeel, Inc., 1976), Chapter 3; see Wise and Ross, 184-192. John McCone who replaced Dulles was a far right-wing business tycoon with interests in Bech-tel, Standard Oil of California, and Curtis-Wright Corporation.

44. See Peter Dale Scott, "The Kennedy Assassination and the Vietnam War," in Peter Dale Scott, Paul L. Hotch, and Russel Stetler, eds., *The Assassinations: Dallas and Beyond* (New York: Vintage, 1976); the information regarding the escalation of troop levels comes from a talk given by John Judge in San Francisco, July 24, 1987. His mother was the Deputy Chief of Staff for Personnel.

45. Prouty, vii, 416.

46. Most of the information from this section is drawn from an affidavit filed for a federal civil lawsuit prepared by the Christic Institute which is available at 1324 North Capitol Street, Washington, DC 20002. All quotes in this section are taken directly from the affidavit unless otherwise indicated.

47. The Shooter Team has been linked by many, including Daniel Sheehan of the Christic Institute to John Kennedy's assassination. See also the reference to the Torbitt document in the footnotes of Chapter 4.

48. Kruger, 146.

49. Marshall, Scott, and Hunter, 8,9.

50. See Noam Chomsky, *On Power and Ideology* (Boston: South End Press, 1987),13.

51. Policy Planning Study (PPS) 23, Feb. 24, 1948, FRUS 1948, I (part 2).

52. Richard L. Rubenstein, *The Cunning of History* (New York: Harper & Row, 1978), x, 64.

53. Gregory Shank, "Contragate and Counterterrorism: An Overview," *Crime and Social Justice*, Nos. 27-28, iii.

54 Edward S. Herman, "U.S. Sponsorship of International Terrorism: An Overview," *Crime and Social Justice*, Nos. 27-28, 15,16.

55. Rubenstein, 53.

56. Taken from Sklar, "Trilateralism: Managing Dependence and Democracy,"
37. The references to trilateralist thinking are from Michael J. Crozier, Samuel

P. Huntington, Joji Watanuk, *The Crisis of Democracy* (New York: New York University Press, 1975).

57. Crozier, et. al., 91-114.

58. Dillion Anderson quoted by Peter Thompson, "Bilderberg and the West," in Sklar, 186; see *The Nation*, "A Mini-C.I.A.," August 15/22, 1987.

Chapter 6

1. John Judge, in a talk given in San Francisco, December 1987.

2. Nelson W. Polsby, *Congress and the Presidency* (Englewood Cliffs, New Jersey: Prentice-Hall, 1986), 139.

3. Perhaps you might want to study the process yourself; Polsby's work is a good place to begin.

4. Thomas Ferguson and Joel Rogers, (ed.), *The Political Economy* (New York: M.E. Sharpe, Inc., 1984), 180.

5. This example was used by Ralph Nader to illustrate the power of corporations in a talk delivered at the University of California in November 1982.

6. Mark Green, James M. Fallows, and David R. Zwick, *Who Runs Congress* (New York: Bantam Books, 1972), 36

7. Ira Katznelson and Mark Kesselman, *The Politics of Power* (New York: Harcourt Brace Jovanovich,1987), 159.

8. Green, 61, 62.

9. Thomas Ferguson and Joel Rogers, *Right Turn: The Decline of the Democrats and the Future of American Politics* (New York: Hill and Wang, 1986), 121. For a discussion of the relation between political parties and corporations, in addition to Ferguson and Rogers, see Gerald John Fresia, *There Comes A Time: A Challenge to the Two Party System* (New York: Praeger, 1986).

10. Ferguson and Rogers, 30; Green, 31.

11. William E. Connolly, *Politics and Ambiguity* (Madison, Wisconsin: The University of Wisconsin Press, 1987), 21.

12. *Business Week*, June 10, 1980; cited in Connolly, 22.

13. Louis Fisher, 1975, 202,203.

14. Fisher, 226; see Chapter 5 for the selling of drugs and covert financing.

15. Martin A. Lee, "How the Drug Czar Got Away," *The Nation*, Sept. 5, 1987, 191.

16. The information concerning the Pentagon's "black budget" and the projects funded by it is taken entirely from a three part series by Tim Weiner, "The Pentagon's 'black budget,'" *San Jose Mercury News*, February 15, 16, and 17, 1987.

17. The following example is taken from Ferguson and Rogers, 146-154.

18. Ferguson and Rogers, 151.

19. Harvey Wasserman, "The Politics of Transcendence," *The Nation*, August 31, 1985, 146.

20. Joan Cocks, "Wordless Emotions: Some Critical Reflections on Radical Feminism," *Politics and Society*, Vol. 13, No. 1, 1984, 32.

21. Qoted by William Connolly, *Legitimacy and the State* (New York: New York Universtiy Press, 1984), 2.

22. Connolly, 2, 3.

23. Cocks, 40.

24. Information about the "Pledge" is drawn from *Basta: A Pledge of Resistance Handbook,* (Philadelphia, PA: New Society Publishers, 1986); the nonviolence section of the manual was adapted from previous handbooks such as those produced by The Diablo Blockade/Encampment Handbook and The Livermore Weapons Lab Blockade/Demonstration Handbook. The following groups were represented at the initial meeting: Witness for Peace, Fellowship of Reconciliation, American Friends Service Committee, SANE, the Emergency Response Network, the Nuclear Weapons Freeze campaign, the Committee in Solidarity with the People of El Salvador, the National Network in Solidarity with Nicaragua, the Chicago Religious Task Force, the Presbyterian Church, Maryknoll, the Interreligious Task Force on Central America, Mobilization for Survival, Sojourners, World Peacemakers, the Mennonite Church, the Central America Peace Campaign, and the Episcopal Peace Fellowship.

25. It may be worth noting that I have signed the Pledge, participated in Pledge workshops and affinity groups, and I have been arrested in Pledge organized nonviolent actions of civil disobedience.

26. G.W.F. Hegel, *The Phenomenology of Spirit,* trans. A.V. Miller (Oxford: Clarendon Press, 1977), 399-400.

27. For a discussion of this subject see William E. Connolly, *The Terms of Political Discourse* (Lexington, MA: D.C. Heath, 1974), 193-198.

28. Examples such as this one used in this section are based on my own personal experience.

29. Stephen B. Oates, *Let the Trumpet Sound* (New York: Harper & Row, 1982), 212, 226, 461.

30. *Guardian*, New York City, August 26, 1987, 5.

31. Robert Henri, *The Art Spirit* (New York: J.B. Lippincott Co., 1960), 225.

32. Katznelson and Kesselman, 45.

33. W. E. Connolly, *Appearance and Reality in Politics* (New York: Cambridge University Press, 1981), 52, 53.

34. Walter Dean Burnham, *The Current Crisis in American Politics* (New York: Oxford University Press, 1982), 52.

35. I am grateful to Ken Dolbeare for the suggestion of linking Freedom Voting to a more complete program which gives voters something to vote for.

36. With the exception of numbers 4 and 5, these points were quoted directly from Keven Phillips and Paul Blackman, *Electoral Reform and Voter Participation* (Washington, D.C.: American Enterprise Institute, 1975), 23, 26, 33.

37. Burnham, 121.

38. For information regarding Agent Ryan, see Letters, *The Nation*, November 14, 1987; the statement regarding human beauty is a paraphrase of an idea of Roque Dalton's.

Chapter 7

1. I.F. Stone, "Covert Loophole," *The Nation*, September 5, 1987.

2. Sheldon S. Wolin, "What Revolutionary Action Means Today," *Democracy*, Fall 1982, 27.

3. Donald R. Pfost, "Reagan's Nicaraguan Policy: A Case Study of Political Deviance and Crime," *Crime and Social Justice*, Nos. 27-28, 67, 70.

4. Sara Evans, *Personal Politics* (New York: Vintage Books, 1980), 134, 206.

5. *The Progressive*, June 1987, 7.

6. David Viscott, *The Language of Feelings* (New York: Pocket Books, 1976), 39.

7. Pfost, 82.

8. Edward S. Herman, "U.S. Sponsorship of International Terrorism: An Overview," *Crime and Social Justice*, Nos. 27-28, 10.

9. For further information regarding the safety of nuclear power, see: Helen Caldicott, *Nuclear Madness* (Autumn Press, Inc., 1978).

10. "Your Salad Could Be Killing You," *In These Times*, Oct. 14-20, 1987, 8-9.

11. Edward S. Herman, "U.S. Sponsorship of International Terrorism: An Overview," *Crime and Social Justice*, Nos. 27-28, 21.

12. See Vincent Harding, *There Is A River* (New York: Vintage Books, 1983), 323-236.

13. Howard Zinn, *A People's History of the United States* (New York: Harper & Row, Inc., 1980), 128, 129.

14. Noam Chomsky, *On Power and Ideology* (Boston: South End Press, 1987), 13.

15. Walter Dean Burnham, *The Current Crisis in American Politics* (New York: Oxford University Press, 1983), 260.

16. See Chomsky, Lecture 2.

17. Gregory Shank, "Counterterrorism and Foreign Policy," *Crime and Social Justice*, Nos. 27-28, 36-41.

18. CJ Grossman, The McCarran-Walter Act: War Against Margaret Randall and the First Amendment," *Crime and Social Justice*, Nos. 27-28, 220, 225; Vince Bielski, Cindy Forster, and Dennis Bernstein, "The Death Squads Hit Home," *The Progressive*, October 1987, 18.

19. Howard Zinn, *Disobedience and Democracy* (New York: Vintage Books, 1968), 20, 26.

20. From a *New York Times* report quoted by Ravi Batra, *The Great Depression of 1990* (New York: Simon and Schuster, 1987).

21. The following section was inspired by the concepts and poetry of Dennis Brutus and David Viscott, a therapist, who may from time to time be heard to say, "The doubt is false. The belief is real."

Index

397-